ROGER STEVENSON
JANUARY, 1994

JOHN W.B. GIBBS is a Director of Financial Training Publications, Ltd., in London, England.

ROBERT W. MCGEE has a law degree, a masters in taxation, and a CPA and CMA certificate. He has written several articles for professional publications and three forthcoming Spectrum Books on finance.

John W.B. Gibbs
Robert W. McGee

FINANCIAL DECISION-MAKING IN BUSINESS

Planning and Control Techniques to Increase Your Profits

A SPECTRUM BOOK

Prentice-Hall, Inc., Englewood Cliffs, N.J. 07632

Library of Congress Cataloging in Publication Data

Gibbs, John W   B
    Financial decision-making in business

    (A Spectrum Book)
    British ed. published under title: A practical
approach to financial management.
    Includes index.
    1. Business enterprises—Finance.   2. Corporations
—Finance.   I. McGee, Robert W., joint author.
II. Title.
HG4026.G5 1980   658.1'55   80-11770
ISBN 0-13-315994-9
ISBN 0-13-315986-8 (pbk.)

Editorial/production supervision and interior design by Frank Moorman
Cover design by Tony Ferrara Studio, Inc.
Manufacturing buyer: Barbara A. Frick

© 1980 by Prentice-Hall, Inc., Englewood Cliffs, New Jersey 07632.
Originally published as A PRACTICAL APPROACH TO FINANCIAL MANAGEMENT
by John Gibbs, by Financial Training Publication, Ltd., London, England.

A SPECTRUM BOOK

10   9   8   7   6   5   4   3   2   1

Printed in the United States of America

PRENTICE-HALL INTERNATIONAL, INC., *London*
PRENTICE-HALL OF AUSTRALIA PTY. LIMITED, *Sydney*
PRENTICE-HALL OF CANADA, LTD., *Toronto*
PRENTICE-HALL OF INDIA PRIVATE LIMITED, *New Delhi*
PRENTICE-HALL OF JAPAN, INC., *Tokyo*
PRENTICE-HALL OF SOUTHEAST ASIA PTE. LTD., *Singapore*
WHITEHALL BOOKS LIMITED, WELLINGTON, *New Zealand*

Contents

v

Preface

This book is essentially practical, so that it can provide an effective guide for financial managers or others interested in financial decision-making. The book is not an esoteric guide on one particular area of specialization nor is it concerned with deep mathematical analysis. The coverage is broad and the language used is simple so that the nontechnically oriented reader is able to obtain the maximum benefit.

The book is aimed at an audience that includes the general reader who is interested in learning more about the financial decision-making process, students taking a course in financial management, as well as anyone involved in making financial decisions, such as chief financial officers, corporate controllers and treasurers, financial analysts, etc. Investors and lenders will also find the book to be beneficial and informative.

The book is organized into five broad topical areas. The first of these is concerned with the dual (and somewhat conflicting) financial objectives of liquidity and profitability. The second section expands on the liquidity objective, concentrating on cash flow, working capital management, sources of short-term finance and foreign trade and exchange.

The third segment concentrates on sources and costs of long-term capital and illustrates the use of accounting ratios. Section four discusses the factors involved in determining whether a particular investment, acquisition or merger should be made. The last section gives an overview of the basic business law and taxation concepts a financial manager should be familiar with.

Because the contents of the book are arranged by topic the reader is able to zero in on a particular problem area with a minimum of wasted effort.

Introduction

Financial management may be defined as the process involved in the attempt to ensure that financial resources are both obtained and used profitably and effectively for the best accomplishment of the objectives of the organization to which it is applied.

A financial resource enables its owner to spend money. For example, a bank overdraft of a given amount carries as much spending power as the equivalent sum in cash. Unpaid suppliers (creditors) are a resource, because reputable businesses can gain large lines of short-term credit from this source.

The way in which any manager ensures that something will happen is by planning and control. He forecasts the likely outcome of particular actions intended to assist the achievement of his objectives. If the forecast is satisfactory, those actions are adopted as an operating plan. Thereafter, the manager keeps watch on the implementation of the plan and on the results achieved, so that if these deviate from his forecast, he can either modify the plan or the manner in which it is being implemented. In other words he will be controlling the day-by-day operations of the business.

Note that planning and control are closely bound up together. In some cases particular aspects of planning or control can be isolated for discussion, but in practice there is continual interplay between these two manifestations of management activity. Control involves replanning. Planning is ineffective unless it is linked with the means of control.

In the above context the role of the financial manager could be considered under the following main headings:

1. Planning the financial strategy of the business, that is to say, deciding on the financial objectives of the organization and reviewing from time to time in the light of updated forecasts the main areas of financial policy— how much money shall be used, and in what types of enterprise it shall be disposed.
2. Planning and controlling the use of funds in the finance of working capital, including self-financing through the normal mechanism of trade credit.
3. Planning the sources of finance other than self-financing of working capital, and obtaining such finance when required.
4. Planning and controlling the use of funds for long-term investment, whether inside the business in the form of fixed assets, or by purchase of investments in other businesses.

These four main headings are shown in the following chart.

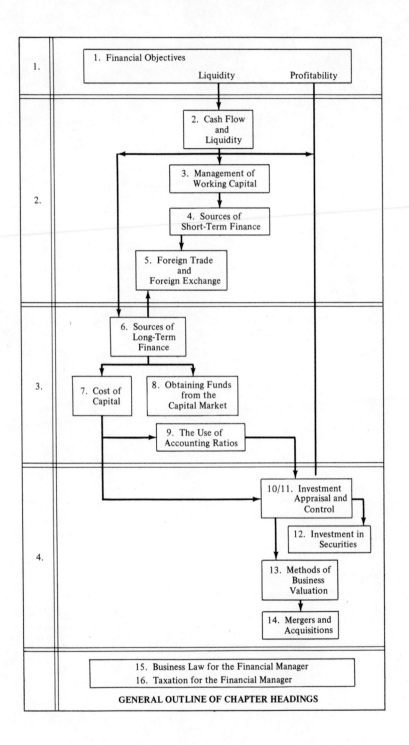

1.

1. Financial Objectives

Liquidity   Profitability

2.

2. Cash Flow
and
Liquidity

3. Management of
Working Capital

4. Sources of
Short-Term Finance

5. Foreign Trade
and
Foreign Exchange

3.

6. Sources of
Long-Term
Finance

7. Cost of
Capital

8. Obtaining Funds
from the
Capital Market

9. The Use of
Accounting Ratios

4.

10/11. Investment
Appraisal and
Control

12. Investment in
Securities

13. Methods of
Business
Valuation

14. Mergers and
Acquisitions

15. Business Law for the Financial Manager
16. Taxation for the Financial Manager

GENERAL OUTLINE OF CHAPTER HEADINGS

Financial Planning

Business Management and Objectives

Many alternative interpretations have been given of the nature of management, and people have listed in different ways the various functions that they attribute to managers. For our present purpose it is sufficient to recall that two of the major functions of management are:

1. Planning.
2. Controlling.

Planning, again in broad terms, means developing, defining and evaluating:

1. The goals or objectives of the organization.
2. The alternative strategies that might lead toward the goals.

In other words, deciding what the business is aiming to do and how it proposes to do it.

"To make money" is the easy answer to the question: "What are the objectives of business?" This is true in that those who participate in a business enterprise do so in the hope of increasing their wealth—their ability to command real resources—and the common measure of this ability is money. But it is inadequate because no business has an automatic right to increases in wealth. Any increases are due to people (customers) wanting the product or service that the business is providing. Every business undertaking, therefore, must have two main sets of objectives:

1. Marketing objectives—what it proposes offering to the world that is unique, special or in high demand.
2. Financial objectives.

And these two are inextricably linked. Financial objectives will not be achieved unless there are adequate marketing objectives. Marketing objectives will be fruitless unless they lead to financial gains, and will be unachievable unless they have financial support.

What are the financial objectives of a business? "To make a profit" some people will say: "To stay in existence" say others. Both are right if we define their meanings correctly.

Profit and Cash Flows

The profit arising from any venture is the difference between the amount of cash introduced by the venturers and the amount of cash they receive back either as distributions during the life of the project or as a terminal distribution when all the assets related to the venture have been realized and all creditors have been paid. Over the life of the venture, there is no profit other than cash. Similarly over the life of any business or any company there is no profit other than the difference between cash introduced by the proprietors or shareholders and the cash they eventually withdraw. This can be illustrated with a simple example.

EXAMPLE

Mr. X buys some shop furniture and fixtures for $1,000 and runs a retail business for three years. His reported results (ignoring taxation) are:

Year	Sales	Purchases and expenses	Depreciation	Net profit or (loss)
	$	$	$	$
1	500	360	333	(193)
2	1,200	690	333	177
3	1,500	900	334	266
Total	$3,200	$1,950	$1,000	$250

By the end of the third year, when the business is discontinued, his fixed assets have been fully depreciated and he has earned a net profit of $250. Taking each year separately, in Year 1 the business showed a loss, but Years 2 and 3 showed increasing profits.

Now assuming that debtors take three months to pay, and that purchases and expenses are paid on the average two months late, the cash flows year by year over the life of the business would have been as follows:

Year	Cash received from debtors			Cash paid to creditors			Net cash flow in or (out)
			$			$	$
1	¾ X 500	=	375	5/6 X 360	=	300	75
2	From Yr 1		125	From Yr 1		60	390
	¾ X 1200	=	900	5/6 X 690	=	575	
3	From Yr 2		300	From Yr 2		115	560
	¾ X 1500	=	1,125	5/6 X 900	=	750	
4	From Yr 3		375	From Yr 3		150	225
							1,250
				Less initial outlay			1,000
				Cash gain			$ 250

(Note that depreciation is ignored since it does not represent a cash flow.)

In brief, the incremental cash received over the life of the business (in the example $250) is, and always must be, the same as the total profit, although year by year the cash flow is likely to be completely different from the reported profit figures. The attempt to break up the continuous life of a business into short-term profit reporting segments can give a misleading view in relation to long-term trends.

There is thus a sense in which it is true to say: "Look after the cash, and the profits will look after themselves." It is the financial manager's particular responsibility to look after the cash, and this is the main theme of this book. We shall begin, in Chapter 2, by looking at the control of "cash" in the narrow sense of the word, but our concern will quickly widen to cover the whole field of the management of "funds," i.e., both actual and potential cash resources— cash and those items readily convertible into cash in the ordinary course of the business. The sources of funds are the profits of the business plus all those liabilities incurred in acquiring the assets which it employs, and including, of course, the ultimate liability to shareholders in respect of the capital which they have subscribed.

The Need for Profit

It is agreed then that in order to achieve the desirable increment of cash one of the business objectives should be to make a profit. But the question remains:

"How much profit?" The answer to this question depends on the purpose for which the profit is to be used. Three possible purposes will be considered:

1. Stability.
2. Growth.
3. Reward.

Stability

The assets used in the business will require replacement from time to time if the business is to continue to exist in its present form. Stocks of goods and materials will have to be renewed as they are sold or used in making products or providing services. Fixed assets will become worn out or obsolete and new assets will be needed to replace them.

Under a historical accounting system profits are stated after charging the use of assets based on their original cost, but the profit figure itself has to be sufficient to cover any enhanced costs of asset replacement over and above the previous purchase costs. It is one of the purposes of accountancy reform currently under debate in relation to the system of *current cost accounting* to ensure that "profits" are declared only after making full provision for the replacement of existing assets. If this is done then all declared profits will be available for purposes other than the maintenance of a stable asset base.

The term "stability" can be used in another sense. If a particular type of business is subject to significant fluctuations in activity, then higher profits in periods of peak output will help to ensure that funds will be available to help the survival of the business during times when sales are low. In this sense stability is closely allied to liquidity, which will be discussed in a later paragraph in relation to the business objective of "staying in existence." It will already be clear that staying in existence, while it may have its own problems, is ultimately dependent on making a profit.

Business Growth

Returning to the purposes for which profits are required we come now to growth. There have been, and probably still are, a lot of misguided ideas about the nature of growth. A manager may say "we have to invest another $100,000 in equipment and machinery next year," and refer to this as growth, but it is possible that having spent the $100,000 he will not have any more items of equipment or any greater productive capacity than he had previously. All that has happened is that the prices of replacement equipment and machinery are higher than those previously in force. In other words, the $100,000 reflects only the impact of inflation. Real growth, like real profit, only exists after the physical substratum of the business has been preserved, although as noted previously the accounting methods for reflecting this are still under review.

Let us assume, however, that the $100,000 buys additional physical equipment, i.e., there has been an effective growth in capital employed. Is this growth relevant to the financial objectives of the business? Not unless it is going to enable more profit to be made than would otherwise have been possible.

Similarly, growth in sales quantity is only relevant to the company's financial objectives if the additional sales improve the total profit above what would otherwise have been available.

Bear in mind here that without growth in assets or sales the business might actually have lost business to a competitor, and this factor would have to be taken into account in deciding whether growth was justified.

The question we started with was *how much* profit do we need for various purposes including the finance of growth?

Growth, whether real or inflationary, cannot in most businesses be financed entirely out of profits. At some stage there will be need for additional funds from outside the business, i.e., for additional long-term capital. Some companies attempt to retain sufficient profits to finance "normal" growth; that is to say, excluding such big steps as the introduction of a new product, a change in technology, or the acquisition of another business. Whether this is possible will depend on the normal amount of profit and the normal rate of growth for that particular business. Whether it is desirable will be related to the company's dividend policy, and this brings us to our third need of profits—for the purpose of reward.

Rewards to Participators in the Business

Who looks to the company's profits for reward? Let us start by considering what are the essential ingredients in a business. As with other theoretical matters there are different possible answers, but on this occasion we shall consider three:

1. Ideas (for products or services, and for the market to be served).
2. Skills (in carrying out the necessary activities).
3. Money (capital).

In the case of the private business all three ingredients may be provided by the same person (the proprietor), and there is no doubt that in whatever capacity he is regarded any profit belongs to him.

The larger business will obtain its ideas in one of two ways: either by employing people to develop them or by buying them from outside. The most obvious example of outside purchase is when an inventor registers his innovation with the patents office and then allows other people to use it on payment of a fee. This fee may be a lump sum or may be a periodic payment related to the benefits obtained from the invention by the user. In the latter case, the inventor is taking a financial risk that the invention may not be successful, so he asks for a share of the profits, having in mind that this share may be zero. It will never be less than zero, however. He is still a supplier to the business and not a participator.

Skills are also purchased by the larger business, for wages and salaries. The employees at all levels of responsibility receive their monetary reward at a fixed negotiated rate, though sometimes there may be an element of profit sharing. The rate of remuneration does not fall below a fixed minimum while the company continues operating.

The risk taken by employees is that their skills will cease to be required, and to this extent they are risk-takers in the business. In theory, should one job cease the employee can take his skill elsewhere, but in practice this possibility is reduced for various reasons, such as the employee's reluctance to move, his age, and the nonavailability of suitable work. For these reasons among others, government economic policy in the United States includes particular concern for the preservation of employment, and there is considerable support for the idea that employees should become more closely involved in the management of business.

Lastly the ingredient "capital." Broadly speaking, money can be invested in the larger business in one of two forms (these will be considered in detail later). First, there is borrowed money (loan capital). The lender is entitled to a fixed rate of interest and to repayment of his loan at a fixed time. In some cases particular assets are earmarked as security for the loan repayment. In some cases, if the company defaults on the loan contract the lender will have the right to appoint a receiver to run the business temporarily with the object of paying the lender his dues. Such lenders are merely suppliers of capital with preferential rights to repayment, running very little risk as long as the value of their security is not eroded. Other lenders may give unsecured loans in exchange for a high rate of interest. They, like most suppliers of goods and services, are taking a risk that the company may not be able to pay them. But unlike the employee whose commitment is potentially lifelong, the lender is only at risk for the agreed limited duration of his loan.

Does the company need any other source of long-term capital? The answer in nearly every case is "yes," for three main reasons:

1. The business may need to buy land, buildings and other fixed assets having a long life. It would be undesirable to finance these solely with loan capital which might have to be repaid before the end of that life, and which might not be renewed or replaced. There is need for a capital fund which will never be repaid while the company continues to exist.
2. The business may have periods of high profit and of low profit. Typically

the early years of a new business may not be profitable. Loan interest is payable regardless of profit or loss. There is need for a source of capital that will only be remunerated when profits are available.

3. If a business is unsuccessful and is discontinued, then there must be (and is) a defined sequence in which various classes of creditors are paid out of the proceeds of realization of the assets. The secured lenders have recourse to the proceeds of those assets charged as their security.

Certain liabilities are given preferential treatment. All the remaining creditors rank equally—unless the suppliers of a certain part of the long-term capital were willing to defer their claims and thus give the trade creditors a better chance of some distribution. If this were not the case, suppliers would be less willing to trade with the business.

We have thus defined contributors of capital who cannot look to the company to repay them until the company is wound up, and then only if there is a surplus after meeting all other liabilities, and who will only get any intermediate reward for their investment if profits have been made and cash is available. These people are the ordinary shareholders, and because they take the risk of complete loss they are rewarded with the whole of any profits made. For this reason they are regarded as the "owners" of the company, and it is they who appoint a board of directors to decide the policy of the company and to oversee its implementation.

Answering the question "How much profit?" in relation to the shareholders, the answer would appear to be "as much as possible." In brief, the managers of the business should aim to maximize the wealth accruing to the ordinary shareholders, subject to the constraints of satisfying the demands of other interests, significantly the lenders and the employees.

Maximizing the shareholders' wealth means more than making the maximum profits. It also means using those profits as dividend distributions and retentions in the business in such a way that between the time the shareholder buys his shares and the time he sells them he gets the greatest possible total benefit. Now this idea raises two extremely difficult problems:

1. Deciding what is the shareholder's own preference between a dividend now and a capital gain in the future.

2. Knowing what capital gain any shareholder will in fact obtain, since very few shareholders bought their shares direct from the company, and fewer still (if any!) will hold them throughout the company's life. The majority of shareholders will buy and sell through the stock exchange, and share prices on the stock exchange are subject to many influences which are not under the control of the managers of the company.

These problems will all be discussed in detail in a later chapter. It will be sufficient for the moment to point out two views on shareholders' rights which differ from those expressed above:

1. Although shareholders theoretically control the board of directors through their votes at shareholders' meetings, in practice very few shareholders bother to vote. Under these circumstances the directors need not attempt to maximize wealth but should seek only to satisfy the shareholders' reasonable dividend requirements, having regard to what other companies are paying, and should then use the residual profits for the long-term development of the company considered as an entity in its own right. This view would not apply when a working majority of a company's shares was in the hands of large institutions which did in fact take an active interest in the management of the business.

2. Ethically there is no reason why the shareholders should be entitled to all residual profits, but if not, then who should be entitled to them? There are many parties interested in the business, as described above. The importance of each will depend at any time on their relative bargaining powers, on the political system of the country and the social attitudes current within the community. The managers of a business must take all these factors into account. They must try to determine the goals of the various interested parties, and build these goals into an acceptable statement of current objectives.

Profit Targets for Managers

Having broadly outlined some of the theoretical considerations affecting the amount of profit required, it is necessary to define some practical working rules for profit planning and control. As a starting point it must be assumed that profits are earned for shareholders. Now profit maximization is not a sound objective in isolation from the amount of shareholders' capital that has to be used in achieving the profit. The true aim, therefore, is to maximize profit per unit of shareholders' funds employed. What is this unit? It cannot be the amount of money paid by shareholders for their shares because the board does not know this. It might be the current market value of the company's share capital, but this could be misleading because market prices fluctuate frequently for a variety of reasons. We are left with two possibilities:

1. Profit per share, also called earnings per share.
2. Earnings per $1 book value of shareholders' capital employed.

The calculation of earnings per share is useful for internal purposes as demonstrating a trend (we hope a favorable one), but as a figure it is not comparable between different companies because a share in one company can have a higher or lower value than a share in another company. If our company is in competition with other companies for shareholders' funds, then something more is needed.

The best consistent measure available to the company of the intrinsic value of its shares is the value of the net assets they represent, i.e., the balance sheet figure of shareholders' capital employed. The usefulness of this figure will depend on the bases used in valuing the assets, but accepting for the moment that there is this problem of valuation, the broad objective of profitability will be expressed as the maximization of:

$$\frac{\text{Earnings attributable to common shareholders}}{\text{Balance sheet value of shareholders' capital employed}}$$

The advantage of this particular formula is that it can be developed for use below board level. The board, guided by the chairman, will decide on the proportions of shareholder and loan capital to be used, and will calculate a weighted average rate of return required on the total capital employed. They will then entrust to the managing director the achievement of this rate on the funds entrusted to him. We now have the familiar internal objective:

$$\frac{\text{Profit before loan interest and tax}}{\text{Total capital employed}}$$

Where there are some funds invested outside the business, or there are items of income and expenditure related purely to financial policy such as dividends and interest receivable, these can be segregated, leaving the formula for the rate of return on operating assets:

$$\frac{\text{Operating profit before tax}}{\text{Operating capital employed}}$$

And this last forumula can then be expanded following the traditional Dupont pattern into:

$$\frac{\text{Operating profit before tax}}{\text{Sales}} \times \frac{\text{Sales}}{\text{Operating capital employed}}$$

And so on by consecutive analysis into a detailed system of ratio analysis.

Keeping the Business in Existence

It is now time to return to the second financial objective suggested at the beginning of this chapter, i.e., "to stay in existence." We have already considered the requirements of this objective in the long term, namely that there shall be sufficient profits to ensure replacement of the assets used in the business. In the short term there is the further need for the business to pay its way—to meet its liabilities as they fall due. The degree to which this need is satisfied is called the "liquidity" of the company. The control of liquidity involves planning and controlling all cash flows, and the amounts invested in the various current assets of the business. We shall study these subjects in detail in Chapters 2 and 3.

The Development of Business Strategies

Once the objectives of the business have been defined, as discussed above, there is a responsibility on managers to decide how these objectives shall be achieved. There are three levels of decision involved:

1. *Broad decisions,* such as those involving the development of a new product, the adoption of a new technology, entry into a new market or expansion of the scope of the business through acquisition of other businesses, are referred to as strategic decisions and are normally formalized in long-range plans, possibly revised annually.
2. *Detailed investment decisions* within the agreed strategies, such as to spend money on a marketing campaign, to purchase particular fixed assets, or to authorize a particular research project—each of these decisions will be made in the light of a financial appraisal, taking account of the profitability of the proposal, the ability to finance it and the likely effect on reported results (the techniques of investment appraisal will be dealt with later).
3. *Operating decisions* reflected in short-term plans or budgets for the business as a whole and for each area of functional responsibility.

Financial Control

The process of control incorporates feedback of data on actual achievement and the follow-up of revealed divergences (variances) from the plan in the sense of:

1. Analysis of causes and responsibilities.
2. Action either to realign future performance with the plan or to modify the plan for future use.

Financial control uses these procedures, and their application to particular problems will be described as each aspect of financial management is dealt with in the chapters that follow.

Summary

A summary of the contents of this chapter is given in the following chart.

We first defined the main functions of management as planning and control. Planning involved developing objectives and then strategies to achieve these objectives. The two fundamental objectives were the marketing objective—what we exist to provide—and the financial objective—what we hope to gain from the marketing objective.

Two aspects of the financial objective were suggested, i.e., to make a profit and to stay in existence.

We then asked why we should make a profit, and decided that it might be

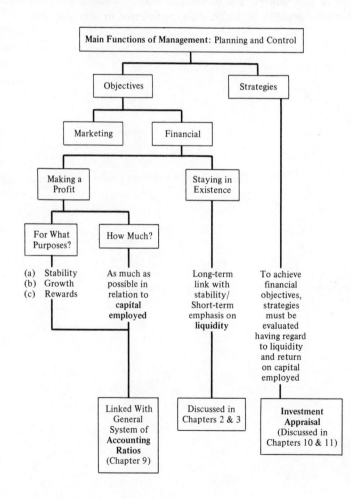

to ensure the stability of the business, or to achieve growth, or to provide a reward for those who were taking the risk of business success or failure.

It was argued that the principal risk-takers were the ordinary shareholders, and on balance we considered that the purpose of profits was to maximize the shareholders' wealth. This in turn was rationalized to mean maximizing the rate of return on shareholders' capital employed. This rate of return concept was used to develop internal measures of financial control, the principal operating ratio being the relationship of operating profit to operating assets employed, from which a comprehensive range of interpretive ratios could be developed.

Our strategies, involving the appraisal on investment proposals, would have to be justified by reference to the rate of return they would yield. Fuller consideration of this subject, and of the problem of financial survival (which was linked with the liquidity of the business), is deferred to later chapters.

Cash Flow
and Liquidity

Business Cash Flows

The primary purpose of cash in a business is to make possible those transactions necessary to set up the business and run it day by day. Before discussing the control of cash, therefore, it is helpful to look at the various transactions in respect of which cash will be received or disbursed. These are summarized in the following diagram. We shall refer to this several times, but for our immediate purpose the important features are as follows:

1. The total cash available in hand or in the bank at any time is represented by the large box in the center left of the diagram.
2. The cash balance with which the business was first established will have been obtained by an injection of capital, as shown in the top left-hand corner of the chart.
3. During the course of the normal trading, manufacturing or service operations of the business, cash will be paid out for the purchase of goods, materials and supplies, for wages and salaries, and for various other expenses such as traveling, postage, insurance and so on.

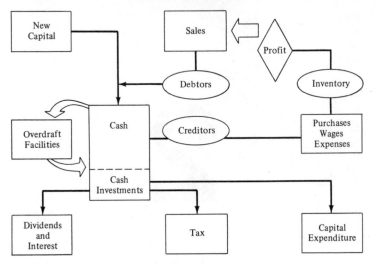

BUSINESS CASH FLOWS

4. The marketable items or services emerging from this expenditure will be sold to customers who will pay for them and thus reinstate the cash balance.

5. If this cycle of events happened instantaneously, then so far as operating transactions were concerned there would never be any shortage of cash. Unfortunately, for nearly every business this is not the case. Various delay factors are interposed, and these are shown in circles on the diagram. Unless this is a cash-and-carry business, customers will not pay immediately, and there will be debtors outstanding at any time. In many businesses the items purchased are not sold again immediately. In a retail or wholesale business it will be necessary to hold shelf stocks of goods from which the customers can select. In a service business there will be stocks of the material used in performing the service, so that work is not interrupted by a shortage of supplies. In a manufacturing business there will at any time be items in process of manufacture, i.e., work in progress. So inventory is another factor delaying the recovery of cash outlays. These two factors, adverse to the cash flow, can normally be offset by a delay factor in payments: the business will owe money to creditors.

6. The net effect of these delays will have been mitigated because one must hope that sales values will have been in excess of the relevant outlays; i.e., there will have been a markup for profit. This profit however has to cover three further items, listed under 7 to 9 below.

7. The majority of businesses will require fixed assets—land, buildings, machinery, motor vehicles, etc. (The outlay on these is shown at the bottom right of the chart as capital expenditure.) This disbursement has

14

to be made before profits can be earned, and will only be recouped over a prolonged period of time, the recovery being represented by a "depreciation" charge in arriving at the profit markup. Although it is not shown on the chart it is possible to impose a delay factor on the acquisition of fixed assets in various ways which will be discussed in Chapter 4, "Sources of Short-Term Finance," in brief by renting or leasing the assets instead of outright purchase.

8. Profit, after allowances for capital expenditure, will give rise to demand for tax. The tax payment will probably occur sometime after a profit has been earned, but will eventually be a complete loss to the cash system of the business.

9. The suppliers of capital to the business must be remunerated. Interest payments will be required periodically and regularly, although dividend payments will be made only if the profits are considered sufficient to justify them. But both types of payment will again be losses to the cash system.

Cash flows will be managed, therefore, by controlling:

1. Working capital—the control of debtors, stocks and creditors is the subject of Chapter 3.
2. Profit margins.
3. Capital expenditure—the appraisal of capital expenditure projects is the subject of Chapter 8.
4. Taxation—tax management is a highly specialized subject outside the scope of this book.
5. Interest and dividends dependent on the capital structure of the company, which is the subject of Chapters 6 and 7.

Cash Forecasting

One objective of cash management is clearly to ensure that the business does not run short of cash. There must always be enough cash available to meet liabilities as they fall due. Equally the business should not be wasteful of cash. The financial manager must be alert for opportunities to make use of any cash temporarily in excess of current needs.

To ensure that these aims are met it is necessary to know in advance as accurately as possible when cash shortages or cash surpluses are likely to occur, so that action can be planned to deal with these eventualities. Cash management depends on cash forecasting.

The most convenient type of cash forecast for this purpose is the receipts and payments forecast, because it is built up in the same form as that used for recording actual transactions in the books of account. A typical form of receipts and payments forecast is illustrated in the following chart, and it covers a period of six months with monthly figures.

The first item, collection of debts, is derived from two sources:

1. The outstanding debtors list at the commencement of the forecast period. Such lists should be under continuous review as part of the company's credit control procedure, and it should be possible to enter the expected collections under the various future months.

2. Estimates of sales invoicing over the six months ahead. The invoice estimates will be converted into collection estimates, using the company's normal credit period, with adjustments for any major items to which

FORM OF RECEIPTS AND PAYMENTS FORECAST

Company	RECEIPTS AND PAYMENTS FORECAST						
	Six months .... 19......						
$	Weeks	1	2	3	4	5	6
Collection of debts	Total						
Due now							
Future invoicing by months							
Other income							
Total in							
Payments on bought ledger							
Creditors now							
Future purchases by months							
Weekly payroll							
Monthly payroll							
Pension contributions							
FICA							
Petty cash payments							
Periodic payments (rents, electricity, etc.)							
Bank charges							
Other payments							
Total out							
Bank overdraft:	Opening						
	Closing						
Limit $							

special credit terms apply or where delays may be anticipated. The collaboration of the sales department will be needed in developing these forecasts.

Other cash receipts may include cash sales (probably extrapolated from past experience), interest receivable at known due dates, and dividends receivable as far as these can be forecast.

A major item of cash outflow will be payments to suppliers. It will be convenient for control if all items dealt with through the purchase ledger are grouped together, though various managers will be involved in forecasting transactions of different types.

Basically the purchasing manager must be required to prepare a forecast of purchase orders due to be placed month by month.

Similar to the debtors forecast, the payments to creditors forecast will start with a list of accounts payable outstanding at the commencement of the forecast period. This and the purchases forecast will have to be converted into a forecast of payment due dates, using the credit period normally taken but adjusted for any special credit terms agreed to by the purchasing manager. The payments forecast should be made initially strictly in accordance with these credit terms. Any deviation from them in order to improve the cash position at any time would be the subject of a later decision after all other possible courses of action had been taken into account.

The remaining payments will be forecast under the headings most suitable for comparison with source documents, for example:

1. Net wages and salaries for comparison with payrolls.
2. Petty cash items in total for comparison with the petty cash books.
3. Special check payments and bank standing orders (analyzed by type of expense to ensure that none is forgotten), which will probably be compared with analysis columns in the main cash book.

Each month net cash inflow or outflow is calculated and adjusted on the previous month's cash balance to give the new month-end balance. It is thus possible to see whether at any time surplus funds will be available. If, on the other hand, the forecast shows excess demands which cannot be met from the available cash or overdraft facilities, then it will be necessary to review the forecast and to make plans for modifying the timing of particular cash flows so as to restore an acceptable balance. Some possible ways of doing this are given in the next section.

A monthly control report should be prepared. This will have the same line analysis as the forecast, and will set out the forecast and actual cash movements on each line and the variances between them. These variances must be analyzed by cause and responsibility so that action can be taken to improve cash control for the future.

Modifying the Forecast Cash Flows

When a cash forecast shows unsatisfactory cash balances throughout, it will probably be necessary to consider ways of obtaining additional capital. But if cash shortages are forecast only as short-term features within a general satisfactory trend, each item in the forecast should be scrutinized for possible modifications to either:

1. Timing, or
2. Amount.

The possibility of changes in amount should be dealt with first, because an improvement in total collectibles or a reduction in total payables is of greater benefit to the business than the mere shifting of an item from one time period to another.

In relation to sales income, forecast sales quantities and prices could be reviewed, but care must be taken that this leads to a new figure which is genuinely expected to occur, and is not just a change from a moderate to an optimistic forecast.

Because of the variety of possibilities (and often their relatively small amounts), miscellaneous receivables may have been ignored but it is possible that in total they could have a significant effect on the cash position. Three particular examples are:

1. Sales of scrap, possibly after sorting and cleaning.
2. Disposals of underutilized fixed assets.
3. Sales of surplus inventory.

In each case the potential sales proceeds have to be compared with the opportunity cost of relinquishing the asset.

In attempting to reduce the amount of proposed expenditure a good starting point is to classify the various items between those that are essential to current operations and those that are discretionary. Discretionary expenses may include such items as subscriptions and donations, books and publications, advertising and publicity. Such expenditure can be reduced without causing short-term damage to the business.

Even the forecast expenditure on essential items may be excessive in amount. Purchases of productive or salable materials may have been related by traditional rules to output requirements taking account of desirable inventory, but they may still be capable of reduction. It is sometimes necessary to impose limits on the total value of purchase orders to be placed each period. This will result in a closer scrutiny not only of quantities requisitioned but also of the production methods and materials specified, and of the inventory that is really essential to survival, and it may cause the buyer to involve himself more fully in the wider aspects of business management.

There is nothing like a shortage of cash (real or induced) to get every manager reviewing the effectiveness of his expenditure (though there must be strong central coordination to ensure that short-term savings do not lead to long-term losses).

Adjusting the timing of forecast cash flows involves:

1. Ensuring that responsibilities have been delegated for fast and effective action on overdue or disputed customer accounts, and that the cash forecast incorporates the collection of such items at target dates.
2. Scheduling the essential payments in such a way that the cash balance is preserved with the least impairment of good relations with the creditors.

The Profit/Cash Forecast

An alternative form of forecast begins with the forecast profit for the period, and then converts the profit into a cash flow by adjusting the various delay factors noted in our earlier diagram (i.e., changes in debtors, inventory and creditors) and the noncash depreciation figure. An operating cash flow having thus been defined, other items such as dividends, interest, tax payments and payments for fixed assets will be adjusted to arrive at the net cash flow for the period. A simple form of profit/cash forecast is illustrated in the diagram on page 20.

This type of forecast is often helpful in explaining gains or losses of cash to nonfinancial managers, since it starts with a profit figure they can recognize from other accounts. It is the form commonly used for the cash budget when presented as part of the master budget of the business, although it is less satisfactory for control purposes than the receipts and payments forecast. In fact the detailed calculations needed for a receipts and payments forecast may have to be carried out before the profit/cash forecast can be established.

Sometimes the profit/cash forecast is a mere statement of differences between two balance sheets, as shown in the example on page 20. This is not completely satisfactory because it does not reveal actual cash flows, such as the payment of tax and dividends and cash aspects of additions to or deletions of fixed assets.

The Statement of Change in Financial Position

When a general manager is faced with a set of historical accounts his almost invariable questions will be:

PROFIT/CASH FORECAST Period ending		
		$000
Net income		276
Add: Depreciation		22
		298
Changes in working capital		
Inventory increase	(57)	
Accounts receivable increase	(32)	
Accounts payable increase	29	
Accruals and prepayments	5	(55)
Operating cash flow		243
Interest and dividends received		10
		253
Interest paid	14	
Dividends paid	17	
Taxation	116	(147)
		106
Fixed asset purchases (less sales)		72
		34
New permanent capital		—
INCREASE/(DECREASE) IN LIQUID BALANCES		34
Cash and short-term investments		
At beginning of period		49
At end of period		83

1. How much profit have we made?
2. Where has all the money gone?

Because of the normal discrepancy between profits and cash flow it is common to include in management reports a historical profit/cash conversion statement in similar form to the profit/cash forecast outlined above. In the historical form it is usually referred to as a statement of Change in Financial Position, or the Source and Application of Funds Statement.

The Accounting Principles Board has issued an opinion, making this a mandatory financial statement.

The objective of such a statement is to show the manner in which the operations of a company have been financed, and in which its financial resources have been used.

A comprehensive illustration follows.

EXAMPLE

The management of Hatfield Corporation, concerned over a decrease in working capital, has provided you with the following comparative analysis of changes in account balances between December 31, 1976 and December 31, 1977:

| | December 31, | | Increase |
Debit Balances	1977	1976	(Decrease)
Cash	$ 145,000	$ 186,000	$ (41,000)
Accounts receivable	253,000	273,000	(20,000)
Inventories	483,000	538,000	(55,000)
Securities held for plant expansion purposes	150,000	—	150,000
Machinery and equipment	927,000	647,000	280,000
Leasehold improvements	87,000	87,000	—
Patents	27,800	30,000	(2,200)
	$2,072,800	$1,761,000	$311,800
Credit Balances			
Allowance for uncollectible accounts receivable	$ 14,000	$ 17,000	$ (3,000)
Accumulated depreciation of machinery and equipment	416,000	372,000	44,000
Allowance for amortization of leasehold improvements	58,000	49,000	9,000
Accounts payable	232,800	105,000	127,800
Cash dividends payable	40,000	—	40,000
Current portion of 6% serial bonds payable	50,000	50,000	—
6% serial bonds payable	250,000	300,000	(50,000)
Preferred stock	90,000	100,000	(10,000)
Common stock	500,000	500,000	—
Retained earnings	422,000	268,000	154,000
Totals	$2,072,800	$1,761,000	$311,800

Additional information:

During 1977 the following transactions occurred:

• New machinery was purchased for $386,000. In addition, certain obsolete machinery, having a book value of $61,000, was sold for $48,000. No other entries were recorded in Machinery and Equipment or related accounts other than provisions for depreciation.

- Hatfield paid $2,000 legal costs in a successful defense of a new patent. Amortization of patents amounting to $4,200 was recorded.
- Preferred stock, par value $100, was purchased at $110 and subsequently canceled. The premium paid was charged to retained earnings.
- On December 10, 1977, the board of directors declared a cash dividend of $0.20 per share payable to holders of common stock on January 10, 1978.
- A comparative analysis of retained earnings as of December 31, 1977 and 1976, is presented below:

	December 31,	
	1977	*1976*
Balance, January 1	$268,000	$131,000
Net income	195,000	172,000
	463,000	303,000
Dividends declared	(40,000)	(35,000)
Premium on preferred stock repurchased	(1,000)	—
	$422,000	$268,000

Required:

1. Prepare a statement of changes in financial position of Hatfield Corporation for the year ended December 31, 1977, based upon the information presented above. The statement should be prepared by using a *working-capital format.*
2. Prepare a schedule of changes in working capital of Hatfield Corporation for the year ended December 31, 1977.

The first step is to compute the change in working capital. Working capital is defined as current assets minus current liabilities. The computation can be made in schedule form, as follows:[*]

Current Assets	*1977*	*1978*	*Increase (Decrease)*
Cash	$145,000	$186,000	$ (41,000)
Accounts receivable	253,000	273,000	

[*]Material from the Uniform CPA Examinations and Unofficial Answers, ©1978 by the American Institute of Certified Public Accountants, Inc., is reprinted with permission.

Current Assets	1977	1978	Increase (Decrease)
Less: Allowance for uncollectibles	14,000	17,000	
Net accounts receivable	$239,000	$256,000	(17,000)
Inventories	483,000	538,000	(55,000)
Current assets	$867,000	$980,000	$(113,000)
Current Liabilities			
Accounts payable	$232,800	$105,000	$ 127,800
Cash dividends payable	40,000	—	40,000
Current portion of 6% serial bonds payable	50,000	50,000	—
Current liabilities	$322,800	$155,000	$ 167,800
Working capital	$544,200	$825,000	$(280,800)

Working capital decreased by $280,800. When a comparison of changes in noncurrent items is made, the same figure should result.

Increase or Decrease in Noncurrent Items			
Assets			
Securities held for plant expansion		$150,000	
Machinery and equipment	$280,000		
Less: Accumulated depreciation	44,000	236,000	
Leasehold improvements	—		
Less: Amortization allowance	9,000	(9,000)	
Patents		(2,200)	$374,800
Liabilities and Equities			
6% serial bonds payable		$ (50,000)	
Preferred stock		(10,000)	
Common stock		—	
Retained earnings		154,000	94,000
Net difference			$280,800

When presented in a source and application format, the changes would appear as follows:

Sources		
Working capital provided from operations:		
Net Income		$195,000
Add (deduct) items not requiring working capital:		
Depreciation expense	$ 89,000	
Loss on sale of machinery	13,000	
Patent amortization	4,200	
Amortization of leasehold improvements	9,000	115,200
		$310,200

Increase or Decrease in Noncurrent Items		
Other sources:		
Machinery sale	48,000	$358,200
Applications		
Legal fees	$ 2,000	
Machinery purchase	386,000	
Preferred stock purchase	11,000	
Cash dividends	40,000	
Purchase of securities	150,000	
6% serial bonds payable	50,000	639,000
Net decrease in working capital		$280,800

Cash Balance Required

The purpose of this example was to ensure the availability of a cash balance. The question may be asked whether it is possible to define the amount of cash which ought to be held at any time.

Cash is needed for three reasons:

1. To finance transactions (which was the main theme of the previous paragraphs).
2. As a precaution—a safeguard against inaccuracies in cash forecasts—bearing in mind that every forecast by its very nature will be inaccurate.
3. For speculative purposes—to take advantage of any profitable opportunities that arise. This need is probably only significant in businesses which are inherently speculative. In other cases there would probably be advance warning of the need for cash, and special financing arrangements could be made.

What average cash balance then should be held to finance normal transactions, including any necessary margin of safety? The word "normal" is important because it may be assumed that small deviations from the norm will be covered by overdraft facilities.

This is a question closely akin to one we shall be asking about inventory in Chapter 3, and attempts are sometimes made to establish a similar equation based on:

1. The "holding cost" of cash (i.e., the opportunity cost of keeping the cash uninvested).

2. The "procurement cost" of cash (i.e., the transaction cost of converting securities into cash, or otherwise obtaining new funds).

The estimates used in such calculations are likely to be suspect, and the model to which they give rise is only applicable when the demand for cash is reasonably consistent from period to period.

Other mathematical models have been suggested by various authors, but they tend to be mainly of academic interest only.

A simpler approach to the definition of the required cash balance is by the use of ratios.

One such measure is the ratio between the sales for a period and the opening cash balance:

$$\text{Cash turnover} = \frac{\text{Sales for period}}{\text{Initial cash balance}}$$

This is sometimes called the cash velocity. (The resemblance to the inventory turnover ratio will be obvious.)

As with all management ratios one is looking for consistency period by period within the company, or a trend of improvement which, in this case, would be higher sales per unit of cash held. If, for example, the cash velocity last period was:

$$\frac{\text{Sales}}{\text{Initial cash balance}} = \frac{\$180,000}{\$9,000} = 20x$$

Then an increase of sales to $225,000 without a change in cash holding would increase the velocity to $25x$. In other words, the cash balance would have been kept to $9,000 instead of rising to $225,000/20 = $11,250, so there would be a saving of interest or a gain at the opportunity cost rate on $2,250. Again, like other ratios this ratio cannot be used in isolation. An increase in sales without an increase in cash balance might mean that the company had become less able to pay its debts as they fell due, signifying that it was overtrading. It might be possible to use this ratio for comparison with an average for the industry, but probably not with individual firms within the industry since special factors might affect the balance held by a particular firm at its year-end date (especially if the business were seasonal, or if the firm under review were accumulating cash for a specific project).

Going outside a particular industry we can find an enormous range of velocity ratios, ranging from about $6x$ (General Electric 1974) to nearly $80x$.

A second ratio quite often found is that between the cash balance and the total current assets:

$$\text{Proportion of cash held} = \frac{\text{Cash balance}}{\text{Current Assets}}$$

A wide range of figures between different industries will be found. Based on transaction analysis or past trends, the company could set a minimum proportion of cash holdings to current assets with the object not of using this as an absolute limit but of giving an opportunity for reviewing the reasons for any deviation from the norm.

In general the use of simple ratios has limited value in cash planning. There is no adequate substitute for detailed cash forecasts, possibly linked with a financial model of the business as a whole.

For the outside observer, and to some extent for the board of a company, useful information can be derived from a trend of liquidity ratios incorporating not merely cash but also those elements of working capital which are readily convertible into cash. This concept of liquidity was built into the source and application of funds statement previously described.

Liquidity

When analyzing a company's balance sheet without access to detailed cash flow information, it is customary to calculate two ratios as indicators of the company's ability to pay its way:

$$1.\ \textit{Current ratio} = \frac{\text{Total current assets}}{\text{Total current liabilities}}$$

$$2.\ \textit{Quick ratio} = \frac{\text{Total quick assets}}{\text{Total current liabilities}}$$

Looking back to the cash flow chart at the beginning of this chapter, total current assets would be inventory (and any work in progress), accounts receivable, cash and short-term cash investments, in other words, those assets which are continuously becoming available as cash in the ordinary course of the operating cycle.

Current liabilities would be the accounts payable for operating supplies and expenses (as shown) plus any payables for credit expenditure, taxation, interest and dividends and possibly loan repayments falling due within the relevant period. In the case of most companies, this would normally be one year.

Taking one year as the "current" period, the current ratio is an adequate reflection of liquidity as demonstrated at that point in time, unless, for example:

1. The operating cycle is so long that part of the inventory or work in progress will not be converted into sales until after the end of the year (as might be the case with a public works contractor).
2. Because spasmodic customer demand is linked with a high level of service from inventory, it is necessary to hold some inventory which will not be turned over within the year (e.g., a capital equipment supply business).

3. The figure for receivables includes contract retention moneys, or items under dispute which will not be collected within the year.

If such features exist, then this should be known from the nature of the business, and one would expect to see a higher current ratio than in businesses with fast-moving inventory and restricted credit terms.

How should a bank overdraft be treated? Any outstanding overdraft is in fact a current liability since it is repayable on demand, but there are two possible arguments against this treatment:

1. If the business is profitable and is generating sufficient cash flow to keep within an agreed overdraft limit, then often the overdraft will be allowed to remain as a medium-term source of finance, when it should be ignored in liquidity calculations.

2. If the outstanding overdraft is less than the agreed limit available, then at that point the intention would appear to be **not** that the overdraft should be repaid but that additional cash will be made available—if the overdraft is ignored, the cash balance from time to time would vary according to the extent to which the limit had been utilized.

A workable rule would appear to be to treat the nonutilized limit as cash, and to include the total overdraft as a current liability. Where the extent of the limit is not known, it may be more informative to make two calculations of current ratio, one including the existing overdraft as a current liability, and a second calculation ignoring it.

Example of Current Ratio Calculation

	Year 1 $000	Year 2 $000
Current assets:		
Inventory	500	900
Accounts receivable	300	600
Cash	80	280
	$880	$1,780
Current liabilities:		
Accounts payable	290	540
Bank overdraft (total limit: $1,000)	—	1,000
	$290	$1,540
Current ratio:		
1. Ignoring overdraft	3.0 : 1	3.3 : 1

	Year 1 $000	Year 2 $000
2. Including overdraft		1.2 : 1
3. Year 1, adding limit to cash balance and treating it as a current liability	1.4 : 1	

The comparison at 1, or the comparison of 2 with 3 both suggest that there is evidence of deliberate liquidity planning. But to confirm this it would be necessary to validate the inventory, accounts receivable and accounts payable figures by calculating such asset management ratios as were available; for example, the trend of accounts receivable to sales, and of inventory to sales or to cost input figures (if they were available).

However they are compared, the figures in the example show an ability to meet current liabilities out of current assets.

At what figure should the current ratio stand? There is no answer to this, but it should be consistent within the same company, and it may be measured against an industry average, since there should be a norm for any particular type of business.

The liquid (or "quick") ratio is based on the assumption that inventory will not be converted into cash quickly enough to meet the time scale for the payment of the accounts payable, and the business must therefore look to its accounts receivable and cash balance to cover the current liabilities. The comments made about bank overdraft facilities apply equally to this ratio, except that in practice the bank may well be prepared to look to the realization of inventory to cover its repayment; in this case the unused overdraft limit is a quick asset but the total overdraft limit is not a quick payable.

The traditional yardstick was that the quick ratio must not be less than 1:1, but bearing in mind the enormous range of realizability of inventory (and of accounts receivables) and the quality of the outstanding liabilities, there can be no general rule. Many companies are found operating successfully with liquid ratios of less than 1:1; again there will be a norm for a particular business or type of business.

Ratios give rise to questions, but they do not provide final answers. The only test of liquidity is the detailed time matching of transactions as was done in the cash forecast.

Investing Surplus Funds

If the cash forecast for a business shows surplus funds becoming available, then plans should be made for putting them to use. If such surpluses appear to be a continuing feature of current operating conditions then thought should be given to plans for expansion, since it is assumed that the business can make more profitable use of the money internally than by investing it outside (other than perhaps in an acquisition of a trade investment). However, the surpluses may be transitory, either because they are being accumulated deliberately for some purpose, such as the purchase of equipment, or the payment of taxes, or because the business is seasonal and the funds will eventually be required to finance off-peak activities.

It is important to schedule in detail, with frequent reviews, how much money will be available for various periods of time, so that it can be put to the best possible use. Small amounts which are required to be kept liquid are probably best placed on deposit with a bank or other facility. The rate of interest will be low, but only short notice is required for withdrawal. When large sums are available there is a greater range of investment alternatives. Commercial paper and treasury notes are liquid, as are negotiable certificates of deposit issued by the commercial banks.

The purpose of this type of investment is to squeeze extra profit out of money which is normally in use in the operation of the business. It does not give full scope for portfolio planning, which is essential when funds are available for investment over a long period. (This point will be discussed in detail in a later chapter after the factors influencing the market price of stocks have been reviewed.)

The main principle involved in planning the investment of short-term cash surpluses is to match investment maturities with cash needs. Before considering investment, therefore, it is necessary to have reliable cash movements forecast, so that one knows with reasonable certainty how much cash will be available for what periods of time.

The second principle is to invest for as long as possible, because interest rates are higher for longer periods. Opposed to this principle is the need to have a margin of safety; this may be a bank overdraft arrangement or may take the form of slightly more liquidity in the investment portfolio than the forecast strictly requires.

The size of the fund available for investment will have an effect on how profitably it can be used, both because large funds can bear the cost of a professional investment manager and because such funds can be placed directly on the money market rather than through the company's bank or brokerage firm.

At one time considerable profits were made by using bank overdraft arrangements to provide cash for investment at short term outside the business. Quite apart from the risk of speculative losses this is now regarded as a misuse of bank finance, particularly when the amount of credit is limited (unless, of course, a bank loan is made specifically to finance an investment project).

Cash Management in a Group of Companies

Within a group of companies it is often considered desirable for cash to be managed by a central department which will:

1. Gather in all surplus funds from the various companies and redistribute them in accordance with the investment opportunities which best serve the group objectives.
2. Dictate the dividend distributions of the subsidiary companies to ensure that funds are retained where they are needed within the group.
3. Arrange the investment outside the business of funds which are temporarily surplus to group needs.
4. Negotiate centrally any bank overdraft limits, and the raising of new long-term capital.

With regard to internal investment it sometimes appears that priority is given to projects from those companies which are already profitable (since they are able to show better incremental returns than those which are currently less successful); and it is argued that the loss-making companies may well have the greater need for investment so that they can break through into profitable operations. The argument is probably not valid if the group has a clearly defined long-range corporate plan and if it is using the best available techniques of investment appraisal, such as those which will be discussed in Chapter 10. It must also be borne in mind that the least successful companies may be those which at present have the weakest managers, so that an organization decision must take priority over investment decisions.

In relation to overdraft limits, the argument for group central negotiation is that only one banker will be involved who will be well informed on the whole of the group's activities, and that all the resources of the group will be available as security. This does, however, put the whole group at risk if credit limits are reduced. If the various companies have a good local relationship with the banks they have used individually in the past, it can happen that the total of locally negotiated overdrafts is greater than could have been obtained centrally, while the withdrawal of one overdraft limit still leaves the other companies untouched.

If one bank is used by the whole group with local accounts for the various companies, then agreement can be reached that in calculating bank charges all the accounts are consolidated, so that overdrafts in one area are offset against credit balances in other areas. If there is only one central bank account, then to avoid loss of interest in respect of cash-in-transit, arrangements should be made for immediate notification of deposits at branch banks. Some groups require accounts receivable payments to be made to a central cash office, but it is not always easy to obtain full compliance from customers and it can hamper de-centralized credit control procedures.

The payment of accounts payable centrally is easier to arrange, though it may involve delays in payment if invoices have to be approved by local offices. Whether centralized purchasing is beneficial will depend on whether the advantages of standardized specifications and the negotiation of bulk discounts are offset by a loss of specialized purchasing skills for a diverse range of products and by delays in the procurement of urgently needed supplies.

The majority of the foregoing comments will apply equally to a single company having divisional profit centers in scattered locations.

Summary

Having looked at the transaction requirements of a business, we have reviewed various management ratios designed to give indications of the adequacy of cash balances and of the working capital structure. Although these will give warnings of deviations from what is regarded as a normal position, they are not instruments for the control in detail of cash availability. For this purpose cash forecasting is essential, as is the review in detail of actual cash movements against the forecast.

The receipts and payments forecast is most suitable for control purposes, but the profit/cash forecast is often helpful in presenting the facts to managers. This type of presentation is also used for a historical source and application of funds statement.

In planning cash availability, account must be taken of the need for a safety margin and, where appropriate, of funds for speculation.

All surplus cash should be put to use, possibly by short-term investment.

In a group of companies the group central office is often best able to exercise control in the interests of the group as a whole.

In Chapter 3 we shall consider the control of the other elements in working capital (i.e., accounts receivable, accounts payable and inventory), and in Chapter 4 we shall begin to consider outside sources of finance.

3

Management
of Working
Capital

Questions About Working Capital

Working capital, apart from cash balances which were the subject of Chapter 2, comprises inventory of various kinds (raw materials, work in progress and finished goods) and accounts receivable balances, primarily the outstandings receivable from customers; in other words the current assets of the business, which are offset by the current liabilities in arriving at the figure of net working capital.

In managing working capital three questions have to be asked:

1. How much working capital should a business hold?

2. What proportion of the total current assets should be in the different forms of current asset?

3. How should working capital be financed? This question will be touched on briefly in the present chapter but is dealt with in more detail in Chapter 4.

Working Capital Ratios

It is possible to take an overall view of the level of working capital by establishing ratios linking working capital or its constituent parts with other aspects of the business, and having decided on normal or desired relationships to monitor deviations from the norm. Such variations may in fact be fully justified, but it is good to make sure that the causes are known and the effects evaluated.

A commonly used ratio is:

$$\frac{\text{Working capital}}{\text{Total assets}} \quad \text{or, alternatively,} \quad \frac{\text{Working capital}}{\text{Fixed assets}}$$

This ratio was selected as one of the five key predictors of corporate bankruptcy in a study by E. I. Altman published in 1968 (the others, in broad terms, being return on total capital employed, sales to capital employed, retained earnings to capital employed, and a form of gearing ratio, i.e., market value of equity to book value of total indebtedness).

The implication is that a high proportion of working capital to total assets gives the business greater freedom to adapt to changing circumstances, to realize assets and invest the proceeds in different ways, or to boost sales by a temporary rundown of liquidity. What is a normal ratio, however, will depend on the type of industry; for example, continuous flow production of chemicals or steel will need a relatively high investment in fixed assets. Neither investment in working capital nor investment in fixed assets is an end in itself. One needs to look at those assets in relation to what they produce—output, sales and profit. Nevertheless, as part of a general system of ratio analysis the ratio of working capital to total assets contributes another control indicator, and deviations from trend in this ratio require investigation.

A cluster of ratios normally calculated when interpreting business accounts is:

Accounts receivable:Sales

Inventory:Sales

Accounts payable:Sales

Together giving—

Net working capital:Sales

Cash is ignored in the above analysis. Whereas in the absence of some change of policy one might expect accounts receivable, inventory and accounts payable to vary in sympathy with sales, cash has a variety of uses and can also appear in the guise of overdrafts without appearing in the balance sheet. It is therefore better dealt with separately and in detail.

It should be noted that while the accounts receivable:sales ratio can also be expressed in physical terms (i.e., so many days' sales outstanding), this cannot be done for inventory or accounts payable because they are stated at cost whereas the sales figure is at selling price. The inventory and accounts payable ratios therefore merely express relationships, that is, they indicate the rate of variability of these items with sales value.

Inflation normally has a distorting effect on these ratios because selling prices are likely to change at different times and by different amounts than costs; even the accounts receivable figure will be at old sales values that are likely to be different from those used in reporting the comparative value of sales. If possible it is helpful to express all the items at standard prices or, if there are homogeneous units of sales, the ratios can then be expressed in $ per unit of sales.

These ratios, if consistently expressed, are considered useful as indicators of the amount of working capital needed per $1 sales; they act as warning signals for investigation if they show marked deviations from either a standard or from previous trends.

The Working Capital Cycle

The working capital cycle (or operating cycle) is the length of time between a company's paying for materials entering into inventory and receiving the inflow of cash from sales.

Taking the business's accounts (either historical or budgeted), the time cycle can be calculated in the following way:

Basic data	Average amount outstanding	Average value per calendar day (365 days)
	$	
Inventory: Raw materials	80,000	
Work in progress	60,000	
Finished goods	40,800	
Accounts receivable	100,100	
Accounts payable	(70,400)	
Average working capital	$210,500	
Sales		$1,540
Cost of sales		$1,200
Purchases of raw material		$ 640

Working capital cycle

				Days
Raw material holding:	Raw material inventory	$80,000		
	Daily purchases	$640	=	125
Less: Credit taken:	Accounts payable	$70,400		
	Daily purchases	$640	=	110
				15
Production period:	Work in progress	$60,000		
	*Daily cost of sales	$1,200	=	50
Finished goods turnover:	Finished goods	$40,800		
	Daily cost of sales	$1,200	=	34
Customer credit period:	Accounts receivable	$100,000		
	Daily sales	$1,540	=	65
Total Cycle				164

*Alternatively, the daily cost of inputs to work in progress.

The above analysis is carried out:

1. To improve our previous working capital ratios for control purposes—accounts payable and inventory are now related not to sales value but to purchases.
2. To emphasize the total time lag within the operating cycle, and to indicate the relative significance of its constituent parts as a starting point for efforts to reduce the working capital tie-up by action appropriate to each element.
3. To provide a series of days' equivalents which can be used in budgeting or forecasting to translate sales and costs budgets into budgets of working capital values.

When a new business is commenced, the finance required for working capital will build up progressively as materials are first procured, then labor is applied in manufacture and finished inventory is accumulated. Once a steady level of production and sales is achieved, each cycle will overlap the others, giving a constant total of days' tie-up. However, many businesses do *not* enjoy steady and continuous production and sales; some businesses are seasonal and others spasmodic. In reviewing the working capital cycle from time to time it is necessary to remember these variations in the level of activity.

Having looked at working capital as a whole, we have already begun to study its constituent parts, namely, accounts payable, accounts receivable and inventory. We shall now look at these individually in greater detail.

The Control of Accounts Payable

The number of days' credit taken from suppliers is to a large extent under the control of the business, and may be varied from time to time. It is generally important, however, to be consistent in one's credit policy. A company may be a slow payer, but if the supplier knows he will get paid regularly he may accept this delay. He may nevertheless reimburse himself by increases in price, which will then in effect include the interest charge which the paying company would have incurred if it had borrowed money to pay its accounts earlier.

Although the practice of offering cash discounts for prompt settlement has diminished in recent years, some cash discounts may be available. Whether it is beneficial to take advantage of these will depend on:

1. Whether the annual discount rate compensates for the opportunity cost of early payment.
2. If so, whether this gain is counteracted by the extra cost of handling quick-payment invoices separately from the mainstream routines of invoice processing.

For example, a company normally pays its suppliers in the third month after the month of invoicing, but is now offered 2½% discount for payment within thirty days in respect of invoices totalling $10,000 per month. It estimates that the cost in staff overtime of handling these invoices separately from the normal batches would be $15 per month. The bank borrowing rate is 12½%. It can be calculated that:

1. In order to pay these particular invoices two months earlier than at present, the company will need $20,000 more funds which, at 12½% per annum, will cost $2,500 per annum.
2. Each month it will gain a cash discount of 2½% × $10,000 = $250 or $3,000 per annum.
3. By taking advantage of the discount it will gain $(3,000–2,500) = $500 per annum less $180, the cost of additional overtime.

   If it is company policy to take cash discounts, then there should be management reports showing the discount received month by month as a percentage of total purchase values.

The credit period taken should be as long as possible subject to consideration of the following factors:

1. Increases in purchase prices, or deterioration in service, to compensate the supplier for the slow payment of his bills.
2. Possible disruption of the business if creditors cut off supplies.

3. Inability to obtain new sources of supply because of the company's poor credit rating.

4. The need not to put suppliers out of business due to shortage of cash—this danger is mainly confined to small suppliers, and some companies make a practice of paying these more quickly than the other creditors.

5. The cost of dealing with telephone calls, letters and statements in respect of overdue accounts.

A periodic management report should be made stating the average credit period taken in paying suppliers this month and in previous months.

Control of Accounts Receivable (Credit Control)

The object of giving credit is to increase sales, while the object of increasing sales is to increase profit.

Some of the reasons why increased profit may not be earned are illustrated in the following example.

EXAMPLE

A company conducts a cash sales business with average annual sales of $120,000. The marginal contribution from these sales is at the rate of 25% on sales value. Inventory, less accounts payable applicable thereto, is currently $10,000. The sales manager states that by giving one month's credit to all customers he could boost the annual sales by 33-1/3%; alternatively, he could double them if two months' credit were given. The cost of operating the necessary credit control procedures is estimated at $6,000 per annum in either case. Bad debts would probably be incurred, estimated at 1% of sales value if one month's credit were given, or 2% of sales value if customers were allowed two months to pay. The company's cost of capital is 15%.

The first year's results under the three alternatives are tabulated below:

Sales	No credit	One month's credit	Two month's credit
Sales	$120,000	$160,000	$240,000
Accounts receivable	–	13,333	40,000
Inventory (less accounts payable: 1/12 of sales value	10,000	13,333	20,000
Total	$ 10,000	$ 26,666	$ 60,000

Sales	No credit	One month's credit	Two month's credit
Increase in working capital through granting credit		$ 16,666	$ 50,000
	$	$	$
Marginal contribution	30,000	40,000	60,000
Less Cost of:			
Credit control		(6,000)	(6,000)
Bad debts		(1,600)	(4,800)
Relevant comparable profits	$ 30,000	$ 32,400	$ 49,200
		$	$
Increase in profits		2,400	19,200
But the company requires a return of 15% on the increase in capital employed, i.e.,		2,500	7,500
The net advantage (or disadvantage) of the proposed changes in credit policy is therefore		($100)	$ 11,700

Note that we have not shown an "interest" charge on the increased working capital because in due course the increase in inventory and accounts receivable will in effect be financed out of the improved profits, and no specific borrowing may be needed. However, regardless of how the working capital is financed it must still produce the required rate of return.

This example makes the fairly obvious points that giving credit involves costs, including the opportunity cost of additional capital employed. In some cases these costs will cancel or outweigh any gains from increased business. In some cases the granting of credit may not increase the sales of the business, but may be justified because it will prevent a loss of sales to a competitor.

The above tabulation will immediately suggest three subjects for management reports in connection with credit policy:

1. Accounts receivable expressed in relationship to sales—either as a percentage or as a number of weeks' sales. This provides an overall confirmation that the business is effective in carrying out its own credit policy.

   With a seasonal business, however, these calculations could be misleading. If $240,000 annual sales occurred at $50,000 per quarter for the first three quarters of the year, and $90,000 in the last quarter, then accounts receivable of $40,000 at the end of the year would represent only $\frac{40,000}{90,000} \times \frac{52}{4}$ weeks, i.e., approximately 5.8 weeks' sales.

Another disadvantage of overall averages is that they may conceal the fact that some long-overdue receivables are being compensated by quicker collections from other customers. For management control in detail there is no substitute for a complete listing of receivable accounts, analyzed by age, compiled every month.

2. Bad debts as a percentage of sales value, or reported in detail.
3. Credit control costs. We shall look at these again after discussing the operation of a credit control system.

Credit control involves three types of action:

1. Deciding the normal credit period to be allowed.
2. Establishing credit limits for individual customers.
3. Implementing the system (that is to say, ensuring that credit limits and the credit period are not exceeded).

Deciding the Credit Period

If a business is offering a unique product or service, or one for which demand exceeds supply, there may be no need to offer credit terms at all. In other cases the starting point in deciding credit policy is a review of the credit terms offered by competitors, and from this basis the credit terms of the particular business will be developed.

Longer credit may be offered if this will enable the business to capture a larger share of the available market, or to break into a new market. The initial effect of granting longer credit may be adverse because of the extra costs involved, but it is necessary to look to the longer term where, among other possibilities, selling prices may be increased because competitors have been eliminated in the "credit war." (This, of course, assumes an absence of statutory restraints.)

Shorter credit may be imposed if demand is inelastic, so that the quantity sold will not be affected simply by changes in credit terms.

Establishing Credit Limits

The fact that the business has a credit policy does not mean that credit terms will be granted to every customer. It is not always easy to decide whether a particular customer is "creditworthy" in the sense that he has both the ability and the inclination to pay at the due date. Many companies require cash with order from new customers until their creditworthiness has been established.

In assessing the creditworthiness of a customer two things are necessary:

1. Facts about his business, in particular whether it is profitable, whether it is generating or has access to sufficient cash to meet its liabilities, and whether it has suitable assets available to cover the claims of unsecured creditors in the event of liquidation. In brief, it is necessary to analyze the accounts of the business. It is helpful also if the customers will supplement these with the sort of information they do not give; e.g., the current order book, any plans for future development, and the condition and market value of the assets.
2. Opinions about the business and the people running it, either formed from personal contacts (salesman with buyer, accountant with accountant, or at director level) or obtained from third parties such as business associates, mutual acquaintances or employees changing jobs.

If the customer is a publicly held company the latest annual report will be available and should be inspected. Privately held companies may have audited statements available for inspection.

If the analysis of annual reports or audited financial statements shows consistent or improving ratios (i.e., there is evidence of purposeful financial management), the assumption is commonly made that such good management will continue.

There is often delay in having financial statements published, and in cases of doubt it is desirable to ask the customer to provide the most recently audited statements even if they have not yet been published.

Other sources of information are:

1. Reports from credit bureaus or Dun and Bradstreet—these make use of other creditors' experience as well as of published data.
2. Reports from the relevant trade association, if one exists.
3. Trade references from other companies with which the customer has done business.
4. Bank references—these may not give a lot of information but they tend to use a series of standardized replies, and experience with these will indicate the relative credit rating of the customer in question.
5. Reports published in trade journals or the financial press dealing either with the customer company or with the type of business in which it is engaged.

In assessing the creditworthiness of overseas customers, reports from bankers are an important source of information. It is also necessary to weigh the risks of the customer being prevented from paying either through political or exchange control restrictions. On all these matters the World Trade Institute or the international department of many banks can usually give guidance.

If the customer's creditworthiness appears to be established, the next stage is to decide the amount of credit he will be given.

Theoretically there are three possible ways of doing this:

1. *The income or cash flow method,* which requires knowledge of the amounts of cash becoming available to the customer, and how he proposes spending them, thus indicating his ability to pay the supplier's invoices— this method is possible between a bank manager and his client seeking an overdraft or loan, but seldom in business life.

2. *The capital structure method,* under which the value of uncharged assets in the customer's last balance sheet is estimated, and the credit limit will be a percentage of this value. This is a necessary calculation when the proposed value of future transactions will involve a major increase in the customer's total indebtedness, but it is not an indicator of liquidity, and is not particularly relevant to small transactions in the ordinary course of trade.

3. *The requirement method,* which is almost always used in practice. If the customer is creditworthy then we should be able to rely on him to pay any amounts arising from the ordinary course of business. The amount of credit granted, therefore, is based on the value of business which the customer expects to place with the supplier each month. The forecast monthly sales to the customer are multiplied by the number of months' credit laid down as company policy to given that customer's credit limit. If, for example, a customer proposed placing orders totaling $1,500 per month with a supplier whose credit terms required payment by the end of the month following the date of invoice (say, two months' credit), the credit limit granted him might be 2 X $1,500 = $3,000 outstanding on the ledger account at any time.

For customers of international repute it may be decided that no limitation of credit is necessary, but the financial difficulties of several major companies in recent years must be a warning against the automatic granting of unlimited credit.

Processing Incoming Orders

The amount appearing on the customer's ledger account at any time will, of course, result from posting the orders he has placed, so that if the value of orders in any period were to exceed the original forecast this might not become apparent until after posting. At that time the outstanding balance on the ledger would suddenly be found to be in excess of the agreed limit.

To safeguard against this possibility an order register may be kept for each customer, showing the value of orders placed for delivery in particular months. Each incoming order will then be checked against the register to confirm that it will not cause the credit limit to be exceeded. This could be a cumbersome procedure, and normally it would only be used for:

1. New customers until their compliance with credit limits had been established.
2. Customers who had consistently failed to adhere to their credit limits in the past. (It might be better in such cases to withdraw credit facilities completely.)

All incoming orders should be checked to ensure that they are placed on the customer's official order form and authorized by somebody purporting to have the power to place that type of order.

Sales Invoicing

As far as the customer is concerned, the company's credit period does not begin until he receives an invoice. Even then his accounting procedures probably involve a monthly cutoff date for the receipt of invoices, so that any invoice received after, say, the 28th day of the month will be treated as belonging to the succeeding month.

It is important, therefore, that delays in invoicing be kept to a minimum. The causes of delay are nearly all within the control of the company, and may include:

1. An inflexible routine in the sales invoicing department (perhaps invoices are issued only on certain days in the month).
2. A requirement for approval or signature of sales invoices by members of the sales staff who are often away from the office.
3. Failure to agree on prices for special work.
4. For jobbing work, and in other cases where prices are linked with costs, excessively slow procedures for calculating costs.

Debt Collection

There must be no slackness in pursuing the collection of debts. In most businesses purely formal reminders are ineffective, and therefore a waste of money. When an account has passed its due date there should be early personal contact with the customer either by telephone or a salesman's visit or by a letter addressed to a named person in the company. If necessary there may be a follow-up at a higher level of authority, and this should be followed by a threat to cut off supplies.

The value of legal action against debtors needs to be assessed. When this stage is reached, the likelihood of the customer's paying is sharply reduced, and additional legal costs may never be recouped. On the other hand the action may deter potential future defaulters.

From the point of view of the salesman every customer is valuable. From the financial officer's standpoint the marginal contribution from goods sold to a late payer will be eroded by financing and clerical costs until a stage is reached when the business would be more profitable without sales to that particular customer.

Monthly lists of outstanding debts were mentioned above, and a simple form for such a report is illustrated below:

Outstanding debts report as at .... 19......						
Last month's total		This month's total	Age of debt			
			Current	1 month	2 months	over 2 months
$ 1,247	J Brown	$ 1,973	$	$	$	$
	Inv 1681		502			
	1573			786		
	1549			600		
	1302				85	
425	G Green	437				
	Inv 1644		12			
	1099					425
	Etc.					
$ 22,665	Total	$24,118	$15,678	$6,029	$1,929	$482
	% of total		65%	25%	8%	2%

Overdue debts should be the subject of formal discussion between the sales and financial managers. The reasons for delayed payment should be noted, and decisions should be made on the action to be taken in each case and the people responsible for taking it.

Although the salesman's job is not complete until his customer has paid the money due, it is often advantageous for the more rigorous collection procedures to be handled by finance staff, leaving the salesman free to exercise his persuasive influence with the customer's buying department.

Costs of Credit Control

The costs of credit control are now seen to include the costs of:

1. Assessing and reviewing creditworthiness.
2. Checking incoming orders.
3. Sales ledger keeping and invoicing.
4. Debt collection.

These costs may occur in various departments of the business, but there should be some means of identifying them and collecting the total cost, which will have to be taken into account in reviewing the benefits of the credit policy.

Cash Discount

An alternative or supplement to a formal credit policy is to offer a discount for prompt payment. In considering this possibility it is important to bear in mind that:

1. Customers who normally pay promptly will now become entitled to a discount, although there will be no improvement in the timing of their payments.
2. Some late payers will nevertheless deduct a discount from their settlements, and there may be some practical difficulty in recovering these incorrect deductions.

As an illustration of these points, consider the following:

X Company has monthly sales of $90,000. About half of its customers pay their accounts within the month of invoicing, one-third in the following month, and the remainder during the second month after invoicing. It has been decided to offer 1¼% discount for payment within the month of invoicing. During the first six months of the new policy, collections are improved so that on average three-quarters of the customers pay in the first month, this improvement coming entirely from those customers who had previously paid in the month after invoicing. The current cost of capital is 15% a year. Ignoring any additional clerical costs is the change in policy financially justified?

The answer is *no,* as shown in the following calculations:

	Month		
	1	*2*	*3*
Collections:	$	$	$
Old system	45,000	30,000	15,000

	Month		
	1	2	3
New system	67,500	7,500	15,000
Discount: 1¼% X $67,500	$843.75		
Interest saved: 15/12% X			
$(67,500 − 45,000 = 22,500)	$281.25		

The proposal therefore is *not* justified.

Financing Accounts Receivables

There are various other ways in which a business can speed up its collection of cash without requiring the customer to pay any earlier. The most common examples are:

1. *The use of bills of exchange* given by the cusomer and discounted by the supplier. These are used to a small extent in domestic trade, but are very common in export business. The rate of discount will, of course, depend on the status of the customer.

2. *Factoring the accounts receivable.* In its simplest form this means selling the collectible accounts to a finance house (the factor) who will then be responsible for sales accounting and collection procedures. The factor will, if required, advance up to about 80% of the value of the debts immediately at a financing charge of about 3% above the clearing banks' base rate. The service charge for sales accounting and debt collection may be up to 2½% on sales value. For an additional fee, factors will also offer 100% protection against bad debts.

   As comprehensive service, factoring may justify its cost, but purely as a source of finance it is expensive. It is in any case only suitable for businesses in which the credit risks arise primarily from assessments of creditworthiness. It is not suitable for the sort of specialist engineering or service business in which accounts can be disputed on the grounds of errors in specification or poor quality of work.

3. *Discounting.* The discounter will advance up to 80% of approved accounts, against a bill of exchange given by the supplier. No services of any kind are performed. This facility is not available to very small companies, and is expensive.

For the sake of completeness in dealing with customer credit we have here digressed briefly into the field of short-term finance, which will be dealt with in greater detail in Chapter 4.

Personal Guarantees

A form of protection against bad debts is to take a personal guarantee in support of the customer's account. The value of personal guarantees varies considerably and they are likely to present two problems:

1. It may be more difficult to assess the creditworthiness of an individual guarantor than of the trade customer.
2. The guarantor does not normally expect to be called upon to pay, and there may be difficulties in obtaining money from him when the need arises.

These problems do not occur to the same extent when the guarantor is another company, often the parent company in the customer's group.

Control Of Inventory

The financial decisions relating to inventory have certain special features, but looking first at salable inventory (finished goods) we can postulate that the object of holding inventory is to increase sales, and that the object of increasing sales is to increase profit. We can then create a simple model similar to that for accounts receivable.

EXAMPLE

The Y Company makes cash sales from inventory, and obtains an average rate of marginal contribution of 25% on sales value. When it holds inventory equivalent to one month's cost of sales it achieves sales of $100,000 per annum.

It is estimated that by doubling the inventory available an increase of 25% in sales value could be achieved; alternatively, if three months' inventory were held then sales could be increased by 35% from the present level. The effect on profits of these two alternatives, including any relevant changes in costs, is illustrated as follows:

	One month's inventory	Two months' inventory	Three months' inventory
	$	$	$
Sales	100,000	125,000	135,000
Cost of sales	75,000	93,750	101,250
Contribution	$25,000	$31,250	$33,750
Value of inventory holding	$6,250	$15,625	$25,312

46

	One month's inventory		Two months' inventory		Three months' inventory	
Contribution, brought forward	25,000		31,250		33,750	
Costs of processing purchase orders:						
	$		$		$	
Buying department	6,500		6,000		5,800	
Costs of inventory holding:						
Warehouse premises costs	5,000		7,500		7,500	
Storekeeping costs	4,000		5,000		6,500	
Inventory losses (½% X cost of sales)	375		469		506	
Insurance—1% X inventory values	63		156		253	
Cost of capital tied up in inventory (15%)	937	16,875	2,343	21,468	3,797	24,356
Relevant net profit		$8,125		$9,782		$9,394

This somewhat exaggerated example draws attention to three points which are relevant to any further discussion of the financial implications of inventory policy:

1. There may be a point beyond which further increases in inventory will not give rise to sufficient additional sales and gross profit to justify the additional costs involved.
2. Purchase order processing costs per unit or dollar value of purchases (and possibly even in total, as shown) are likely to diminish as inventory holdings are increased, because instead of having to place frequent orders for the renewal of inventory, the company is now placing less frequent bulk orders; i.e., one negotiation, one order and one progress action cover a large quantity of any particular item.
3. Inventory holding costs naturally increase with the size of inventory holdings because:

   a. *Inventories occupy space* which has to be purchased, rented, or converted from some other use—that space has to be equipped with racks or containers, and it requires light and heat.
   b. *Inventories need people* to put them into the warehouse, to withdraw

47

them when needed (picking and packing), to record them, check their
condition and ensure they are not lost.

c. *Inventories lose value* if they deteriorate, are wasted in handling, pil-
fered, destroyed or allowed to become obsolete—it may be desirable to
insure against some of these risks.

d. *Inventories tie up money,* involving interest charges or opportunity costs.

Why should increased inventories give rise to increased sales? One reason
would be that the business was offering a wider range of goods—it was diversify-
ing its range. Another could be that with the existing range the business was
offering a better level of service; i.e., it was less frequently out of stock of an
item when it was required.

Inventory Service Levels

In deciding on an inventory policy it is necessary to define the level of service to
be offered to the customer, in the sense of the percentage of orders which can be
satisfied immediately from stock. This will depend on the nature of the business.

In some cases the firm will be a monopoly supplier of certain goods, or
may offer particular advantages of quality, reputation, reliability or after-sales
service. Where such distinguishing features exist, it is possible that the customers
will be prepared to endure occasional delays in meeting their requirements, so
that it would not be necessary to hold sufficient inventory to ensure immediate
delivery.

In other cases quick delivery may be an essential feature of success in
achieving sales. This would be the case, for example, if there was strong competition for a limited market, or if the failure to supply a spare part for installed
equipment would cause significant loss to the customer while the equipment
was out of use.

Between these two extremes delivery delays may cause some loss of business and thus of profit earned; but there will be a level of service at which the
cost of holding additional inventory will exceed the amount of additional profit
which could be earned by having the inventory available.

When the required level of service has been defined, the next problem is
to decide how much inventory is needed to meet that requirement. This will be
the *minimum* holding, and not the average holding which will be influenced by
the inventory holding costs illustrated in the previous section.

Patterns of Procurement and Inventory Holding

Assuming that an item is in constant demand and there are no difficulties in
obtaining supplies, it would be normal to take a supply into inventory and then
use it up steadily until it was exhausted, when a new supply would be obtained.

Taking the example from the section on control of inventory where sales were to be $135,000 per annum, assume that this represents 135,000 units of an item of stock at $1 each. If demand is steady, the monthly usage of this item would be 11,250 units.

Now it would be possible to buy all 135,000 units at the beginning of the year and to use them progressively as shown in the following diagram:

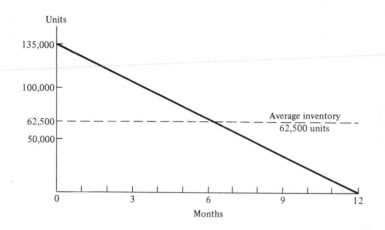

If this were done then:

1. There would be only one purchase, so the related costs in the buying department would be low.
2. The average inventory would be 62,500 units, so there would be 62,500 × 12 = 750,000 unit-months to influence the costs of inventory.

An alternative action would be to buy twice during the year, as shown in the next diagram. This would double the procurement costs, but would reduce the average inventory to 31,250 units so that inventory costs would be determined by only half the previous number of unit-months.

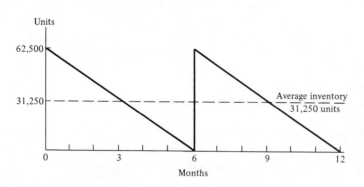

There is obviously a very large choice of procurement and inventory patterns; what is needed is to find that pattern which keeps total procurement and holding costs at the lowest possible level.

In doing this we shall find the "economic order quantity" for the particular item of inventory under review. The combination of the various items of inventory into the total business inventory will be discussed later.

Economic Order Quantity

The economic order quantity calculation is easiest to explain by reference to the following chart:

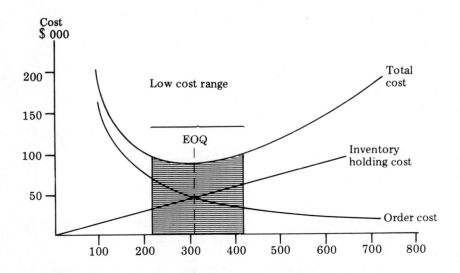

Order quantity within annual total quantity of 800.

The total annual demand for the item under review is forecast at 800 units. Along the horizontal axis are the various purchase order quantities which might be used to make up this total. If the purchase order quantity were 200 units, for example, this would mean that four orders would have to be placed during the year, obviously at three monthly intervals; if the purchase order quantity were 400 units then only two orders would be placed, one every six months. If a large number of small purchase orders are placed during the year, then the ordering costs per unit (and per annum) will be high, but if a small number of large orders is placed (towards the right of the chart), the ordering costs will be low.

The larger the quantity ordered each time, the higher the average inventory will be, and therefore the higher the inventory holding costs. The economic order quantity is at the point where these total costs are lowest.

The economic order quantity (EOQ) is usually calculated by a formula based on differential calculus. Textbook presentations of the formula are not uniform in the symbols they use, though identical in the answer they give.

Two common forms are:

$$\bar{Q} = \sqrt{\frac{2\,C_s\,d}{C_h}} \qquad\qquad \text{EOQ} \doteq \sqrt{\frac{2\,S\,D}{C\,I}}$$

Where:

$\bar{Q}$ = procurement order quantity

d = annual demand

C_s = cost of placing an order

C_h = cost of holding one unit for one year.

Where:

D = consumption rate per annum

S = ordering/handling costs per order

C = purchase price per unit

I = inventory carrying cost per annum as % of purchase price.

There are two important things to note about the above graph:

1. Although a mathematically precise EOQ can be calculated, in practice there is likely to be a range of order quantities (indicated by shading on the chart) within which total costs remain at a low level. The choice of order quantity within this low-cost range may not significantly affect the overall financial plan.

2. The key factor in the calculations is usually the cost of capital (interest on inventory); in times of high interest rates this is likely to outweigh all the other variables. The inventory holding cost line on the chart will slope very steeply, and one's conclusion will be that inventory should be kept to the lowest figure possible having regard to any practical difficulties in obtaining frequent replacement supplies.

Optimum Order Quantity

The last comment above is a reminder that suppliers do not like handling small orders. The purchase price per unit, therefore, may vary with the size of the purchase order, and this will require a modification to our EOQ calculation.

The supplier might for example, impose a "minimum order value," so that for quantities below this limit the cost per unit would, in effect, be higher than normal. This would either impose a lower cutoff limit on the size of order placed, or would introduce an upward curve at the lower end of the holding cost line on the EOQ chart, since insurance and interest charges per unit would be relatively high until the small order limit was reached. For larger orders, on the contrary, there might be quantity discounts, and these would cause one or more downward steps at those points on the holding cost line where they began to operate.

This possibility is illustrated on the following chart on which is shown a point of minimum total cost which differs from the position of the EOQ as originally calculated. This point is sometimes distinguished as the "optimum order quantity." The chart could alternatively be drawn to include actual purchase prices as well as the procurement and cost.

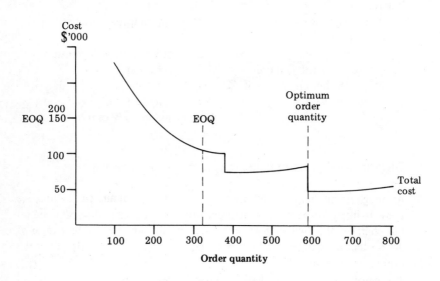

Safety Margins in Inventory

So far we have assumed that a company will be placing purchase orders at regular intervals of time for a fixed quantity (the economic or optimal order quantity) of any particular item. The possibility of doing this depends on demand remaining constant from period to period, and on supplies being available as and when required.

Sales demand, however, could show fluctuations around the normal level, so that in a period of high demand the available inventory could be used up before fresh supplies were due to arrive. Similarly, in some periods deliveries from suppliers could be delayed so that even the normal sales demand could not be satisfied.

Against both these contingencies, it is necessary to hold a safety margin of inventory (see the following diagram of inventory holdings). If it were necessary to hold a safety margin sufficiently large to cover the simultaneous occurrence of a peak in demand and a delay in supplies, then the minimum inventory (shown in the diagram as 42,500 units) would form the greater part of the total inventory.

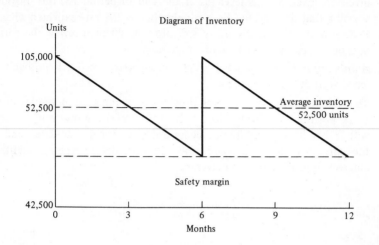

Very little can be done to correct for random delays in supply, but it may be possible to anticipate changes in the trend of demand and to modify the purchasing procedure to meet them in one of the following ways:

1. To order in economic order quantities but at varying time intervals according to the rate of demand currently being experienced or anticipated in the near future—this is known as the fixed order quantity or reorder level system (for reasons which will be explained below).
2. To order at regular intervals but in varying quantities determined by the current rate of demand—this is the fixed interval, or periodic review, system.

Modified Ordering Systems

The reorder level system involves deciding a level of inventory at which new purchase orders shall be placed. This will be decided in relation to the normal rate of issues during the normal purchasing lead time. The quantity to be ordered is constant, and an order for that quantity will be placed whenever stock falls to the predetermined reorder level. The system thus responds quickly to variations in demand, though there is a danger that in doing so it may reflect purely short term or random fluctuations in sales.

The diagram on page 54 illustrates the operation of the reorder level system, including the use of:

1. *A maximum inventory level.* This would correspond to the normal peak holding under stable conditions (as at the beginning of period 6). If the inventory exceeds this level (as at the end of period 13) this provides a warning that demand has been running below the rate expected when the EOQ was fixed. The inventory specialist should then review the correctness of his standard purchase order quantity.

2. *A minimum inventory level* which, as suggested above, is probably the amount of the safety margin.

The minimum inventory level provides a warning of potential out-of-stock position. When inventory falls to that level the inventory specialist will review his outstanding purchase orders and their due dates, and also the current trend of demand, and can then decide whether additional emergency procurement is necessary.

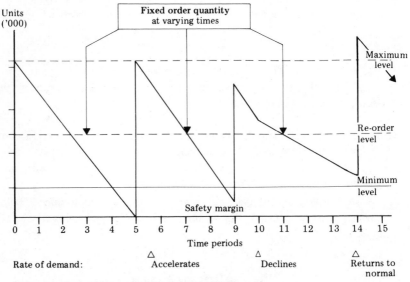

Order quantity (within annual total quantity of 800)

Under the periodic review system, purchase orders are placed at fixed intervals of time, but the quantity ordered can be modified to meet the rate of demand indicated by current experience. This gives an opportunity for analyzing the trend of demand, and various techniques such as "exponential smoothing" can be used in forecasting this trend. The system does not respond rapidly to immediate needs, and it may therefore necessitate a larger safety margin than the reorder level system.

It is, in fact, common experience that the reorder level system gives slightly lower average inventory levels, and it is sometimes thought to be the cheaper system to operate because reordering is triggered automatically at the reorder level. Reorder levels, however, require reviewing in the light of changes in the rate of demand. Any system can appear cheap in the short run if it is operated in a slovenly manner.

Infrequent and Seasonal Demand

In most inventories it will be necessary to carry items which are slow moving in the sense that units of demand are separated by significant intervals of time. These items may have high individual value but because they are demanded infrequently they will probably contribute only a small percentage of the total annual value of sales. The normal Pareto distribution of inventory will show that about 20% of the line items carried would contribute 80% of the total annual usage, though this relationship will vary between different types of business.

It may be decided not to hold inventory of some slow-moving items, but to procure them as and when they are required. If inventory is needed, however, the amount held will probably be limited to the quantity most likely to be next demanded, the occurrence of the demand being the signal for further procurement action. The quantity held may, however, be increased if the purchase price per unit is sufficiently lower for large quantities so as to offset any increase in holding costs for a larger inventory holding. This could occur, for example, when the supplier imposed a minimum order value.

There should be a regular review of slow-moving items to identify inventories which have become technically obsolete or for which the demand has diminished to the point where inventory holding is no longer justified.

In some businesses (for example, women's fashion wear), it is necessary to place orders for the full seasonal requirement well in advance of the demand occurring, with a high probability that repeat orders will not be obtainable. In such instances the purchase and sale of each batch will be a separate project or venture dependent heavily on accurate forecasting of demand quantities and selling prices. In this case, the evaluation procedures applicable to inventory holding for continuous demand will not apply.

Bulk Buying and Hedging

Of similar nature will be decisions:

1. To purchase goods in bulk in advance of demand in order to protect the business against anticipated price rises or shortages of supply.
2. To purchase commodities forward at a fixed price for future delivery.
3. To combine forward purchase options with forward sales options, so as to

limit losses arising from price changes (including changes in currency exchange rates).

4. To purchase foreign currency forward against specific overseas purchases, so as to minimize the effect of changes in exchange rates.

These are financial decisions quite separate from the routine problems of inventory control, and would be evaluated as investment projects.

The Total Inventory

The techniques described in the foregoing paragraphs all relate to single line items of inventory; the assumption has been made that if each item is held at its own economic level then the overall holding of inventory will be correctly balanced. This would be true provided that two conditions were satisfied:

1. That there was enough space available to hold all the inventory required.
2. That enough money could be found to finance it.

Neither condition is likely to be fulfilled in practice, so some form of mathematical program might be used to constrain the ideal unit quantities within the limiting factors. There are, however, a number of simple pragmatic approaches to inventory reduction, and these include:

1. Modifying the service level offered, either generally or in relation to selected items.
2. Letting the company's suppliers act as inventory holders (possibly by placing bulk orders with schedules of call-off dates linked to sales demands).
3. Discontinuing those items which are the least profitable, having regard to their marginal contribution and relevant fixed costs per unit of the limiting factor.

Raw Material Inventory and Work in Progress

So far, in considering inventory control we have been discussing salable inventory, but the same principles apply to inventory of raw materials. The main difference is that demand for raw materials is not direct from the outside customers but indirect through the production plans of the factory using the raw materials.

In considering the scheduling of production the "economic batch quantity" (EBQ) corresponds to the EOQ for purchased items. Manufacture in small batches will be more costly than in larger batches because there will be greater repetition of planning and progress actions and of the setting up and breaking down of machine tooling, and also because there will be less opportunity for an efficient momentum of work to be established. However, these batch processing costs (like procurement costs of inventory) will change inversely to the holding costs of the work in progress (floor space, insurance, interest on capital, etc).

A big problem with work in progress is that work passes in sequence through a series of operations. What is an economic batch for lathe work may not be economic for drilling, milling, or assembly operations. Applying an EBQ calculation to one operation in isolation can cause bottlenecks in the flow of production—creating excessive holdings of partly completed work because it could be produced cheaply in a large batch, even though there will be no demand for that work for some time ahead.

A similar problem is that of keeping skilled workpeople steadily occupied, since their wages are basically fixed in relation to time, even though outside customer demand may be seasonal or erratic.

Because these problems are concerned with the uneven timing of cash flows they are best solved by the use of discounted cash flow techniques. If, however, there is a capability of a rate of production which is in excess of a *steady* rate of demand (internal or external) then the problem is to decide what is the economic length of a production run, the facilities then being switched to other work until the next run is required. The EBQ formula can be adapted to this type of situation, and is then modified to:

$$Q = \sqrt{\frac{2\,C_s\,d\,p}{C_h(p-d)}}$$

where:

Q = batch quantity
d = demand per period
p = production capability per period
C_s = setup costs per batch (or other relevant fixed costs)
C_h = inventory holding costs per unit per period.

As an example of this calculation, assume that production of a component is at the rate of 120 units per week, but the rate of usage is 80 units per week only. Setup costs are $600 per batch, and holding costs are $5 per unit per week held. The approximate calculation of the economic batch quantity will be as follows:

$$\text{Economic batch size} = \sqrt{\frac{2 \times 600 \times 80 \times 120}{5\,(120 - 80)}}$$

$$= \sqrt{\frac{11,520,000}{200}}$$

$$= \sqrt{57,600}$$

$$= 240 \text{ units}$$

Two hundred forty units will take two weeks to produce and will satisfy three weeks' demand. The available free time between batches is one week.

Summary

The investment of any money in a business, whether in fixed assets or working capital, has to be justified in the light of the overall financial objectives of the business; whatever investment decision is under review there must be constant reference back to its impact on the business as a whole.

Within this context, possible ways of comparing the effects of alternative decisions are:

1. Formulas (for the choice of a credit period or an inventory level, for example) based on a static cost structure.
2. Discounted cash flow calculations and related methods of investment appraisal.
3. More complex modeling systems.

Once a decision has been taken, the adherence to the plan and the effect of changes in parameter on target result areas can be checked by using such asset management ratios as accounts receivable:sales, accounts payable:purchases and the various relationships between inventory holdings and input or output figures.

4

Sources
of Short-Term
Finance

The Need for Short-Term Finance

A business will often discover from the preparation of a cash budget or a cash forecast that its needs for cash in implementing proposed courses of action are in excess of the amounts of cash becoming available in the ordinary course of events. We have discussed already in connection with cash forecasting how changes might be made, either to the timing of proposed inflows and outflows, or to the amounts of certain items, without detriment to the overall plan. Such actions, however, will not always be sufficient to close the gap between applications and sources of cash, and it will then be necessary to consider means of obtaining funds from outside the business.

In deciding how to obtain this finance, two questions must be asked:

1. For what *purpose* is the money needed? It might be, for example, to support an increase in sales with the necessary investment in working capital; it might be for investment in fixed assets, or on a larger scale, for the acquisition of another business, or for the routine replacement of assets in times when progressively increasing prices are outstripping the company's ability to generate finance from its existing activities.

Some of these purposes will be self-financing in the long run. With stable prices, an increase in sales should eventually yield sufficient profit to finance the related working capital. An investment in fixed assets similarly should not be made unless the forecast benefits will repay the investment as well as provide the required rate of return on capital employed. Looked at in isolation, such projects would require the injection of capital for only a limited period.

Other requirements may be for very short periods, measured in days or weeks rather than years, such as cover for fixed costs during a period of low activity, or the spreading of heavy individual outlays—taxation payments for example—over a period of time. At the other extreme, as a business grows its assets structure will take on new permanent forms, and to dismantle that structure would involve the discontinuance of the business. Funds then become involved permanently in the business.

The question of purposes therefore is interlinked with the second question:

2. For what *time span* is the money needed?

Having answered these two questions it is possible to start matching up the requirements of the business with the various types of finance available. In some cases the nature of the assets involved suggests a form of specific finance. Accounts receivable, for example, can be financed directly by factoring or discounting, as was described in Chapter 3. Where inventories are held to be processed for a particular customer, then that customer may be willing to buy the inventories and provide them as "free issue" to the processor. In most cases, however, money will be needed for the general development of the business, and having decided whether this is a short-term or a long-term need the financial manager will aim to select the source of capital which meets his time requirements at the lowest cost.

The expressions "short-term," "long-term," and "medium-term" have no precise connotation. If pressed for a definition one might say that short-term is up to five years, medium-term from six years up to the starting point for long-term capital, which would be defined in relation to the fixed asset life or the research-to-exhaustion cycles of the business—anything from ten years upwards.

As a convenient basis for discussion we will regard long-term capital as the share capital of the business plus loans for more than about seven years. Any other capital sources we will deal with now under the heading of short-term finance.

Borrowing Short and Investing Long

It is a cardinal rule of financial management that you do not borrow at short-term and use the proceeds for investment in assets which will not be realizable by the repayment date of the loan. The obvious reason is that if funds are not available to repay the loan when due, then the business may find that it has either to renegotiate a loan under unfavorable conditions or to sell an asset which is needed for the continuity of the business.

Noteworthy examples of the dangers of this practice have been those finance companies which in past years accepted short-term deposits from the public and invested them in projects for property development. When property values fell and there were few willing buyers, these institutions were faced with the prospect of selling their assets at a loss in order to meet depositors' withdrawal requirements, thus putting themselves at the risk of insolvency if heavy withdrawals were made.

Savings and loan associations, on the other hand, prosper by breaking this rule. They also take short-term deposits and lend the money on mortgages of property repayable over long periods. The reasons why they do this are:

1. Many of their depositors keep their life savings in the association and have no intention of withdrawing them.
2. Other depositors keep their money there because this gives them favorable treatment should they require a mortgage.
3. The mortgage advances are in relatively small amounts spread over a large number of people, so that the risk of large-scale default in repayment is small.
4. The security for most of the advances is residential home properties, which is less susceptible to diminution of value than other types of property development.

So, every rule has exceptions and this is one based on very special circumstances.

When there is a shortage of long-term finance, it may be necessary for short-term money to be used for long-term investment, and this has happened to commercial and industrial companies in the United States during the last few years when bank borrowing has taken the place of equity finance. Both borrower and lender are at risk in such a transaction, and should have some agreement about the renewal of the loan when it falls due.

Bank Credit

In rare cases a long-term bank loan may be obtained for the purchase of fixed assets, but banks do not consider this a proper use of the predominantly short-term funds at their disposal, so the normal forms of bank credit are the short-term loan and the bank overdraft.

The interest charge in either case will be a small percentage above the bank rate, but whereas loan interest is charged on the full amount of the loan agreed upon, overdraft interest is only payable on the actual balances outstanding day by day.

From the point of view of the borrower the flexibility of overdraft financing and the relatively low interest rate are attractive, but the danger of overdraft financing, and the advantage from the banker's point of view, is that overdrafts are legally repayable on demand. Normally, however, the bank will agree that an overdraft shall not be called in for a defined period of time, and when credit conditions permit, banks are generally prepared to continue financing a client whose business is profitable and shows a regular turnover of funds.

Banks prefer self-liquidating loans, in other words, those used for a purpose which will automatically generate cash for repayment of the loan. Examples of these would be:

1. Finance for a specific contract.
2. Finance for the purchase of inventories which are not likely to lose their value, and which can be pledged as security.
3. Finance for seasonal business, such as crop loans to enable a farmer to purchase seed.

It is important that the business should produce reliable cash forecasts, both to support an application for bank credit and to ensure that cash would be available to meet repayments if required.

Trade Credit

A great deal has been said about trade credit in Chapter 3 from the points of view both of taking credit from suppliers and of minimizing the credit granted to customers, including such possibilities as discounting and factoring.

Although difficulties in obtaining finance from other sources may drive a business into taking extended credit from its suppliers, it must always be borne in mind:

1. That this makes the business highly vulnerable to pressure from the suppliers, including possible action to cut off supplies.
2. That it can make the business dangerously illiquid if credit is being taken without properly negotiated terms.
3. That trade credit, which appears to be interest-free, may in fact be very expensive, either through discount foregone or through hidden costs of high prices, poor service and loss of reputation.

Among the forms of supplier finance not mentioned elsewhere is the provision of loans for the purchase of equipment. Oil companies, for example, may make loans for upgrading gas station facilities. Often such loans are cheap and for long periods, but they can have the disadvantage of limiting the independence of the business receiving them.

In the case of a business carrying out long-term contracts, customer finance is often obtained in the form of progress payments or installment payments against work in progress. From the point of view of the financial officer the object is to ensure that all costs of the contract, including the cost of capital tied up in work in progress, are covered in the contract price. The timing and amount of the desired installment payments would be established by a net present value calculation of the various cash flows resulting from the contract (a technique dealt with in Chapter 10).

Acceptance Credits and Bank Bill Finance

Acceptance credits are made available by syndicates of banks and factors, normally through the intermediary of a merchant bank. They are in effect long-term overdrafts, usually for a period of around five years. Drawings up to the agreed limit are by bills of exchange drawn under the credit, and as these are "fine" bills they can be discounted at a very low rate. The due date on a bill should coincide with the time funds become available from the transactions for which the finance was required.

Commercial Bills of Exchange

A commercial bill of exchange is drawn by a supplier on his customer with the object normally of discounting it, so that the supplier gets access to cash earlier than the customer has to pay it. Unless the bill has been "accepted" by the customer's banker or an accepting factor, the ability to discount it will depend on the general financial and commercial standing of the two parties, and the rate of discount will be considerably higher than for fine bills. Although bills of exchange are used for some types of domestic transaction, their main importance is in connection with export trade.

It may also be possible to discount a postdated check given by a customer of good reputation.

Loans from Clearing Banks, Merchant Banks and Discount Houses

Where money is needed for a specific project which will yield profit over a period of years, an overdraft which could be recalled is often not the most suitable source of finance. It may be preferable to seek a loan for a fixed period from one of the "secondary banks"—merchant banks or discount houses. In recent years the clearing banks have also begun to enter this field, offering loans of from $2,000 upwards for periods between one and seven years.

Rates of loan interest can be high, but will depend in part on the borrower's financial standing, the asset cover available and the profitability of the proposed venture.

Leasing

Leasing is a convenient source of finance for the purchase of the plant and equipment. The lessee has the use of the equipment with a relatively small initial down payment, and he obtains tax relief on the interest paid and in the form of depreciation allowances. The company's funds are thus kept available for other profitable uses. There is freedom to commute future payments at any time, and most contracts will include "skip" arrangements whereby installments may be omitted at certain times of year when sales are low.

For leasing to be used:

1. The equipment purchased must be easily identifiable.
2. It must have an effective life in excess of the life of the agreement.
3. Its disposal value at any time must be in excess of the amount outstanding under the agreement.
4. It must generate sufficient earnings to meet the installments as they become due.

Equipment Leasing

Almost any type of fixed asset from about $100 upwards can be leased, the contract period running from 1-3 years in the case of contract leasing of motor vehicles, 3-5 years for office equipment, and up to 15 years or more for heavy industrial equipment.

Contracts vary considerably, but in most cases there will be two rental periods: an initial period of high rentals from which the lessor will aim to recover the capital cost of the equipment and make his profit, and a second period, terminable when the lessee desires, in which rental charges are very low. Some agreements include insurance, maintenance, breakdown replacements, and an option to purchase the asset at the end of the rental period. This last option may not be of interest to the lessee if his object is to have the use of up-to-date equipment for a short period until it becomes obsolete, or if the equipment is only needed for part of its potential working life.

The whole cost of leasing is allowed for taxation purposes as a business expense, with some restrictions.

As a general rule leasing will be more expensive than financing an outright purchase by means of a fixed-term loan.

Until recently the leasing agreement had the advantage that no asset or liability appeared on the lessee's balance sheet, so that his borrowing power was not affected by the transaction. As a simple example of this, suppose a company's fixed assets appear on the balance sheet at $5,000 and it is considered prudent to borrow up to 40% of that value, i.e., $2,000. If an additional asset costing $1,000 is obtained on credit, and the outstanding liability under the agreement is $800, then the new borrowing limit will be reduced to 40% X ($5,000 + $1,000) = $2,400 *less* the $800 outstanding, leaving $1,600 only.

Under a leasing contract there would have been no entry on the balance sheet other than a current liability for any arrears of payments under the contract. FASB-13 now requires that capital leases be recorded as both an asset and a liability on the balance sheet, so it is no longer possible to "hide" leases from potential creditors. Even operating leases require that a schedule of lease payments be disclosed.*

Sales and Leaseback

A possible source of urgently needed funds is the sale of property to an insurance company or other institutional investor and its immediate leaseback to the vendor. There was in the early 1970s a period when credit was short but property values were rising, and under these circumstances sale and leaseback transactions benefited both parties to the contract. In earlier years sale and leaseback deals were a common means of raising funds for business expansion by the acquisition of other companies.

The benefit to the vendor arises from his ability to use the sale proceeds more profitably than in property ownership. In striking a balance of advantage one has to take account of the following factors:

1. The vendor may be subject to capital gains tax on the transaction.
2. He has relinquished the ability to use the property as security for further financing.
3. The rent payable may seem reasonable initially, but in a long leaseback it will be subject to periodic review.
4. There may be restrictions on future alterations to the property; it is no longer under the control of the former owner.

---

*The Financial Accounting Standards Board (FASB) replaced the Account Principles Board (APB) in 1973 as the principal accounting rule-making body. As this book goes to press the FASB has issued nearly forty Statements and a similar number of Interpretations. Many of the recent Statements and Interpretations have been in the area of leases.

In considering the relative advantages of borrowing on mortgage or sale and leaseback it is interesting to ask why the company concerned ever purchased its premises in the first place instead of renting suitable accommodation.

Among the reasons might be:

1. It was difficult to find "suitable" rentable accommodation—its requirements were perhaps somewhat specialized.
2. Rental charges are a perpetual fixed cost of the business, and they are subject to periodic review (possibly every seven years) when they are likely to be increased.
3. Once the property has been acquired the owner can modify, adapt and expand it to meet the changing requirements of his business.
4. The premises can provide excellent security for borrowing as and when required.
5. Whereas under a rental contract the costs of maintenance are incorporated into the regular rental payments, with owned premises the amount and timing of maintenance work is at the discretion of the owner.

A decision to borrow money by mortgage therefore is a decision to make use of one of the advantages of ownership.

A decision to sell and leaseback is a decision to relinquish all the advantages outlined above in exchange for the once-and-for-all receipt of a lump sum in cash, which will probably be subject to capital gains tax. It falls therefore under one of two categories:

1. It is a last resort effort to obtain cash at any price.
2. It is a wonderful opportunity to increase profits by reinvesting the sale proceeds at a higher rate of return than was represented by the advantages outlined above. This can sometimes be the case, but careful investigation is needed to ensure that one is not trading off long-term stability against a short-term speculative gain.

In making a final decision it is worth also considering the alternative of outright sale and removal elsewhere. It will often be found, however, that a sale with continuing tenancy will command a higher price than a sale with vacant possession, and if the premises are at all specialized or are in one of the older industrial areas there may be no bidders for vacant premises except perhaps the local or federal government for the purpose of demolition.

Short-Term Finance from Government Sources

Government financial aid to industry takes different forms from time to time dependent on the current economic problems of the country; managers should be alert to new developments. The Small Business Administration is a major source of finance, especially for small, closely held companies.

Interest Rates

Reference has been made earlier to the relationship between certain borrowing rates and either the clearing banks' base rate or the factor's base rate.

Following is a form which can be used for recording information about interest rates, which will be found under the heading "Money Market Rates" in the financial pages of some newspapers.

Two items not mentioned previously, and not of direct interest to the business borrower or lender are:

1. Interbank market—these are the rates on borrowing by banks from each other.
2. First class factor houses—the rates at which rental and similar companies can borrow from banks and institutions.

MONEY MARKET RATES

Date reported:

	Over-night	2 days	1 week	1 month	2 months	3 months	6 months	12 months
Bank minimum lending rate (Last changed:								
Clearing banks base rate								
Factor base rate								
Discount market loans Open Close								
Treasury bills discount Buying Selling								
Prime bank bills discount								
Trade bills discount								
Local government bonds								
Secondary market $ CD								
Local government market								
Interbank market Open Close								
First class finance houses								

5

Foreign Trade and Foreign Exchange

Finance of Foreign Trade

Many export sales are made for cash or on credit terms up to sixty days, in respect of which the exporter does not need to obtain outside financial assistance to any greater extent than he would for domestic sales.

A high proportion of export sales, however, will involve giving prolonged credit, so that in addition to the common problems of:

1. Ensuring that a customer is creditworthy.
2. Obtaining payment on the due date.

Export trade more frequently than domestic trade will pose the problems of:

3. Financing the order over a long period of credit.

Wherever possible of course the export price should include a loading for the cost of finance, but under competitive conditions this will not always be possible.

Where it is possible to establish creditworthiness without much difficulty and where political barriers to payment are not envisaged (such as changes in exchange control regulations or import licensing, or wars or political upheavals) it is possible to conduct overseas business in the same way as domestic business, on "open account," and this is standard practice within the European Economic Community.

Trading on open account means trusting a customer to pay for goods or services supplied in accordance with agreed credit periods. The customer is not expected to provide any collateral security, nor are any third parties associated with the transaction for the purposes of guaranteeing the payment of amounts due. The common methods of settlement will be:

1. By telegraphic transfer.
2. By mail transfer from the debtor's bank.
3. By personal check if exchange control regulations permit this.
4. By banker's draft issued directly in favor of the creditor's bank or through a correspondent bank in the supplier's country.

A common method of strengthening the likelihood of eventual collection is to draw a bill of exchange on the customer, usually for a period between 30 and 80 days. This can be submitted for acceptance through the supplier's agent with the bills of lading attached, so that these documents of title are not released to the customer until he has accepted the bill. This is known as a documentary bill.

When there is no doubt about the customer's integrity the bills of lading will be sent directly to him. The bill of exchange he accepts is then referred to as a "clean" bill.

The supplier may hold bills of exchange until maturity, or he may obtain immediate finance either by discounting the bills through his bank or by obtaining a loan from the bank on the security of the bills.

If the customer is not well known there may be difficulty in making use of his bills in this way except perhaps at a very heavy rate of discount. (This comment does not apply if the account has been insured.) As a method of ensuring payment this method is not completely satisfactory. A bill of exchange is only a postdated check, and it can be dishonored by the customer; i.e., he will fail to provide funds to meet it on the due date. If this happens and the supplier has previously discounted the bill, then the discounter will have recourse to the supplier to meet the bill.

A method which gives greater assurance of payment is for the customer's bank to issue a *letter of credit* in favor of the exporter and send it to their correspondent bank in the exporter's country.

This may be done in relation to a specific transaction, or a "revolving credit" may be opened under which the exporter will be able to draw up to a specified amount at any one time or during any one period.

A simple letter of credit, however, is only a payment instruction issued at

a point in time. The instruction could be countermanded before payment
became due. For this reason the letter of credit should be expressed as "irrevocable." The correspondent bank can then be relied on to carry out its terms provided the customer has made funds available. To overcome this last obstacle the
letter of credit should be "confirmed"by the bank, and the exporter then has absolute assurance of payment provided he carries out his part of the contract (and,
a necessary proviso nowadays, provided the confirming house remains solvent).

The exporter may get his money in one of two ways: either directly from
the correspondent bank as soon as the necessary documents are presented (a
"sight credit"), or by drawing a bill of exchange on the correspondent (an
"acceptable credit").

In some cases the customer will, if requested, make the credit "transfer-
able" to a nominee of the exporter—often the exporter's own supplier.

There are three other methods by which the exporter can be sure of getting his money (apart from credit insurance which is dealt with below) without
any recourse to himself should the customer default. These methods of "non-
recourse" financing are:

1. *Export finance houses* whose business is to give credit to the overseas
   buyer and at the same time give the exporter an irrevocable undertaking
   to pay him against presentation of the necessary documents—invoices,
   bills of lading and other shipping documents.
2. *Confirming houses* who confirm orders placed by overseas buyers and
   again pay the exporter on the production of the documents' title.
3. *Export factors* who offer a complete service package (as already described
   in Chapter 3) in respect of sales on short term of nonperishable consumer
   goods.

Export Credit Insurance

A number of commercial insurance companies will insure the exporter against
the risks of damage to goods in transit and of the insolvency or default of the
buyer, in the same way as for domestic trade. In the United Kingdom the
Government's Export Credits Guarantee Department (ECGD) will also cover
political risks. This organization, which also has access to valuable information
on the credit status of overseas customers, will insure 90% of the risk of customer insolvency or default, and between 80% and 95% of other risks, such as:

1. Introduction of exchange control regulations preventing payment.
2. The buyer's failure to take up the goods which have been shipped, provided that this is not due to any fault of the exporter.

3. Any change in import licensing regulations or export licensing conditions.
4. War or other political risks preventing either the shipment of the goods or their delivery to their destination.
5. Diversion of voyage causing the exporter additional costs not recoverable from the customer.
6. Any other cause of loss occurring outside the country of shipment and not within the control of either the exporter or the buyer.

There is a wide range of policies, falling under four categories.

1. *Comprehensive.* The comprehensive policy can cover either the whole export business of the supplier for periods of 1-3 years or sales to selected markets for one year. Premiums are at scale rates for the various areas of the world, but an average figure where up to six months' credit is given would be 24p per £100 of goods sold. Sales to the U.K. agents for shipment overseas can be included.
2. *Specific.* Specific policies for up to 5 years are issued covering the sale of large-scale capital goods. The premium would be specially negotiated in each instance.
3. *Service.* Both comprehensive and specific policies can be drawn to cover overseas sales of services.
4. *Investment cover.* The political risks attendant on overseas investment can be covered for periods between 3 and 15 years at a premium of 1% of the sum insured.

One advantage of insurance through ECGD is that it gives the exporter access to cheap finance. On the basis of an ECGD guarantee banks will lend money to the exporter at the subsidized rate of ½% above the clearing banks' base rate. The advances will be made either against bills of exchange drawn on the customer or, when transactions are on open account, against promissory notes from the exporter. A fee of 1/8% on the agreed borrowing limit will also be payable to ECGD.

Similar terms apply to loans to the overseas buyer made through the export finance houses mentioned above.

In brief then, ECGD provides:

1. Insurance against loss.
2. Information about credit standing.
3. Finance at cheap rates.

Most other countries, including the United States, do not have government financed programs to protect against political risks.

Eurocurrency

Eurocurrency is any currency owned by a firm or individual resident outside the country where the currency was issued and lent to another nonresident. As dollars have traditionally contributed the largest portion of the eurocurrency pool it is convenient to use eurodollars as an example of this type of currency.

Three questions arise:

1. How do eurodollars come into existence? In brief, through an imbalance of international payments. During the 1960s the United States paid out large sums in foreign aid; and U.S. companies exported dollars for investment in Europe. Currently large amounts of royalties are being paid in dollars to oil producing countries. In addition dollars have left the United States for investment overseas because of lower interest rates on the U.S. home market.

2. How do eurodollars go out of existence? Only when the holder buys an American product and pays for it in dollars, or invests in American domestic securities.

3. What is the use of eurodollars? They are money available to be borrowed. Once they have been acquired they can be converted into any other currency at the appropriate exchange rate.

Transactions in eurocurrency are on a vast scale, and are handled by specialized banking organizations, either consortium banks formed by groupings of traditional banks or syndicates of banks.

A major part of eurocurrency transactions is the continuous interbank lending and borrowing that enables individual banks to keep their currency positions in balance. Among the outside borrowers of eurocurrency will be:

1. Companies needing large sums for investment anywhere outside their home countries.

2. Multinational companies needing large sums for investment outside their base country.

3. U.S. companies operating abroad and unable to get sufficient funds from the United States.

4. National governments and statutory authorities needing to raise more capital than is available in their national markets.

5. Companies, unit trusts and investment trusts wanting to invest in U.S. securities.

The evidence of a deposit of eurocurrency is a "certificate of deposit." These have a life of between three months and five years and carry a fixed rate of interest. They are negotiable documents, and are the instruments used as the basis for most eurocurrency transactions.

It is also possible to arrange long-term eurocurrency borrowing through the issue of "eurobonds." These are for periods not normally longer than fifteen years. The bonds are placed by the issuing bank with other banks and institutions.

Where exchange control permission could be obtained, the two advantages of borrowing abroad to finance domestic activities would be:

1. Access to a larger pool of funds than is available locally.
2. The ability to take advantage of slightly lower interest rates in markets where capital is plentiful.

These advantages are of interest primarily to the borrower requiring very large amounts of money.

The big disadvantage of overseas borrowing is that the loan has to be repaid in the currency of issue. The borrower thus runs the risk of an exchange loss (or the possibility of gain) should either of the currencies be revalued between the time of borrowing and the time of repayment.

It is unlikely that overseas borrowing by individual organizations would have a significant impact on the U.S. economy, but in theory:

1. The requirement for foreign currency to service the loan and eventually to repay it would weaken the dollar in relation to that currency, and this might give rise to an increase in domestic interest rates.
2. If foreign capital were predominant in a company then there would be the risk of the overseas lenders' interests taking priority over the interests of U.S. shareholders, employees, suppliers and customers. This of course is the common fear in relation to the operations of multinational corporations.

Exposure to Foreign Exchange Risks

Whenever a company enters into a transaction under which it is committed to receive or pay foreign currency at some future date, then it exposes itself to the risk of exchange losses.

No standard parities currently operate although there are purposes for which a company may wish to use standardized exchange rates, for example:

1. When it has quoted for a construction contract in a foreign currency, it may wish to report the actual costs incurred using the same exchange rate as was assumed in the quotation, exchange differences being reported separately as largely noncontrolable variances.

2. When a branch or a subsidiary company keeps its records in a currency other than that of the head office, then for the purposes of short-term reporting to the head office it may use standard exchange rates laid down for internal use from time to time.

The financial officer, however, is vitally concerned with the effect of actual movements in rates of exchanges on those outstanding transactions which, being expressed in foreign currency, expose the company to the risk of an exchange loss.

"Exposure" is a question of fact in each case. To take a very simple example, if a company is importing goods which are to be invoiced in a foreign currency, then from the time a commitment is entered into, the company is exposed to the risk that the home currency will become devalued (will depreciate) in terms of the currency in which payment has to be made. For example, if machinery had been imported from Germany at a price of DM120,000, and if the exchange rate then slipped from 2.30 (1 DM = 43½ cents) to 2.00 (1 DM = 50 cents), the company would have to pay more than it had expressed to the extent of $\frac{120,000}{2.30} - \frac{120,000}{2.00}$, or equivalently,

$$120,000 \times (.50 - .43\frac{1}{2}) = \underline{\underline{\$7,800}}$$

Protection against the type of exposure is obtained either by requiring the overseas supplier to quote in the buyer's currency or at a fixed rate of exchange or by *buying forward* (to the time when the supplier's invoice has to be paid) the necessary amount of foreign currency. A premium is charged on such forward transactions (which you can see quoted in the financial press where exchange rate tables cover both "spot" and forward rates), but the buyer has now fixed the total amount of home currency he has to find.

With regard to export sales, the seller is protected when these are invoiceable in the home currency, but there may be good reasons for quoting and invoicing in a foreign currency, for example:

1. To match up against imports priced in the same foreign currency.
2. Where the selling company is a subsidiary company, to ensure that the sales proceeds are in the currency of the parent company.
3. As a hedge against weakening of the home currency. For example, if a sale to Germany were priced at $920 at a time when the exchange rate was DM2.3 = $1, the seller would receive merely $920 even if the exchange rate had meanwhile weakened to 2.0. If, however, the price had been quoted and invoiced at DM920 $\times$ 2.3 = 2,116 then the proceeds at the new exchange rate would be worth $\frac{2,116}{2.0}$ = $1,058.

However, a debt owing in a foreign currency does expose the seller to the risk of exchange rate changes causing a diminution in the amount of home currency eventually received.

Suppose now an inventory of trade goods has been consigned to a foreign currency area for sale. Again the consignor is exposed to the risk that the sale proceeds when eventually remitted will have less value in home currency than was expected when the venture was begun.

If the home business has provided long-term finance for overseas operations, possibly for the purchase of fixed assets, then there is no immediate expectation of the repatriation of such funds, and if fluctuations in exchange rates occur they have no direct effect on the liquidity of the home business other than through later distributions of profit from the foreign business or any accruing requirement for funds to replace the fixed assets. There is, however, the contingent risk of loss on the total home currency investment, and it may be desirable to reduce this by gearing up through foreign currency borrowing to finance foreign currency operations.

We have now got to the stage of envisaging a foreign company subsidiary to the home company, and it is of interest to look at the exposure position from the point of view of the foreign subsidiary. Clearly, if there is risk of the deterioration of the foreign currency this would increase the load of liabilities to the home company, since fewer home currency units would be obtainable for one foreign currency unit. It would then be desirable from the points of view both of the foreign company and of the group as a whole that the foreign operation be made as self-sufficient as possible. This could be done in various ways, as follows:

1. The foreign company should look for local substitutes for imported materials and supplies, and to the extent that this cannot be done, it should increase its selling prices before the full impact of currency devaluation is felt on its costs.

2. If exchange control regulations permit, and if the effect of the impending currency deterioration has not yet been fully reflected in forward currency rates, it should buy currency forward to cover anticipated liabilities to the home company.

3. Any outstanding liabilities to the home company should be settled while the cost in local currency is relatively low, and if possible the payment of dividends and management fees should be brought forward.

   Similarly, imported materials should be stockpiled, and contracts for the import of fixed assets should be expedited.

In order to take these actions, it may be beneficial to defer payments in the local currency, to press local debtors for payment, and to borrow in local currency.

You can see that there are a number of actions that companies might be taking when they are dependent on imports or are borrowing from abroad, even though they may not be subsidiaries of companies in other countries. Unfortunately, some of them are inhibited by exchange control regulations or price controls.

The Multinational Company

A multinational company can be defined as one having a substantial proportion of its sales, profits or assets abroad. Typically, it will operate in a number of different countries and there will be a significant volume of intertrading between them. It will thus be exposed not only to interacting risks of exchange fluctuation but also to exchange controls and other trade barriers such as were mentioned in connection with export trade above.

In such an organization there will be a need for the continuous review of the deployment of liquidity and the protection of assets exposed in foreign currency not only in the parent company but in each subsidiary. The financial officer may well need to delegate these responsibilities to a full-time "treasurer" acting in a central coordinating capacity.

The management accounts of each company in the group should include a balance sheet or net assets position analyzed to show the exposed position on each currency in which balances are outstanding, as in the example on page 77.

Historical statements, however, are not sufficient for control purposes and at least two forecasts will be required at frequent intervals:

1. A cash forecast from each company, possibly (as this is a summary for the treasurer) in the form of a source and application of funds statement, showing sources and applications in each relevant currency.
2. A forecast of the exposure position in each currency, possibly covering three or four quarterly periods ahead.

Currency Translation

What bearing do these financial management considerations have on the preferred method of currency translation, i.e., the conversion of foreign currency accounts for the purpose of incorporation into a head office or holding company consolidation?

In FASB-8 (dealing with foreign currency translation) the Financial Accounting Standards Board laid down a set of rules determining how specific items should be translated. As a general rule it can be said that historical rates should be used for all items that are reflected on the financial statements at

Balance Sheet of one of the group companies
(Expressed in $000 Equivalents at the Exchange Rates on December 31)

	U.S. $	German DM	French francs	Belgian francs	£	Total $
Share capital and reserves	3,650					3,650
Loan capital	800	250				1,050
Total capital employed	4,450	250				4,700
Current assets						
Inventory	876					876
Accounts receivable	900	460	230	178	666	2,434
Cash	90		32			122
	1,866	460	262	178	666	3,432
Current liabilities						
Accounts payable	754	300	112		500	1,666
Taxes payable	690					690
Dividends	240					240
	1,684	300	112		500	2,596
Net current assets	182	160	150	178	166	836
Fixed assets	3,864					3,864
Total	4,046	160	150	178	166	4,700

historical or acquisition cost. Current rates should be used for all other items. More specifically, historical rates should be used to translate prepaid expenses, most inventories, marketable securities, fixed assets and corresponding accumulated depreciation, intangible assets, deferred income items, and most stockholders' equity accounts, such as retained earnings and capital stock. Current rates should be used to translate cash, receivables and payables, and accrued expenses. Revenue and expense items are generally translated at the average rate for the period, since revenues accrue and expenses are incurred ratable during the period.

Much criticism has been made of FASB-8 because adherence to its provisions may result in an unfair presentation and may be misleading to the average reader. There is a very real possibility that the rules regarding the reporting requirements for foreign operations and foreign exchange will be modified in the near future.

Sources
of Long-Term
Finance

In Chapters 6 to 8 we shall be considering possible sources of long-term finance and their relative costs. Readers must be aware, however, that the availability of funds for investment will be strongly influenced by the general state of the economy, and that severe inflationary or deflationary conditions can distort the normal pattern of business finance.

The Need for Long-Term Finance

Long-term finance is required from outside the business:

1. When it is first established, in order to acquire any necessary fixed assets and to provide the initial working capital. As we have seen in discussing cash management, one of the objects of the business is to make profits; and if it does so then in due course return flows of cash will be received. This cash, however, will be needed to pay taxes, to distribute dividends,

and to replace the existing assets when necessary. If any surplus remained, it would usually be more profitably used in expanding the business than in paying back the investors. The initial injection of capital, therefore, should be regarded as sunk in the business permanently or for a long time.

2. When expansion of the business is required at a greater rate than can be financed out of retained earnings. The need for long-term finance is sometimes evidenced by a declining current ratio. When sales are expanded there will usually be an increase in the supporting inventory and in the outstanding receivables; and if increased credit is taken from suppliers correspondingly, the current ratio will decline.

For example, the working capital of Company A last June was as follows.

	$
Inventory	8,765
Accounts receivable	6,125
Cash	310
	15,200
Less: Accounts payable	7,600
Net current assets	$7,600

Following a 30% increase on sales, inventories were increased by $4,000 and accounts receivable by $3,000, both financed by taking $7,000 extra credit from suppliers. There was no significant change in the cash balance. The current ratio declined from 2:1 to 1.5:1 approximately, i.e.,

Ratio last June
  15,200/7,600   = 2:1

Ratio now
  (15,200 + 7,000)/(7,600 + 7,000) = 22,200/14,600 = 1.5:1

The business may be "overtrading," i.e., trying to achieve too much with the limited capital available. This situation is exaggerated if trade credit is used to finance the acquisition of fixed assets. Under these circumstances new long-term capital is needed to "fund" the short-term debt.

3. When the replacement costs of inventory or fixed assets are increasing at a faster rate than "profits" and it is not possible either to increase selling prices or to reduce costs sufficiently to give the necessary cash flows for the replacement of the assets.

The two main sources of long-term finance are:

1. Venture capital, remunerated in accordance with the success or failure of the business and bearing the risk of ultimate loss (the equity capital).
2. Loans, having a fixed or determinable date for repayment, and entitled to a predetermined rate of interest.

The Private Business

For proprietorships or partnerships the venture capital will be provided from the personal funds of the proprietors, including such amounts of profit as they choose not to draw out but to leave invested in the business. These amounts are commonly represented in the balance sheet of the business divided between the proprietors' "capital" accounts, i.e., the amounts intended to remain permanently invested, and their "current" or drawings accounts, which are the undrawn profits. The distinction may be somewhat artificial because:

1. There is nothing to prevent the proprietors reducing the amount of capital invested if they so desire.
2. In any case from the point of view of the creditors of the business there is no distinction between the proprietors' business and personal assets; both are available in the last resort to discharge the business liabilities.

The sources of loan capital for the private business are virtually the same as for an individual in his private capacity—mainly bank loans, loans on mortgage of property, loans secured by insurance policies, and loans from friends. The ability to borrow money will, however, be improved because business assets (equipment, inventory and accounts receivable) will be available as security, and because the flow of profits will, one hopes, be greater (though perhaps less secure) than a salaried income.

Long-Term Capital for Companies

From the point of view of the providers of venture capital, a big advantage of forming a company is that their personal liability is limited to the amount they agree to subscribe. From the point of view of lenders and other creditors the advantages are mainly:

1. That the company has a separate legal entity, and its assets cannot be withdrawn by the individual proprietors.
2. That annual statements are available, and in the case of a public company,

a form 10-K, so that a good deal of information is available about the business affairs.

Because of these advantages it is usually easier for a company than for a private individual to obtain both venture and loan capital.

Some partnerships are formed with unlimited liability on the members. From the lenders' point of view these combine the advantages noted above with the ability to pursue claims against individual members. From the point of view of attracting venture capital the publication of financial statements is not required, although audited statements may be made available to potential lenders. This may give a sense of security, but the lack of limited liability can be a deterrent.

In some cases the members' liability is limited by guarantee. This special feature (called a limited partnership) does not have any significant effect on the problems of financial management. We will discuss the long-term finance of companies in relation to those companies where the members' liability is limited.

For these companies the essential venture capital is provided by the common shareholders. In addition there may be various types of secured or unsecured loans. Occupying a somewhat ambivalent position between common stock and borrowing one may find preferred stock; and finally either loan capital or preferred stock may carry the right of eventual conversion into ordinary shares.

Common Stock

Common shares in a company have the following distinguishing features:

1. *Dividends* are payable at the discretion of the directors out of undistributed profits remaining after all prior claims have been met. Amounts available for dividend but not paid out are retained in the company on behalf of the common shareholders. The amount the common shareholders receive will vary from year to year depending on the performance of the company; but because the common shareholders take the risk that no profits will be available they will expect an average rate of return higher than that accruing to other forms of investment.

2. *Capital.* The common shareholders cannot regain the money they have invested except by selling their shares to another investor or by waiting until the business is discontinued. When the business is liquidated the common shareholders are entitled to all surplus funds after prior claims have been met. Shareholders can, of course, liquidate the company if its original objects have ceased to exist or if it cannot be carried on at a profit.

3. *Voting rights.* Most common shares entitle their holders to vote at share-holder meetings. Apart from special or extraordinary meetings of share-holders there must be an annual general meeting at which the prescribed ordinary business is to receive the company's accounts, to declare dividends, to appoint or reappoint directors, and to appoint and fix the remuneration of the auditors (who are appointed by the common share-holders for the purpose of ensuring that the accounts and the directors' report on them do present a true and fair view of the business affairs).

Provided that in every case a company has some common shares carrying the above rights it is possible, on occasion, for a company also to have other common shares with modified characteristics. The most usual of these are *non-voting common shares.* The holders of such shares are not entitled to any say in the affairs of the company, even though they take the same risks as the other common shareholders. Where the prospects of profit were good, some investors in the past have been prepared to relinquish their voing rights in order to partici-pate in those profits.

Retained profits are an important source of new finance for the company, and are particularly attractive to the board—the reasons normally given being:

1. It is easy to retain profits. It is the directors' responsibility to recommend what dividend may prudently be distributed, and by varying their dividend policy they can influence the amount of profit retained. This is true, but may not be in the long-term interest of the business. If at some future time it becomes necessary to issue further shares, then the potential investors will have regard to the size and consistency of past dividends. If the divi-dend history has been poor or erratic, then the new shares will not com-mand a high price. Similarly an unsatisfactory dividend policy will affect the market price of existing shares, and this may result in a failure to maxi-mize the wealth of the shareholders—a point discussed in Chapter 1.

2. Whereas new shares would produce an additional claim to future dividend payments, retained profits do not. There will still be the same number of shares in existence, and the old rate of dividend can continue. Again, this is not true in the long run; if the shareholders are being forced to reinvest their profits the only satisfactory reason is to enable additional profits to be earned in the future, and the shareholders will expect those increased profits to yield additional dividends.

3. Whereas a new issue of shares would involve legal and other costs, no costs are involved in retaining profits. Unlike (1) and (2) above the reason given in this case is correct.

Long-Term Debt

Debt may take several forms. It may be secured by property, such as equipment, a mortgage or other assets, or it may be unsecured, in which case the bond is called a debenture. If the debt matures on one specific date in the future, the bond issue is called a sinking fund bond, in which case the entire debt is paid at maturity. If the bond issue is paid in installments, the bond is called a serial bond. If bonds are registered, periodic interest payments are made to the registered owners. Coupon bonds are not registered, and payments are made to the party presenting the coupon.

Bonds have a stated rate of interest. Frequently, this stated rate differs from the prevailing market rate. When this occurs, the bond is sold at a premium or discount. For example, if the prevailing market rate is 9%, a bond bearing a stated rate of 7% cannot be sold unless it is sold at a discount. If a $1,000 bond having a stated interest rate of 8% is sold for $980, the company paying interest will have to pay quarterly interest of $20, or $80 per year (8% of $1,000). At maturity, the company will have to pay the bondholder $1,000, even though the bondholder (or former purchaser) paid only $980 for the bond. The extra $20 is considered interest expense to the company and interest income to the bondholder. The $20 is taken into income or expense over the term of the bond, using either the interest method or the straight-line method. If the straight-line method is used and the bond has a ten-year term, $2 will be taken in each of the ten years. If the interest method is used, a different amount will be taken in each of the ten years, using whatever constant rate is needed to produce total interest charges of $20 over the ten-year life of the bond.

Regardless of the negotiated redemption terms, a company may at any time purchase its own debentures on the open market and thus terminate its liability on those debentures, or it can make an offer to the debenture holders in the hope of persuading them to take repayment. The reasons why a borrower might wish to call in a debt before its due date for repayment could include:

1. To take advantage of a decline in interest rates. By negotiating a new loan at a lower rate of interest, the company is able to repay the earlier loan bearing a higher interest rate. Redemption under such circumstances could be to the disadvantage of the lender, both because he had been relying on a steady stream of interest and because he might have to reinvest the money at a lower rate of return. These are reasons why early repayment normally involves the borrower in paying a premium in addition to the amount borrowed.

2. To make use of surplus funds. The assumption here is that the saving of loan interest represents a better rate of return on the funds available than could have been obtained by investing them elsewhere. This would appear

to be an unusual situation except in conditions of acute business depression because the net cost of loan interest (after allowing for tax relief) is considerably less than the agreed rate.

3. To release assets which are covered by a fixed charge as security for the loan. The company might, for example, wish to sell an old machine which was covered by the charge, and to lease a new one which obviously would not be available as security.

In deciding whether to make an early repayment it would be necessary to compare the discounted net present values of the alternative courses of action. (This topic is discussed in Chapter 10.)

Preferred Stock

Preferred stock carries the right to a fixed dividend, if profits are available, before the common shareholders get anything. For example, shareholders of 6% cumulative preferred stock having a $50 par value would be entitled to a $3 dividend (6% of $50) before common shareholders receive a cent. A cumulative preferred stockholder who receives no dividend one year is entitled to receive a full $6 per share the next year before the common shareholders receive anything. If preferred stock is noncumulative, a shareholder who does not receive a dividend one year forever loses his right to receive that dividend, although he will still be entitled to receive $3 per share in subsequent years before common shareholders receive their dividends.

Preferred stock may be either participating or nonparticipating. If stock is nonparticipating, the preferred shareholder is entitled only to his $3 per share dividend. Any remaining dividends are paid to common shareholders. If preferred stock is participating, preferred shareholders receive their $3 per share first; common shareholders then receive their dividends, up to a certain limit; any remaining funds are distributed to preferred and common shareholders in the ratio of their respective total book values.

The cost of servicing any capital will be related to the amount of risk the investor takes, and as individuals have various attitudes toward risk there would appear to be a place for preferred stocks in the capital structure of businesses. They offer the investor a degree of risk intermediate between the high security of preferred stock and the open-ended possibilities of common shares. They offer the company a source of capital with a known annual cost, higher than the cost of secured loans (particularly as loan interest is a deductible business expense for tax purposes) but lower than the cost of common shares. In addition there will be no need in many cases for the company to make provision for their redemption.

Any possible future role of preferred stocks is linked with the future of equity shares. Because the common shareholder puts his capital at the greatest possible risk he would normally expect to receive higher rewards than nonrisk investors.

At the present time business risks appear too high to attract equity investment, and common shareholders are often remunerated less well than lenders, or at best with a differential yield which does not reflect the difference in risk-taking. If this business uncertainty were dispelled and if there were a return to the pre-existing yield gap between secured loans and equity shares, then there might be a place for preferrred stocks bearing intermediate risks and having an intermediate rate of return, and this could attract back into industrial investment those funds which are at present placed in banks or government securities. From the company's point of view, provided the preferred stocks were not redeemable, it might be worth paying a premium over debt interest rates. On the other hand if the preferred stocks were not redeemable the company could find itself encumbered permanently with a high rate of annual dividend, whereas loans can be re-funded from time to time to take advantage of changes in the market rate.

It is sometimes suggested that whereas there is a limit to the amount debt funds a company can raise, based on the available asset backing and the profit cover for interest, these restrictions do not apply to the same extent to preferred stocks since they are recognized as a higher risk investment. This may be true, but it seems to come close to implying that a company need not be too punctilious in paying preferred dividends—which is not true if a company is to preserve its financial standing in the market.

Perhaps the only safe conclusion is that there are some companies with a strong asset base but fluctuating profits which are limited in their appeal to lenders but which could attract preference capital and would, under normal yield differential between common stock investments and debt securities, welcome the opportunity of doing so.

Convertible Bonds

Convertible bonds carry as one of the terms of issue the option for the holder to convert his bond within a given time period into equity shares at a specified price. If the option is not exercised then the bond will continue its normal term to redemption. If a majority of bondholders decide to convert, the company may take powers to convert the remaining bonds or to repay them at a pre-determined price.

The period and terms of conversion are not normally obvious in the description of the bonds in the balance sheet. For example, "10% Convertible Bonds 1991/95" will be redeemable between 1991 and 1995 if the holders have not opted to convert, but to find out when that option has to be exercised, one would have to look at the notes to the financial statements or refer to the debenture or trust deed.

The advantages of a convertible bond issue from the company's point of view are:

1. Provided money is plentiful and the company has good prospects, it will be possible to offer convertible bonds at a lower interest rate than ordinary debentures. This can be particularly useful for a business which is just starting up or is developing a new product, because the conversion date can be planned to coincide with the growing availability of profits sufficient to pay acceptable dividends.
2. When money is in short supply the incentive of a future share in profits may encourage lenders who would not otherwise invest in the company.
3. If the company is in need of permanent capital but the market price of shares is currently depressed, then the issue of convertible bonds can be used as a delaying tactic in the hope that the conversion period will coincide with higher share prices, thus giving the company as much money as possible per share issued.

The big advantage from the point of view of the investor is that he can wait to see how the share price of the company moves before deciding whether to invest in the equity. He receives a low-risk security with an inbuilt hedge against inflation.

Conversion rights can be used in various ways apart from the simple loan to equity conversion. Bonds may be converted into the shares of an associated company; convertible preferred stock has been used under special circumstances, and also convertible common shares—the initial issue having no dividend rights but being convertible into shares having a full dividend status. In every case the objects are the same—jam tomorrow for the investor, and cheap money today for the business.

Bonds with Warrants

A device in some ways similar to conversion rights is the issue of bonds which cannot themselves be converted into equity but which are accompanied by "warrants" giving the holder the right to obtain a certain number of the company's common shares at fixed future dates at an agreed price.

Under this arrangement the bonds remain outstanding until the date of redemption. The warrants, which are a separate negotiable security, will be dealt with quite independently of the bonds, and the dates at which the subscription rights may be exercised can be either before or after the bonds are redeemed.

From the point of view of the company this arrangement has the advantages that:

1. Provided the business is successful, two lots of capital are made available.
2. As with convertibles, there is a delay before dividends have to be found for the additional equity.
3. The additional equity will form a base for yet further new bond issues, even though the original bond issue has not yet been redeemed.

For the investor the advantages are the same as the convertibles, but he now has the additional option of keeping his original bond while using his warrant to obtain common shares.

Institutional Sources of Venture Capital

When a company has a good product and substantial growth prospects, then, even though it may be small and unlisted, there are many institutions offering venture capital for the purposes of:

1. Getting it established.
2. Assisting its growth.
3. Rescuing it from financial difficulties.

The common form of finance would be a minority share in the equity (sometimes convertible preferred shares or convertible bonds) supported by substantial loan capital. Some venturers will wish to nominate a director to the board, but others prefer not to involve themselves in the management of the business. Where the intention is to develop the company to the stage where it will obtain a stock exchange quotation, the venturer may forego interest and dividends on his investment meanwhile and look for an eventual capital gain.

Many sources of venture capital are available. Some venture capital firms will lend as little as a few thousand dollars, and many, including some tax-exempt foundations, are willing to provide millions in "seed money" to worthy enterprises. Venture capital firms advertise in financial publications as well as in the business and finance section of major newspapers. The *Wall Street Journal* and *Fortune* magazine often carry such ads.

Capital Structure—Debt or Equity

Because loan interest is treated as a business expense for taxation purposes the true cost of interest is considerably less than the nominal rate. Loan capital, therefore, will often be less expensive than share capital (whether common shares or preferred shares). Short-term loans involve less risk for the lender than long-term loans, so the interest rate on short-term borrowing will be lower than on long-term borrowing.

In making these comparisons one must remember that loans are repayable and new borrowing may have to be negotiated. Short-term loans have to be refunded more frequently than long-term loans. There are transaction costs, therefore, to set against the difference in interest charges.

Nevertheless it is a good starting point in the planning of finance to assume that as much of the total capital as possible will be borrowed, and that as much of the total borrowing as possible will be at short term.

As in most areas of financial management there are rules of thumb—custom and practice—about the debt capacity of a business, i.e., its total borrowing potential, and as these are widely used by financial institutions we had better look at them.

The *debt ratio* is measured by:

Total debt*:Total assets

The traditional ratio is 1:2—borrowing and current liabilities should be covered twice by asset values. These clearly must be realistic values and presumably on a "going concern" basis, which would include a value for intangible assets.

The *borrowing ratio* is customarily a percentage:

$$\frac{\text{(Medium and long-term borrowing + overdrafts)} \times 100}{\text{Net assets employed}}$$

Overdrafts are added to long-term borrowing on the grounds that although theoretically repayable on demand, in practice they often become a permanent feature of the financing of the business. This is a question of fact in each case, but for comparison of one company with another a common method of dealing with overdrafts is necessary. The net assets employed would be total assets less current and short-term liabilities other than overdrafts. One might query whether the overdraft facility still unutilized should not also be included in the total of borrowing. There is no generally accepted figure for this ratio. The ratio for one company would be compared with that for other companies in the same type of business.

The debt ratio is sometimes expressed as:

Total debt:Shareholders' funds

This expresses the relationship between the balance sheet asset value financed by debts and that financed by equity.

If it is accepted that debt should be covered twice by asset values, this expected ratio would be 1:1.

*All loans and other liabilities—current, medium term and long term.

As the proportion of loan capital becomes higher, so the risk of lending increases. At a 1:1 ratio, the value of the assets can fall by 50% before the lenders' security is eroded. If the ratio were 2:1 then a fall in asset value of only 33-1/3% would eliminate any margin of safety.

We now come to a point of difficulty. The ratio of total debt to shareholders' funds is referred to in some texts as the debt/equity ratio or *leverage* of the company. Other writers measure a debt/equity ratio in other ways, as we shall see in a minute.

Because a balance sheet ratio is dependent on the methods of valuation used, and is valid only at a point in time, the debt capacity of a company is sometimes measured in terms of interest cover, i.e.:

$$\frac{\text{Earnings before loan interest and taxation}}{\text{Loan interest payable}}$$

The cover required at any time would depend on whether the business was expanding or contracting, and this may be influenced by the state of the economy generally.

The calculation of interest cover should not be confined to loan interest and should not ignore preferred dividends, since these also are a fixed obligation to be satisfied. The distinction, of course, is:

1. That preferred dividends are payable only if profits are available.
2. They are an appropriation of profits, not a business expense. This, however, is a legalistic approach. A company issuing preferred shares will regard itself as committed to regular payment of the fixed dividend, so the preferred share capital should in some way be included with the loan capital in the gearing of the company. This cannot be done in an earnings calculation because the cover for loan interest is profit before tax, whereas the cover for preferred dividends is profit after tax. What commonly is done, therefore, is to modify the *debt ratio* in either form to read:

Total debt and preferred share capital:Total assets

Or

Total debt and preferred share capital:Common shareholders' funds

And this is then referred to as the gearing ratio.

When the proportion of fixed interest commitments or fixed interest capital is high, the structure is said to be highly geared. Low gearing means a low proportion of fixed interest commitments.

When a company has high fixed annual payments of any kind, then the profits available to the common shareholders can vary widely according to the level of activity.

Interest payments (or preferred dividends) have this type of impact.

EXAMPLE

1. Assume, for Year 1, profits before loan interest of $7,000, with annual interest of $200. (Therefore profits less interest are $6,800.) If in Year 2 profits increase by 50% to $10,500, but annual interest remains unchanged, profits less interest are $10,300 (an increase of 51.5% over the previous year). If profits had *fallen* in Year 2 by 50% to $3,500, profits less interest would have been $3,300 (a reduction of 51.5% over the previous year).

2. Assume the same facts as in (1) above, except that annual loan interest is $700. Then the first year's profit less interest will be $6,300 and the corresponding figure for Year 2 will be $9,800 (or $2,800), which is a change of ±55.5%.

Notice carefully that in this example we do not know how many shares exist, what loans are outstanding or what is the balance sheet figure of assets. We are saying simply that increasing loan interest means increasing the risks (and the opportunities) for the common shareholders.

Advantages of Issuing Loan Capital

We have seen already that:

1. It is cheaper for a company to service loan capital than an equal amount of equity.
2. Provided the earnings will cover the loan interest at all times, then the higher the amount of loan interest the bigger the opportunities for swings in equity earnings.

A further advantage is:

3. That loan capital does not affect the control exercised by the ordinary shareholders.

Limitations on Debt Financing

The extent to which a company can raise loan capital will be influenced by the following factors:

1. The borrowing powers in its articles of incorporation.
2. The security it can offer. Once assets are pledged, further loans can be raised only by offering higher rates of interest to compensate for the lack of security.
3. The profits available and anticipated in relation to fixed interest charges.
4. The cash flows expected to cover both interest and loan redemption.
5. The increasing risk that the lenders will exercise effective control over the business because their priority interests have to be protected.
6. The consequent increasing difficulty of attracting venture capital.

As indicated above there are a number of ratios giving broad indications of the safety limits on debt financing, but there is no substitute in any particular instance for detailed investigation of the above points, including inevitably a long-term cash forecast.

Tax Impact of Debt versus Equity Financing*

There are two basic methods of financing corporate expansion, debt financing and equity financing. Debt financing occurs when a corporation borrows money, usually from a bank or from issuance of commercial paper, and uses the proceeds either to acquire additional plant and equipment or to increase working capital. Equity financing occurs when funds are raised by issuance of stock.

Ideally, a major corporate decision such as whether to raise the needed capital by debt financing or equity financing should be made without reference to tax factors. The tax factor should remain neutral and should not enter into the decision at all. However, given our current tax structure, the tax factor is quite often the most important factor affecting the decision of whether to finance expansion by debt or by equity. This is so primarily because debt financing provides the corporation with interest expense, which is deductible, whereas equity financing requires that nondeductible dividends be paid to shareholders. This leads to the conclusion that, where interest rates and dividend payout rates are identical, it will always be more beneficial for the corporation to finance through debt. It will be more beneficial, in after-tax dollars, to finance through issuance of additional stock only where the dividend payout rate is so much lower than the prevailing interest rate that the lower dividend rate will more than offset the advantage that could be gained if a corporation financed through debt and deducted the interest charges. In such an event, where the stock has a relatively low dividend rate, it might be difficult to convince investors to purchase stock when they could obtain a significantly higher yield by purchasing debt obligations.

*This article by Robert W. McGee appeared originally in the February 1976 issue of *TAXES—The Tax Magazine* published and copyrighted by Commerce Clearing House, Inc., Chicago, and appears here with their permission.

The following example illustrates the relative merits of each type of financing where the prevailing market rate of interest and dividend yield rate are identical and where all other factors are equal.

COMPARISON OF EQUITY FINANCING
AND DEBT FINANCING

Assumptions:

a. borrow $1,000,000 or sell $1,000,000 worth of stock

b. 15% return on investment

c. 9% interest rate on dividend

	Debt	Equity
Pre-tax income @15% of $1,000,000	$150,000	$150,000
Less interest expense @9% (dividend is not deductible)	(90,000)	
Net pre-tax income	60,000	150,000
Less tax @50% (combined federal and state)	(30,000)	(75,000)
After-tax income	30,000	75,000
Less dividend @9% of $1,000,000	–	(90,000)
Amount available for investment	$ 30,000	$ (15,000)

Conclusion: Given similar conditions, debt financing is preferable to equity financing. From this example it can be seen that, where all other factors are identical, it will always be more beneficial to finance by debt.

However, in most cases the market rate of interest and the dividend yield are not identical. In such cases it will be necessary to determine which financing method is more beneficial by comparing the relative merits of each. The following example makes this comparison where the market rate of interest and dividend yield are not identical. The effective tax rate is again assumed to be 50%. The amount of capital required is an unknown.

Assumptions:

a. 10½% interest rate

b. (i) $16 stock price
   (ii) $1.20 per share dividend
   (iii) 1.20/16 = 7.5% dividend return

c. 30% pre-tax return on equity

d. the amount of capital required is unknown (x)

	Debt	Equity
Pre-tax income @30% of x	.3000x	.3000x
Less interest expense @10½% of x	(.1050x)	–
Net pre-tax income	.1950x	.3000x
Less tax @50%	(.0975x)	(.1500x)
After-tax income	.0975x	.1500x
Less dividend @7½% of x	–	(.0750x)
Amount available for investment	.0975x	.0750x

Given these facts it is possible to answer the following questions:

1. How much would have to be borrowed in order to have the same amount available for investment as would be had by a $1,000,000 issuance of stock?

a. Issuance of stock would provide $75,000 available for investment.

b. In order to have $75,000 available for investment going the debt route it would be necessary to borrow $75,000/.0975 = $769,230.77.

2. How much stock would have to be issued in order to have the same amount available for investment as would be had by a $1,000,000 loan?

a. A $1,000,000 loan would provide $97,500 available for investment.

b. In order to have $97,500 available for investment going the equity route it would be necessary to issue $97,500/.075 = $1,300,000 in stock, or 81,250 shares at $16 per share.

3. For every $100,000 available for investment the corporation would have to:

a. Issue $1,333,333 worth of stock, or 83,333 shares
        $100,000/.075 = $1,333,333
        1,333,333/$16 = 83,333 shares

b. Borrow $1,025,641 at 10%
        $100,000/.0975 = $1,025,641
   Proof: $1,333,333/$1,025,641 = 1.3
        .0975/.075 = 1.3

Conclusion: The same result could be obtained for every $1 borrowed or $1.30 of stock issued.

Using these facts it is more beneficial to borrow than to issue stock. The first two columns of the next example illustrate the relative advantage of borrowing $1,000,000 rather than issuing $1,000,000 in additional stock.

	Debt		Equity
Capital raised	$1,000,000	$1,000,000	$1,300,000
Pre-tax income @30% of capital	300,000	300,000	390,000
Less interest expense @10½%	(105,000)	–	–
Net pre-tax income	195,000	300,000	390,000
Less tax @50%	(97,500)	(150,000)	(195,000)
After-tax income	97,500	150,000	195,000
Less dividend @7½%	–	(75,000)	(97,500)
Amount available for investment	$ 97,500	$ 75,000	$ 97,500

In order to have $97,500 available for investment it is necessary to borrow $1,000,000 or issue $1,300,000 in stock. Column 3 illustrates that, in order to have $97,500 available for investment going the equity route it would be necessary to issue $1,300,000 in stock, whereas it would be necessary to borrow only $1,000,000.

From these examples it can be stated that, as a general rule, it will be more beneficial to finance by borrowing than by issuing additional stock. However, if the dividend yield is significantly lower than the market rate of interest it may be more beneficial to finance by issuing stock even though the dividend paid will not be deductible. The next two examples illustrate the interrelationship of the tax rate, dividend yield and the market rate of interest.

EXAMPLE 1

	Debt	Equity
Pre-tax income @30% of $1,000,000	$300,000	$300,000
Less interest expense @10½%	(105,000)	0
Net pre-tax income	195,000	300,000
Less tax @50%	(97,500)	(150,000)
After-tax income	97,500	150,000
Less dividend @5¼%	0	(52,500)
Amount available for investment	$ 97,500	$ 97,500

In Example 1, the dividend yield is 5¼%, the interest rate is 10½% and the effective tax rate is 50%. Given these rates, each $1,000,000 of capital yields a net return of $97,500 regardless of whether the capital is raised through debt or

EXAMPLE 2

	Debt	Equity
Pre-tax income @30% of $1,000,000	$300,000	$300,000
Less interest expense @10½%	(105,000)	0
Net pre-tax income	195,000	300,000
Less tax @45%	(87,750)	(135,000)
After-tax income	107,250	165,000
Less dividend @5.775%	0	(57,750)
Amount available for investment	$107,250	$107,250

equity financing. The interrelationship among the three variables could be stated as follows:

$$d = i(1 - t) \qquad\qquad .0525 = .105(1 - .50)$$
$$i = d/(1 - d) \qquad\qquad .105 = .0525/(1 - .50)$$
$$t = 1 - d/i \qquad\qquad .50 = 1 - .0525/.105$$

where d = dividend yield
i = interest rate
t = effective tax rate

The relationship remains valid when the effective tax rate is other than 50%, as illustrated in Example 2. The dividend yield in that case is 5.775%, the interest rate is 10½% and the effective tax rate is 45%.

The break-even point in the second example can also be calculated by using the same equations.

$$d = i(1 - t) \qquad\qquad .0575 = .105(1 - .45)$$
$$i = d/(1 - t) \qquad\qquad .105 = .05775/(1 - 45)$$
$$t = 1 - d/i \qquad\qquad .45 = 1 - .05775/.105$$

By using these equations it is possible to calculate the break-even point where either method of financing will yield the same net result. Once the break-even point is known it is possible to determine which method of financing is preferable when two of the three factors are known. For example, how low must the dividend yield be before a corporation should use equity financing, given an effective tax rate of 49% and an interest rate of 12½%? In order to determine the break-even point it is necessary to use the dividend formula.

$$d = i(1 - t)$$
$$= .125(1 - .49)$$
$$= .06375$$

The break-even point for dividend yield is 6.375%. If the dividend yield falls below this level the corporation should use equity financing rather than debt financing.

If the market rate of interest is more volatile than the dividend yield it might be more advantageous to compute the break-even point in terms of the interest rate. Given an effective tax rate of 46% and a dividend yield of 7½% the break-even interest rate would be computed as follows:

$$i = d/(1 - t)$$
$$= .075/(1 - .46)$$
$$= .1389$$

The break-even interest rate is 13.89%. If the interest rate falls below this figure the corporation should use debt financing. Example 3 illustrates the comparative results when the dividend yield is held constant at 7½%, the effective tax rate is held constant at 46%, and the interest rate is allowed to vary.

As can be seen, the break-even interest rate is 13.89%. The 12% rate results in a larger bottom line figure and the 15% rate results in a smaller figure than could be obtained by equity financing.

Another factor to consider is the long-run cost of each method of financing. Using debt it is possible to lock in to a given interest rate for a period of years. If rates become more favorable it may be possible to refinance the outstanding debt at a lower rate of interest. In the case of equity financing the dividend pay-out may increase over time, as companies tend to increase dividends more often than reduce them. Other factors to consider would be brokerage and legal fees associated with a stock issuance, and compensating balances required if debt is incurred by bank financing.

If it is expected that the corporation's effective tax rate will change, as a

EXAMPLE 3

	Debt			Equity
Interest rate	12%	13.89%	15%	
Pre-tax income @20% of				
$1,000,000	$200,000	$200,000	$200,000	$200,000
Less interest expense	(120,000)	(138,900)	(150,000)	0
Net pre-tax income	80,000	61,100	50,000	200,000
Less tax @46%	(36,800)	(28,100)	(23,000)	(92,000)
After-tax income	43,200	33,000	27,000	108,000
Less dividend @7½%	0	0	0	(75,000)
Amount available for				
investment	$ 43,200	$ 33,000	$ 27,000	$ 33,000

result of legislation or for some other reason, it may be worthwhile to calculate the differential impact on debt versus equity financing. Using an interest rate of 13.89% and a dividend yield of 7½%, a decrease in the effective tax rate from 46% to 44% would have the effect as shown in Example 4.

EXAMPLE 4

	Debt		Equity	
Pre-tax income @20% of $1,000,000	$200,000	$200,000	$200,000	$200,000
Less interest expense @13.89%	(138,900)	(138,900)	0	0
Net pre-tax income	61,100	61,100	200,000	200,000
Less tax @46%	(28,100)	0	(92,000)	0
@44%	0	(26,900)	0	(88,000)
After-tax income	33,000	34,200	108,000	112,000
Less dividend @7½%	0	0	(75,000)	(75,000)
Amount available for investment	$ 33,000	$ 34,200	$ 33,000	$ 37,000

Given these conditions, a decrease in the effective tax rate would increase disposable income in both cases, but would increase it more in the case of equity financing. In the event of an increase in the effective tax rate, disposable income would decrease in both cases, but it would decrease more in the case of equity financing. As a general rule, all other things being equal, it will be more beneficial to plan for equity financing if a decrease in the effective tax rate is expected, and for debt financing if an increase is expected. Of course, all other things are almost never equal, so a tax rate change will not be as important a factor as would be a change in interest rate or dividend yield for determining which method of financing to use in most instances.

Summary

Some general rules can be made regarding the relationship of dividend yield, interest rate and effective tax rate to debt and equity financing. Where the interest rate and dividend pay-out rates are identical it will always be more beneficial to finance by debt rather than equity because interest costs are deductible, whereas dividend payments are not. Where the interest rate and dividend payout are in equilibrium (the rates may differ but the bottom-line result will be the same regardless of which method of financing is used), a decline in the dividend payout rate will make equity financing less costly than debt financing, and an increase in the dividend payout rate will have the opposite effect. A decline in the interest rate would make debt financing less costly, and an increase would have the opposite effect. A decline in the effective tax rate would increase the bottom line figure in both types of financing, with the larger increase occurring in the case of equity financing. An increase in the effective tax rate would lead to a decline in both bottom line figures, with the smaller decline occurring in the case of debt financing. These rules can be used to aid in determining which method of financing will be less costly in a given situation.

The Cost
of Capital

Importance of the Cost of Capital

The cost of the funds employed by a company will affect:

1. The evaluation of its various investment proposals—whether investment in fixed assets and working capital, or investments in stocks and bonds. The rate of return obtained from such investments must clearly be greater than the cost of the funds employed. The methods of making such evaluations are the subjects of Chapter 10.
2. The best way of overcoming short-term liquidity problems. The various sources of short-term finance were reviewed in Chapter 4, and some indication of the relative costs involved was given.
3. The decision on the best long-term financing structure. We looked at the possible sources of long-term finance in Chapter 6, and talked briefly about capital gearing—the combination of equity and fixed interest capital.

In this chapter we shall attempt to decide what "cost of capital" is relevant when a company is reviewing its investment strategies, making long-term plans and taking particular investment decisions. In Chapter 9 we shall link this cost of capital to the "rate of return on capital employed," which is the primary measure of success in reviewing company accounts, and set out a logical approach to the financial analysis of those accounts.

There is no single agreed method of arriving at the overall cost of capital for a company, but luckily in dealing with practical situations most methods give answers sufficiently similar as a guide for action.

We will approach the problem by looking at the cost of funds from the three main sources of long-term finance—equity capital, retained earnings, and long-term debt.

The Cost of Equity Capital

One approach to establishing the cost of equity capital is to ask what rate of return an investor expects to receive when he puts his money into an equity investment; and at this stage we are considering equities as a whole rather than the particular circumstances of any individual company—we will come back to that later.

It is assumed that there is an opportunity cost of investing in one company rather than another, and unless the rate offered by our company is comparable with that of others then we shall not attract future investment.

The indefatigable British investigators of this field are, of course, A. J. Merrett and A. Sykes, whose book *The Finance and Analysis of Capital Projects,* published in 1963, has established itself as a definitive text. One of their more recent conclusions is that over the period 1965-66 the average rate of return achieved by shareholders in the United Kingdom (taking dividends and capital gains together) was about 9.6% in money terms or 6.4% in real terms (after taking account of inflation). This was after all relevant corporate and personal taxes.

During the 1970s the achieved rate must have declined due to increasing costs combined with government restrictions on both profit margins and dividends, and a return in real terms of 4% before personal taxes might be nearer the current level of achievement. What this means in terms of company earnings will depend on:

1. The rate of inflation.
2. The rate of tax on corporate profits.
3. The amount of profit distributed as dividend.

If we assume a moderate rate of inflation—say 13% per annum, corporation tax at an effective rate of 50%, and a dividend yield of 5%, then to achieve a rate of return of 4% in real terms a company needs to earn 32% in money terms before tax. This is shown in the following example:

		£
On £1,000 invested, the company earns		
a profit of		320
Less: Corporation tax 50%		160
	£	160
To pay a dividend of	50	
Less: Advanced corporation tax (say 30%)*	15	
the amount taken from profits will be		35
leaving retained profits of		£125

*In the United Kingdom a portion of dividend income is withheld before the shareholder receives payment, similar to wage withholding for U.S. employees. The United States currently does not apply withholding to dividends.

The shareholders thus end the year with total wealth £(1,000 + 125 + 50) = £1,175, but with the cost of living increased by 13% this is equivalent to only £1,175/1.13 = £1,040 in real terms. They have thus achieved an increment of 4% on the original amount invested.

Note that in this example we have made the simplification of assuming that the capital invested in the business is identical with the amount of cash paid out by the shareholder to acquire his interest in the company, i.e., that the £1,000 arises from an initial issue of shares. When we come to analyze the results of a business already in existence we assume that the book total of capital and retained profits is about the same amount as the shareholders have paid for their shares on the stock exchange, or for which they could realize their shares if they wanted to invest their money elsewhere. In other words we are assuming that the main determinant of stock prices, certainly in the long run, is the underlying asset value as shown in the balance sheet. If all companies were to state their assets at updated current values there might be an element of truth in this assumption, which in any case is probably at least as reliable as the 4% "guestimated" target rate with which we started.

A very minor approximation compared with those which we have just outlined is the rate of corporation tax. With a standard rate of 50% the actual effective rate will be slightly different because of the impact of capital allowances, disallowed expenses, and the various differences in timing that enter into the company's deferred taxation account.

An alternative approach to the cost of equity capital is to consider what difference in rate of return has to be offered in order to persuade investors to purchase equity shares rather than to put their money into relatively low-risk fixed interest investments.

There seems to be a consensus of opinion that this risk premium is somewhere between 3% and 5% over the gross equivalent of the rate receivable on a municipal bond investment. With a municipal bond rate of 8% tax free (say 12% gross) then earnings for equities should be between 15% and 17% after corporation tax. This is similar to the 16% rate illustrated above.

The Cost of Retained Profits

The rate of return required on retained profits is the same as the rate required on new equity capital. The net dividend paid to a shareholder is subject to further tax in his hands and can be invested by him. If the company had not paid the net dividend it could have invested the money. On that retention, therefore, just as on any other element of equity capital, it must earn the competitive rate discussed in the previous section.

The foregoing statement is not completely true because:

1. The tax liability of some individual shareholders, particularly in the higher ranges of taxation, may be affected by the receipt of dividends rather than the eventual realization of capital gains.
2. The company will in effect save money if it retains profits rather than distributing dividends and having to raise fresh capital.

These ripple effects of the dividend decision, however, are not easy to evaluate, and probably do not invalidate the general conclusion of the statement.

One thing we have ignored in all our calculations so far is the difference in timing of cash effects of different decisions, particularly the deferment of tax liability. This may not be of great importance in the context of the continuing stream of company activities and of the approximate yardsticks we are using. But it can be very important in deciding between the different possible uses of capital funds—different corporate investment projects—which we shall be discussing in Chapter 10.

The Cost of Equity for a Particular Company

So far we have been talking about the average cost of equity for any company in the market for funds, and have reached the conclusion that the return on shareholders' funds as a whole in a company must be competitive with that available

from any other form of investment, after allowing for differences in risk between different investments. We applied this risk differential to the comparison
of fixed interest with equity investments. There will also be differences in risk
between the equity shares of different types of business, and within any class of
business between individual companies.

How do investors themselves rate different companies? In theory by forecasting each company's likely rate of growth. How do they achieve such a
forecast? Largely from the belief that past growth rates will be continued into
the future!

It would appear then that the cost of capital for a particular company can
be discovered by looking at the relationship between its past profit achievement
and the market price per share which resulted from it, in other words by looking
at one or both of two ratios:

1. The *dividend yield,* i.e., the most recent dividend per share:the market
   price per share after the dividend was declared.
2. The *earnings yield,* i.e., the current annual earnings per share:the current
   market price per share.

It is arguable however that the market price of a share reflects not merely
what dividends or earnings have been achieved, but what, starting from that
basis, the shareholder expects to be achieved in the future. In other words he is
forecasting growth rates. The cost of capital, therefore, is better stated as:

3. *Dividend yield plus an allowance for future growth,* for example:

   a. $\dfrac{\text{most recent dividend}}{\text{market price}} + \dfrac{\%\text{ growth rate in}}{\text{dividend expected}}$

   b. $\dfrac{\text{most recent dividend}}{\text{market price}} + \dfrac{\%\text{ growth rate in}}{\text{share price expected}}$

4. *Future earnings yield,* i.e., anticipated annual earnings per share:current
   market price per share.

It may be asked how the market price moves if shareholders are satisfied
with the company's earnings performance but dissatisfied with the proportion of
earnings distributed as dividend. Shareholders may be prepared to accept a low
dividend for one or two years during a period of business development or tight
liquidity, but in the long run they require cash in their pockets comparable with
that obtainable from other investments. On this basis, most of the theoretical
work on the cost of capital has concentrated on the dividend yield plus an
allowance for future growth.

In practice, however, when rating one company against another the most commonly used measure is the earnings yield, not in the form presented above but conversely:

$$\frac{\text{current market price per share}}{\text{current annual earnings per share}}$$
(usually the earnings in the last annual report)

In this form it is known as the *price/earnings ratio,* abbreviated to P/E ratio. The figure "earnings" used is the profit after tax, and the P/E ratio expresses the number of years' earnings represented by the current market price. For example if the relevant earnings of a company last year were $260,000 on 5,200,000 shares, i.e., $0.05 per share, and the market price of those shares today was $0.25, then the P/E ratio would be 5:1 and the market price would represent five years' earnings at the current level. The significance of a P/E ratio can only be judged in relation to the ratios of other companies in the same type of business. If the median P/E ratio for a group of companies was 6, then a ratio of 14 for a particular company would suggest that the shares of that company were in great demand probably because a rapid growth of earnings was expected. A low ratio, say 3 for example, would indicate a company not greatly favored by investors and probably with poor growth prospects.

In most cases it is possible to make valid comparisons of the P/E ratios of different companies using the earnings figures as reported.

The Cost of Debt Capital

The money cost of fixed interest capital is as stated in the loan agreement less the tax relief obtainable because loan interest is treated as a business expense. (This is sometimes referred to as the "tax shield" effect of borrowing.)

The real cost, however, will be considerably less than the money cost in times of inflation because the real cost of interest payments and of the eventual capital repayment in money terms will be reduced as inflation proceeds. For example, if a business borrowed $5,000 for one year at 15% (less tax deduction at 50%) it would pay out at the end of the year the $5,000 capital plus $750 interest, a total of $5,750. Since $375 is saved in taxes (50% of $750), the net interest cost is only one-half of the actual interest paid.

If the rate of inflation for the year had been 15% then in terms comparable with the receipt of the loan the company would relinquish only $5,375/1.15 = $4,675 approximately. The real cost of the loan would therefore have been negative.

Weighted Average Cost of Capital

The overall cost of capital for a particular company will be the weighted average cost of the various forms of capital employed. There are two possible approaches to this calculation, either to weight the costs by the *book value* of the different forms of capital or to weight them by the *market value* of each form of capital.

Take for example a company having 20,000 common shares, $6,000 in 15% long-term debt, and $4,500 short-term loans on which the rate of interest is 9%. The book value of the common shareholders' funds is $19,500. The market price per share is $2.50, and the long-term debt stands at 104. The rate of corporation tax is 50%. The assumed cost of equity capital is 16% after tax.

Using book value weightings, the weighted average cost of capital would be:

Form of capital	Book value	Weighting	Cost after tax	Weighted cost
	$	%	%	%
Equity	19,500	65	16	10.40
Long term loans	6,000	20	7.5	1.50
Short-term loans	4,500	15	4.5	0.68
Total	30,000	100		12.58

If market value weightings were used the result would be:

Equity 20,000	$	%	%	%
X $2.50	50,000	82.3	16	13.17
Long-term loans				
$6,000 X 104	6,240	10.3	7.5	0.77
Short-term loans	4,500	7.4	4.5	0.33
	60,740	100.0		14.27

There is no doubt that the market value approach is the more correct, for the following reasons:

1. The 16% cost of equity capital was based in the first instance on studies of rates of return obtained by investing at market prices.
2. Investments are normally rated by reference to their earnings yield, and the company has a responsibility to maintain that yield.
3. At the present time the historical book values used in preparing balance

sheets do not represent, or purport to represent, a valuation of the capital employed.

4. In evaluating its own investment decisions, such as the purchase of new assets or the development and launching of new products, the business must look for a rate of return appropriate to the true cost of the capital employed in the project.

Although the cost of equity has been illustrated above at the figure of 16%, which we developed as an average cost for all companies, the percentage to be used when making a cost of capital study for a particular company will incorporate a risk rating relevant to the nature of the business and the inflation percentage currently being experienced.

A query might be raised about the correctness of using the market value of long-term debt securities in the weighted average calculation, since the company is responsible only for earning (in the above example) 7½% on the original amount of the loan, and if the market price of the loan is above par, the real implication would seem to be that in relation to this particular company a rate of slightly less than 7½% is acceptable. Possibly the correct solution in calculating a weighted average cost of capital would be to use the market value of equity but the nominal value of long-term debt securities. As a practical point, however, unless the company relies very heavily on borrowed money a small difference in the figure of long-term debt securities used in the calculation will not make any significant difference to the overall cost of capital.

A more serious question is what the calculation should be if the market value of the equity is significantly below the book value. If this is due to a general decline in share prices in a depressed economy then possibly the reduced value must be accepted in making the cost of capital calculation. If, however, it is a sign that shareholders have lost faith in this particular company, a return to normality can be achieved not by targeting a traditional rate of return on the reduced capital value but by looking for an enhanced rate of return. This highlights a key point about the foregoing calculations. They are *not* necessarily target figures. They merely state what is the cost of capital with a given capital structure at a particular time.

What we need both for planning and control purposes is to decide what our average cost of capital will be under future conditions with our future capital structure.

Let us revert to the second "weightings" example and set it out in a slightly different way:

Form of capital	Market/book value	Cost after tax %	$
Equity—20,000 @ $2.50	$ 50,000	16.0	8,000

Form of capital	Market/book value	Cost after tax %	Cost after tax $
Long-term debt securities	6,000	7.5	450
Short-term debt securities	4,500	4.5	202.50
Total	60,500	Average = 14.3	8,652.50

Now suppose we need to raise $17,500 more capital. We decide to do this in the form of 5,000 new common shares, which can still be issued at a market price of $2.50, and $5,000 long-term debt securities. Because for various reasons (which we will discuss in a minute) we reckon that the business will now have a slightly higher risk rating, and possibly because of economic factors affecting the market generally, we expect to have to pay 8.6% for the additional long-term debt securities (giving us a new average rate of 8%) and to uplift our earnings on the equity from 16% to 16½%. The new average cost of capital is therefore forecast as follows:

	$	%	$
Equity—25,000 @ $2.50	62,500	16.5	10,312.5
Long-term debt securities	11,000	8.0	880.0
Short-term debt securities	4,500	4.5	202.5
Total	78,000	Average = 14.6	11,395.0

And the net effect of changing our capita structure, the *marginal cost of capital*, will be:

17,500		2,742.5
	Marginal cost = 15.7%	

In looking at our future business accounts for the purpose of checking that we are achieving the required rate of return on capital employed, we shall need to make use of the forecast average cost of capital, in a manner to be discussed in Chapter 9. In evaluating proposals for capital investment, however, we shall need to use the marginal cost of capital, bearing in mind that if no change in the various element costs occurs then the marginal cost of capital will be the same as the weighted average cost.

In the example just considered, not only was the total capital of the business increased but there was also a change in the capital leveraging—long-term debt securities plus short-term debt securities moved from $\frac{10,500}{60,500} = 17\%$ of the total

capital to $\frac{15,500}{78,000} = $ nearly 20%.

The traditional theory of capital structure is that as the level of gearing increases within a moderate range of gearing ratios, so the average cost of capital will fall. This is because debt finance is cheaper than equity finance, and provided the proportion of debt capital remains small:

1. There will be adequate profits to pay interest, and adequate capital to provide security, so that successive borrowings can be made without increased risk to the *lenders* and without any increase in the interest rate.
2. There will be adequate profits to ensure a dividend after the loan interest has been paid, and no reason why lenders should need to involve themselves with the management of the company provided the conditions of their loans are fulfilled so that successive borrowings can be made without increased risk to the *common shareholders* and thus without any fall in the share price, i.e., without any increase in the effective cost of equity capital.

But as gearing is increased there will come a point at which lenders feel less assured that the company will always be able to service its loan capital, and shareholders become uneasy that the business may be conducted primarily to satisfy lenders' requirements with only a residual regard for the return on equity. At that point the cost of both types of capital will begin to rise, and further gearing will in fact increase the average cost of capital employed.

This belief in a U-shaped cost of capital curve as gearing increases is not universally accepted either as true or as capable of accurate prediction. This has been a fruitful field for academic debate, but the most original contributions now date back eight to ten years.

Abbreviated summaries of three well-publicized theories are as follows:

1. Modigliani and Miller. They maintain that if tax were ignored, the financial structure of the company will *not* affect the average cost of capital (assuming the cost of capital is based on market values for both equity and fixed interest capital).

   Take an example. A company has some common shares and the earnings attributable to them are $.10 per share. The existing share price is $1 so the earnings yield is 10%. The company also has an equal amount of debt capital at an interest rate of 8%. The average cost of capital is 9%. Now if for any reason the share price rises to $1.40, the earnings yield will drop to $.10/$1.40 = 7%. Shareholders will sell their shares and buy debt securities yielding 10%. The price of shares will drop back, the price of debt securities will rise, until stability is again reached at 9%.

   Take another possibility. The company increases its debt/equity ratio. There is now a higher proportion of loan capital at the lower rate of 8%, so one expects the average cost of capital to decline. The shareholders, however, are now at greater risk. Some of them sell their shares in order to buy debt securities, the market price of shares falls, and stability is again restored.

Well, whatever truth there is in these assumptions about the shareholders' willingness and ability to restructure their own investment holdings, our real concern is what happens to the cost of capital *after tax*. Modigliani and Miller agree that because of the tax shield the average cost of capital will fall as the debt/equity ratio increases. They deny any upturn in cost, however, partly because of the "arbitrage" switches noted above, and partly because they believe lenders would stop lending before the upturn occurred. (Remember, again, that this is all based on market values of capital.)

2. Resek. A nice simple position—unless there is some possibility of default on debt securities, the risk to the lender does not increase with leveraging, and there is no need for the interest rate to rise. If there is a possibility of default one assumes that the company ought not to be raising fresh capital anyhow.

3. Brigham and Gordon. Their investigations suggested that shareholders are in favor of leveraging. As the debt/equity ratio is increased, so the cost of equity increases, but not so much as the investigators expected it would.

Generalized cost of capital calculations, however, only provides a starting point for the investigation of what you have to earn for your investors next year, given an imperfect capital market and unstable economic conditions.

Segment Cost of Capital

We said above that an average cost of capital was needed in order to evaluate capital expenditure projects, in fact to provide a cutoff rate when deciding whether a project was acceptable or not. This would be fine if all uses of capital were obviously profitable, but in practice many apparently necessary uses of capital do not yield measurable profits. Among these are:

1. The accommodation and equipment needed for administrative staff. It may be possible to calculate a benefit from employing administrative personnel by comparing the costs involved with the cost of having the same work done by an outside firm, but in many cases this alternative is not available either because the work is confidential or because it is so closely intertwined with the other activities of the business that no outsider could do it. In such cases it is impracticable to measure a rate of return on the capital employed.

2. Research work, as distinct from the development of salable products, is of its nature nonprofit earning. It is not possible to define a rate of return on the facilities employed.

3. Welfare and amenity projects again add to the general profitability of the business in indirect ways. A new cafeteria or playing field does not of itself yield a profit that can be measured.

To the extent that our capital is to be invested in nonprofitable uses, we have to augment the rate of return required from other projects. Suppose for example that our average cost of capital, i.e., the rate of return we shall seek when using that capital, is 14.6%, and 15% of the total is to be used in non-profit projects. Then we have to recover the whole cost of capital from 85% of its uses, on which we shall be looking for a rate of return of 14.6/85 = 17.2%.

Another possibility is that we shall be using capital to buy land and buildings which will be occupied for a variety of business activities. The cost of premises in this instance cannot be taken up into projects for the purchase of the plant and equipment, but is the subject of a separate decision to buy rather than to lease the premises. What rate of return would we expect from carrying on the business of property ownership, as distinct from our business as manufacturers or shopkeepers? Suppose we decide that 30% of our total capital will be used in buying premises, and that a reasonable rate of return for us as property owners is 8%, then, continuing from the calculations in the previous paragraph, we finish up with the following position.

Use of capital	% of total (a)	Rate of return to be achieved % (b)	Weighted rate % (a) × (b)
Administration, research and welfare	15	—	—
Land and buildings	30	8.0	2.4
Other operational uses	55	22.2	12.2
	100	14.6	14.6

The overall cost of capital is in this instance 14.6%, but in appraising most capital expenditure projects we shall have to look for a 22.2% rate of return after taxes.

8

Obtaining Funds from the Capital Market

Advantages of Public Companies

In Chapter 6 we deferred consideration of the various methods by which shares and debentures could be issued to the public. We are now going to deal with this subject. We shall be talking about public companies which either are already listed on a stock exchange or are seeking a listing in connection with the issue.

So let us first summarize the advantages of becoming a public company and of obtaining a listing. Although theoretically separable, the two things almost inevitably go together, and are commonly thought of together when the expression "going public" is used of a company. The advantages of public status are small without a listing.

What is lost when a company goes public?

1. In a private company, there will be close personal contact among proprietors, managers (often the same people) and employees. The public company, appealing to outside shareholders, loses the contact between proprietors and managers other than through formal meetings, and as the object of going public is growth, eventually there may be the penalty of

growth in the loosening of ties with employees. This is not inevitable, but an organization problem is introduced.

2. The private company, within its limited means, can be more enterprising. It can undertake development projects having low immediate returns without the need for quick profits to satisfy absentee shareholders. Against this, of course, the scale of its operation is limited.

3. Usually, the members of a private company are in control of the business. With outside shareholders, and possibly eventually outside directors, the freedom of action of the original proprietors may be restricted. This is a general statement of the particular case in (2) above. Note, however, that it is sometimes possible to make a public long-term debt offering while keeping the common stock unlisted. New members on the board can, however, be an advantage of going public. Private companies sometimes get into trouble because of the lack of management skills among family shareholders.

4. The private company knows who its shareholders are, so it cannot be faced with a takeover from someone who has acquired a large block of shares. Again, is a takeover always a bad thing for the future prospects of a business? Obviously not. In discussing the "advantages" of private or public status, it is important to ask "advantages to whom?" The development of the business as a profitable entity, the employees, the community, or certain existing shareholders or managers?

What are the advantages of a public company with a stock exchange listing?

1. It can get additional capital more easily and in larger amounts than the private company, not only through issues of shares and bonds but also because banks and other short-term lenders will have greater grounds for confidence in it.

2. Its listed shares are acceptable as consideration in merger and takeover transactions.

These two points mean that the business can grow more quickly.

The three points that follow are of more advantage to the members of the pre-existing private company:

3. Subject to the facts of the case, the public company is likely to avoid "closely held company" status for tax purposes.

4. Because the shares are easily negotiable, the members can obtain cash for part or the whole of their interests. This can be important when, for example, one of the members wishes to retire from business.

5. The market price of the shares will often be a readily acceptable basis of valuation for the purpose of estate and gift taxes.

Requirements for Publicly
Held Companies

The Securities Exchange Commission (SEC) requires that all publicly held companies be audited annually by a firm of independent certified public accountants. The CPA firm issues a report based on their audit stating their opinion on the fairness of the financial statements presented by the company. This presentation of opinion by the independent CPA is referred to as the "attest function."

An audit by a firm of independent CPA's adds credibility to the financial statements. Creditors, potential creditors, stockholders, potential stockholders, financial analysts, and government regulatory agencies all rely on the opinion expressed by the CPA. Although the purpose of the audit is to determine whether the financial statements are presented fairly, the auditor is not responsible for detecting errors or irregularities that have a material effect on the financial statements. The audit is not conducted to detect fraud, per se.

There are other long-range benefits associated with an independent audit. Material weaknesses in internal control are often uncovered, and once such weaknesses are uncovered they can be corrected. The auditors also make recommendations to improve effectiveness and efficiency. These recommendations sometimes result in savings that are large enough to pay for a substantial portion of the total audit costs. Tax advice offered by the CPA firm, which has a group of tax specialists, often results in additional savings.

Audit and other legal requirements will be covered in detail in later chapters. Because of the large amounts of money that are generated by the capital market, specialized institutions have emerged to facilitate the flow of funds from supplier to user. Over the years this market has become very complex and efficient, and many different groups are involved.

Role of the Investment Banker

The financial manager is to the general practitioner as the investment banker is to the surgeon or other medical specialist. Whereas the financial manager can handle the day-to-day financial management problems of the company, a specialist has to be called in to handle a major offering. The average financial manager is unfamiliar with the intricate interworkings of the capital market because it is a market he never has to deal with.

Unlike commercial bankers, who lend money, the investment banker acts as a middleman who coordinates the flow of funds from those who wish to invest to those who need the funds. If the investment banker lends at all it is only for a short period of time. Basically the corporation needing funds sells its issue to the investment bankers, and the bankers in turn resell the issue in smaller lots to a variety of buyers. Investment bankers are akin to wholesalers in that they purchase a product (securities) from the original source and sell the product on the retail market. A corporation that sells securities only occasionally does not have the facilities or expertise to float such a large offering without outside help. The expense of maintaining such an organization would be prohibitive. Investment bankers often do not buy the securities directly but merely find buyers, who use the investment banker as an intermediary.

The investment banking firm that handles an offering is called the originating house. Since his name is associated with the offering, the banker must be very thorough in his evaluation of the prospective company. If he sells an issue for a company that later goes bankrupt it will be very difficult to sell a subsequent offering to those same investors. An exhaustive study is generally made of the company's financial statements and management. The originating house often sells a portion of the issue to other investment bankers. The originating house recommends terms and price to the issuing corporation, since it has a more intimate knowledge of the market. Offering attractive terms and price will greatly facilitate a quick sale, which is usually very important to a corporation in need of cash. The originating house also helps the issuing corporation prepare the necessary legal documents that must be filed with various federal and state agencies.

Underwriting an Issue

The investment banker usually obtains an option to purchase the entire offering and agrees to deliver a check to the issuer for the full amount within a week or two of the public offering date. Since most investment bankers do not wish to swallow an entire issue themselves, they will enter into agreement with other investment bankers to share the risk and profits. This way, each banker will be required to sell only a small portion of the total offering. If the entire offering is not sold within the specified time period, the investment banker will borrow short-term funds from a commercial bank and use the unsold securities as collateral.

As an alternative to underwriting an issue, offerings are sometimes sold on a "best efforts" basis, which eliminates the investment banker's risk. Under this arrangement the investment banker sells the issue at a fixed price and receives a commission for his efforts. If the banker does not sell the entire issue, his commission income potential is not fully realized, but he does not bear the risk of swallowing the unsold portion. Small companies often obtain funds in this manner, since investment bankers may be unwilling to undertake the risk of underwriting an issue for a small, relatively unknown company. Some very large corporations sell issues on a best efforts basis because the risk of not selling the entire issue is slight, and paying a commission to an investment banker is cheaper than paying him to assume an almost nonexistent risk.

The investment banker depends on turnover. When an issue is underwritten, the gross profit is often less than 1%. If an issue is not sold out, the investment banker must borrow funds and pay interest until the total issue is sold. This not only ties up his funds, thereby preventing him from participating in other issues, but also creates the possibility of taking a loss on the issue that is unsold.

Investment bankers may be chosen either by public bid or direct negotiation. Although it would appear on the surface that investment banking is a highly competitive business, competition is limited by several factors. Many corporations tend to use the same investment banking firm year after year because the quality of service offered over the years has been consistent, and the cost savings resulting from changing investment bankers is not significant enough to warrant the risk involved of hiring another firm with unproven ability.

Another limiting factor is the fact that many investment bankers tend to specialize in one or two fields. One may specialize in insurance company securities, another in utility issues, etc. Although there may be hundreds of investment bankers to choose from, there may be only a few who have the expertise and resources to handle a particular issue.

Private Placement

A private placement is the sale of a large block of securities to institutional investors directly by a corporation. Generally private placements consist of long-term debt issues. Institutional investors consist primarily of insurance companies, commercial banks, and pension funds. Private placements can usually be made in a very short period of time, and this is one of the primary reasons why corporations use the private placement rather than an investment banker. Private placements do not have to comply with the complex SEC regulations, and this saves both time and money. The interest a corporation must pay on a private placement is usually somewhat higher than the interest that would be paid on a public offering because institutional investors are more shrewd than the general public, and part of the cost savings inherent in a private offering are usually passed on to the investor in the form of a higher interest rate.

Pricing Equity Issues

Within the total amount of money required from an issue, the company has to decide how many shares to issue at what price each. In this decision, it will rely heavily on the expertise and experience of the originating house. Five things have to be considered:

1. Without regard to any other factors, what sort of share price will investors think is appropriate? The decision here is subjective and therefore to some extent arbitrary, but it would be possible to say, for example, that a price of $5 per share would seem excessive to a lot of investors who like to hold plenty of share certificates for their money, and a price as low as 10¢ per share would be regarded with suspicion as an attempt either to sell off useless shares or to spread shareholdings so widely as to avoid concentrations of voting power.

2. What are the market ratings of similar companies already listed? These would be expressed in terms of P/E ratio, dividend yield, and dividend cover. These expressions will be familiar to you, and their significance should become clear in the example that follows a little further on.

3. To what extent should the company try to surpass its competitor's performances to ensure a small premium developing when dealings in the shares commence? The prospect of an increase over the issue price will encourage investors to subscribe to this issue in preference to others, and the achievement of this premium will give the underwriters a small profit on any shares they have to take up. It will also be remembered favorably when future issues are made by the company. The prospect of a large premium, however, is undesirable. It would mean that the company was not getting as much money from the issue as it might. And it would encourage speculators to subscribe for shares with the object of selling them at a profit as soon as dealings commence. This causes an undesirable fall in price. It also means that long-term investors may fail to get the numbers of shares they apply for because speculation has caused an oversubscription.

4. Having regard to the amount of capital to be raised and the forecast of profits available to service it, can the company achieve the required P/E ratio?

5. If the P/E ratio is acceptable, can the number of shares and the price per share be planned to give competitive figures of earnings per share and dividend per share?

If it should prove impossible to meet market requirements in relation to the P/E ratio or the profits per share, and if the forecast of profits cannot be improved, then it will be necessary to consider whether gearing with fixed interest capital can be introduced to achieve the required results.

The foregoing description may perhaps be clarified by an example. It is a fairly long example but in essence extremely simple. In fact, it illustrates what the more mathematically minded might regard as the oversimplified approach to share pricing which is customarily adopted by originating houses.

EXAMPLE

Company X is going public and needs to raise $600,000 by an issue of common shares. Future maintainable earnings for the common shareholders are forecast at $45,000 per annum.

The company has to decide how many shares it shall issue (and therefore at what price).

From the *Wall Street Journal* it extracts the following information about three companies in a similar line of business. (Note: Columns 1 and 4 have been added to help explain the published figures.)

Company	(1) Earnings dollars per share	(2) Dividend dollars per share	(3) Price dollars per share	(4) P/E ratio (3 ÷ 1)	(5) Dividend yield (2 ÷ 3)
A	6.0	3.0	79	13.2	3.8%
B	3.46	1.88	37	10.7	5.1%
C	9.4	2.94	140	14.9	2.1%

Notice three things about these figures:

1. *P/E ratio*. This is a reasonably close grouping. In the full list of food and grocery companies from which these three extracts were made, the P/E ratios fell into three groups: one group under P/E 10 with a mean of about 8.8; a second group with P/Es between 11 and 15, averaging 12.5; and a third small group of randomly higher ratios. Companies A, B, and C, therefore, are representative of the middle group—the plodders rather than the high flyers.

   Our Company X would probably like to achieve a P/E ratio toward the top of this group, but this is not likely to occur immediately on a first public issue unless Company X already has a household name.

   At this stage, therefore, Company X will look for a P/E rating somewhere between 10 and 15.

2. *Share price*. The range here (and in the full list) is enormous. In the full list, however, there is a marked clustering between $50 and $80, with an average of $66.

   Company X does not want to overprice its issue, and might consider a price within the range $60-$70.

3. *Other data.* There is no observable norm for these three companies which are alleged to be comparable in the type of business they conduct.

Company X would like to offer something better than its main competitor, but not unreasonable in relation to the average market data. It would probably set target figures for earnings per share, dividend per share and dividend yield, and then try out a few alternative plans as illustrated below.

Let us assume that Company X's shopping list is as follows:

P/E ratio	not less than 10. Aim for 15
Share price	$60-$70
Earnings per share	$6
Dividend per share	$2
Dividend yield	5%

The stages in developing its issue plan are as follows:

1. P/E ratio. In the absence of factors unknown to us, the opening P/E ratio will presumably equate the value of the issue ($600,000) with the forecast earnings ($45,000), so it will be $\frac{600,000}{45,000} = 13.3$ which is within the desired range.

2. If the issue price per share is to be $60, then the number of shares issued will be $\frac{\$600,000}{\$60} = \$10,000$.

   If the share price is $70 it will be necessary to issue $\frac{\$600,000}{\$70} = 8,571$ shares.

3. If 10,000 shares are issued, the earnings per share will be $\frac{\$45,000}{10,000} = \$4.50$.

   The dividend will be $2.30 and the dividend yield will be $2.30 ÷ $60 = 3.8%.

   We conclude, therefore, that if we issue the shares at $60, the earnings per share and the dividend per share will be slightly better than for Company B in our sample, the dividend yield as good as Company A (the middle performer) but all well below our provisional target.

4. If we issue 8,571 shares at $70, the other figures will be:

Earnings per share	$45,000 ÷ 8,571	= $5.20
Dividend yield	2.6 ÷ 70	= 3.7%

The first figure is better than before, the dividend yield about the same, and still we have not reached our target figures.

5. At this point, therefore, either:
   a. We must try to improve the forecast profit.
   b. We must modify our targets in some way.
   c. We must try to improve the earnings per share by gearing.

It will be noted from the basic data for Company X that the forecast "earnings yield" (the converse of the P/E ratio) is $\frac{\$45,000}{\$600,000}$ = 7.5%, which is after corporation tax (assumed to be at 50%).

If we can raise loan capital at a lower net rate, then gearing can be advantageous to the common shareholders.

Suppose the market rate of interest is 12%, i.e., 6% after taxes.

Let us try to make half of our $600,000 issue in the form of a 12% long-term debt. The earnings for common shareholders will now be forecast at $45,000 less ($300,000 × 6%) = $27,000.

We could now issue 5,000 shares at $60 or 4,286 at $70.

The revised results will be:

	At $60 per share	At $70 per share
Earnings per share		
$27,000 ÷ 5,000	$5.40	
$27,000 ÷ 4,286		$6.30
Dividend	$2.80	$3.20
Dividend yield		
$2.80 ÷ 60	4.7%	
$3.20 ÷ 70		4.7%

The figures at a share price of $70 are very close to the targets we set so the 50% gearing now suggested might be the best solution. We should, of course, try to reduce the gearing below 50% if this would still give acceptable results for the common shareholders, remembering always:

1. That we cannot push the gearing beyond the asset cover available.
2. That high gearing increases risks for both lenders and shareholders, and might therefore push up the interest rate we had to pay and also make investors less willing to pay the price we are suggesting. We are now in the area where we need further guidance from the knowledge and experience of our originating house.

The calculations and comments in this section have related to a first issue of shares by a previously unquoted company. If a quoted company wishes to make further issues, then it already has the market price of its existing shares to guide it. The important thing is to ensure that the old shareholdings do not lose value because of the new issue, i.e., that the equity is not diluted. The approach can be illustrated by considering the valuation problems in a rights issue.

Rights Issues

When considering a rights issue, the company must ensure that the extra earnings achievable on the proposed amount of the issue are at a rate not less than the earnings yield on the existing capital. Take a simple example.

A company has 400,000 common shares already issued. The annual earnings for the common shareholders are $72,000, giving earnings per share of 18¢. The current P/E ratio for the company is 7.5 so that the "market capitalization" of the company is 7.5 × $72,000 = $540,000 ($1.35 per share). The earnings yield (72/540) is 13.3% (nil dividend distribution is assumed). In considering an additional issue of capital the company has to consider two questions:

1. Will additional earnings be at least 13.3% on the amount raised?
2. Will the market recognize this fact and maintain the existing P/E ratio? In most circumstances it is assumed that this will be the case, since the P/E ratio is taken to represent the market rating of the prospects of the company, taking account of its past performance and the quality of the management. The new issue will not affect either of these factors.

Why does the company in our example require additional capital? To carry out particular projects. Let us assume there are three possibilities:

1. Additional capital of $150,000, giving rise to additional earnings of $24,000.
2. Additional capital of $200,000, giving rise to additional earnings of $27,000.
3. Additional capital of $250,000, giving rise to additional earnings of $27,500.

A quick calculation shows that alternative (1) yields 16%, alternative (2) 13.5% and alternative (3) 11.0%. The company might therefore undertake projects (1) or (2), but certainly not project (3).

This conclusion can be expressed in a different way, by looking at the new total of earnings under each alternative and providing capital for those amounts at P/E 7.5. Thus:

Project	Capital raised $000	New total earnings $000	Market capital-ization at P/E 7.5 $000	Increase $000
1	150	72 + 24 = 96	720.0	180.0
2	200	72 + 27 = 99	742.5	202.5
3	250	72 + 27.5 = 99.5	746.25	206.25

The increase in market capitalization is by comparison with the existing figure of $540,000. It will be seen that under alternatives (1) and (2), the increase in the market capitalization is greater than the new capital raised, but that the reverse applies in the case of alternative (3).

Having decided how much capital is to be raised, it remains to decide how many shares this shall represent, and thus at what issue price.

Take our example above. At present the company has 400,000 shares, and the market price of them is $1.35. In implementing Project 2 and raising $200,000, suppose the company decides to issue 200,000 shares at $1 each; the offer will then be one new share for each two shares currently held.

After the issue, the market price (theoretically) should be the weighted average of:

400,000 @ $1.35 (the "pre-rights" price)	$540,000
200,000 @ $1.00	200,000
600,000 shares valued at	$740,000

i.e., the new market price (the "ex-rights price") will be 740/600 = $1.23.

If the $200,000 new issue had been 160,000 new shares at $1.25 each then the ex-rights price would have been

$$\frac{\$740,000}{400,000 + 160,000} = \$1.32$$

These are only two of a number of possible alternative ways of raising the required $200,000. Let us look at the financial effect in each case on a shareholder who originally held ten shares.

	200 shares issued (one for every two now held) @ $1.00	160,000 shares issued (two for every five now held) @ $1.25
The shareholder starts with ten shares valued at $1.35 each	13.50	13.50

	200 shares issued (one for every two now held) @ $1.00	160,000 shares issued (two for every five now held) @ $1.25
He subscribes for:		
1. 5 shares at $1.00	5.00	
2. 4 shares at $1.25		5.00
He finishes up with:		
1. 15 shares @ $1.23	18.50	
2. 14 shares @ $1.32		18.50

Now suppose that the shareholder does not take up his new shares but sells the rights to a third party. The market value of a right is the difference between the ex-rights market price and the price at which the shares can be purchased under the option.

He starts with ten shares valued at:	13.50	13.50
By selling his rights he recovers:		
1. $5 \times (\$1.23 - \$1.00)$	1.15	
2. $4 \times (\$1.32 - \$1.25)$		0.28
He finishes with ten shares worth:		
1. $1.23	12.3*	
2. $1.32		13.2*

*The slight differences are, of course, due to rounding off the ex-rights prices of $1.23 and $1.32 to the nearest penny.

In brief, it does not matter in theory what price is put on the rights. The shareholders will be as wealthy after the issue as before. However, the lower the price at which the rights issue is offered the more valuable will be the rights when they are sold separately. It is normal to price rights issues appreciably below the present market price of the company's existing shares.

The above theoretical prediction of the change in share price consequent upon a rights issue may prove false in practice. The market price of the existing shares in fact frequently falls when a rights issue is announced—the main reasons being:

1. The market may mistrust the company's ability to maintain the existing rate of earnings per share on an increased number of shares.
2. Jobbers may mark down the price in anticipation of some shareholders being forced to sell their rights due to inability to pay for the new shares.

The price may also be marked down because after the rights issue there will be more shares in circulation so they should be relatively easier to obtain; i.e., a buyers' market will develop. This will not always be the case, however. If the company is fast growing, the availability of new shares may stimulate demand so that the price will rise.

To summarize some of the advantages and problems of rights issues:

1. *From the point of view of the company:*
   a. A rights issue is simple and cheap to implement.
   b. It is usually successful.
   c. And if so it provides favorable publicity for the business.
   Offsetting the low cost of issue is the fact that the issue price will be lower than might have been obtained from an offer for sale.
2. *From the point of view of the shareholders:*
   a. They have the option of buying additional shares at a preferential price or of withdrawing some cash by selling their rights.
   b. They can maintain their existing relative voting position.

Capitalization Issues, Scrip Dividends and Stock Splits

A capitalization (or bonus) issue is an issue of additional shares to existing shareholders without the shareholder having to subscribe additional cash. It is a "capitalization of reserves," or stock dividend, and in the company's balance sheet it involves merely a transfer from retained profits to the share capital account. As the shareholders already own the residual assets of the company, and as they already receive the amount of dividend that the directors consider it prudent to distribute, what advantage is there in issuing additional share certificates?

There is still some validity in the "sop to ignorance" reason for capitalizing reserves. With time the accumulated reserves of a company become large in relation to the nominal capital; and the distributed profits appear high when expressed in relation to a small number of shares. An increase in the share base eliminates this appearance of excessive profitability. There is a better reason for a capitalization issue however. Increasing the number of shares does often increase the market capitalization of the company. For example, a company has an issued capital of 800,000 shares and the current market price is 60¢, giving a market capitalization of $480,000. If the directors issue 200,000 bonus shares (making 1,000,000 in all), one would expect the market price to drop to 48¢ to maintain the existing market capitalization. In fact, the price might fall only to, say, 50¢ because investors will believe that the company's earnings will increase to correspond with the increased number of shares. This feeling is based on any company's distaste for having to announce or explain a reduction in earnings or dividend per share. In fact, a capitalization issue is often prefaced by an undertaking to maintain the existing dividend per share.

The issue may therefore be a token of good things to come. It may equally be a token of good things already achieved, in the sense that a company may have made acceptable profits, but because it is short of cash, it issues bonus shares instead of a dividend—a "scrip dividend." The shareholder receiving such shares may either cash in on the improvement in market price, selling sufficient shares to maintain the previous market value on his remaining holding, he can wait for the company to pay the now expected higher dividend next year or he can sell enough shares to pay himself a dividend and hope that the shares he has left will still bring in an unchanged future income because profits are increasing.

Finally, a capitalization issue may be a defense against an expected takeover bid. Because the issue is expected to increase the market value of the business, and because it is likely eventually to increase the number of people holding shares, it may at least force a higher bid than would otherwise have been made.

A somewhat similar device is the "stock split," i.e., the replacement of shares having a high nominal value with a greater number of shares having a lower nominal value. This normally improves the marketability of the shares. This effect is partly psychological: an individual may prefer to buy 400 shares at 25¢ each rather than 100 shares at $1 each because he seems to be getting more for his money. Also, if he has a large number of shares he has greater facility to sell a few of them when he needs ready cash. Small-value shares, therefore, are likely to be traded more actively than large-value shares, and this will tend to put up the price—to increase the market capitalization of the company.

Another reason why the market capitalization may increase after a stock split is that the market, rationally or otherwise, tends to expect that the amount of dividend or of earnings per share will be higher proportionately to the new number of shares than to the old, i.e., that profits will be increasing. Lastly there may be a political motive for the stock split. With a few high-value shares the figures of earnings per share or dividend per share may appear to be excessively high compared with other companies, and may thus give the impression to people without financial training that the business is making excessive profits. In this context there is the possibility of excessive wage claims. With a large number of shares the amount of profit per share will be less.

To summarize:

1. The effect of a stock split is usually to increase market capitalization; i.e., the share price per $1 nominal value will go up.
2. The advantages to the company are that when it needs to raise fresh capital

it will be able to obtain a higher price per $1 nominal than previously. If it is faced with takeover aggression it can demand a higher total price; and it may avoid excessive wage claims.

3. The shareholder benefits from the enhanced market value and in the ability to dispose of holdings more easily.

A stock split is thus often made when a takeover bid is feared and when the company foresees the need to raise fresh capital.

Timing of Capital Issues

From our discussion of the pricing of issues, it is clear that the best time to make an issue is when share prices generally are high, which means equally when interest rates are low. High and low however are definable only in relation to foreseeable trends; and a time of high share prices may be the very time when investors are preparing to sell their stocks. (Stock market trends will be considered in connection with securities in Chapter 12.)

Among other factors to be taken into account in deciding the timing of an issue will be anticipations of changes in taxation, in legislation, in government involvement in industrial affairs, and in national and international economic trends.

9

The Use
of Accounting Ratios

Cost of Capital and Accounting Ratio Analysis

In Chapter 7 we defined the cost of capital as the relationship between the earnings required for a particular category of investors and the current market value of their investment, although it was envisaged that for internal management control it would be necessary to express such earnings in relation to the book value of capital employed. The basic formulas for this translation were given in Chapter 1, with the warning that the usefulness of accounting ratios for particular purposes would depend on the acceptability of the valuation conventions used in arriving at the book value of the assets employed.

The purpose of the present chapter is to review the value of accounting ratios to shareholders and other outside users of published annual reports, and also their relevance to the needs of management control. Some of the subsidiary ratios to be illustrated have already been discussed in connection with liquidity and the management of working capital in Chapters 2 and 3, to which reference will be made.

Because the managers of a business will have access to the full details supporting the accounts under review, we will consider first their use of ratio analysis.

We shall then be in a better position to consider the extent to which financial analysis can be helpful to outside users of the annual reports.

Management Use of Ratio Analysis

Managers can use ratio analysis in planning and controling the company's operations. The main value of ratios is in making comparisons, and in particular of:

1. The company's profitability during the period under review, as compared with that budgeted or achieved in a previous similar period.
2. Any changes in liquidity, and the ability to attract adequate financial resources to ensure its survival.

Even when such comparisons are made it may be misleading to draw conclusions from one ratio in isolation from:

1. Other related ratios. For example, a low rate of profit on sales may be acceptable if the sales value is high in relation to the value of capital employed.
2. The data from which the ratios are derived. For example, a low ratio of current assets to current liabilities may be acceptable if a high proportion of the current assets is held in cash.
3. Explanatory information. For example, low profitability may be acceptable during a period when a company is undertaking new capital investment in anticipation of future expansion. No mention has been made so far of comparison between one segment and another of the same company, or of comparison between different companies. These offer special problems which will be discussed in later sections.

Profitability and Survival

The profitability of a business is measured by linking the profits earned with the value of sales and the amount of capital employed, using three key ratios which are illustrated in the diagram on the following page.

It will be evident that provided the definitions of "profit" and "capital employed" are constant for all three ratios, then ratio 1, the rate of return on capital employed, will be equivalent to the product of ratios 2, the percentage of profit on sales value, and 3, the capital turnover ratio. In a capital intensive business the rate of return on capital employed is regarded as the primary ratio of profitability. In businesses requiring very little capital investment the ratio of profit to sales would be of primary importance.

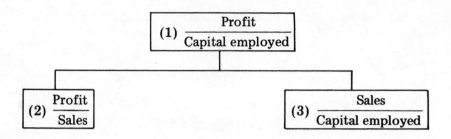

The percentage of profit on sales value can be investigated by reviewing the relationship to sales value of various elements of cost (using "cost ratios"). The rate of capital turnover can be subanalyzed by calculating "asset management ratios" linking different categories of asset value with the sales achieved. With regard to the ability of the business to survive, a variety of measures is available, including:

1. *Liquidity ratios,* indicating the availability of funds in the short term, the key ratio being the relationship between current assets and current liabilities (the "current ratio").
2. *Financial structure ratios,* indicating the borrowing capacity of the business.
3. *Investment ratios,* which make use of stock market prices and indicate the company's potential to common shareholders.

In addition it may be helpful to calculate *rates of growth* in profit, sales, and capital employed. This will help to explain the reasons for existing ratios and will provide a basis for future extrapolations.

Return on Capital Employed

The rate of return on capital employed can be calculated in alternative ways dependent on the type of achievement it is desired to measure. Three main alternatives are:

1. Return on total capital employed.
2. Return on common shareholders' capital employed.
3. Return on operating capital employed.

Return on total capital employed. This is a measure of the success of general management in ensuring that the company's funds as a whole are profitably employed.

The figure of capital employed used in this calculation will include the total shareholders' funds (including any minority interests if a group of companies is under review) plus loan capital and any significant long-term or deferred liabilities, and in this definition it will be equivalent to the net assets (fixed and current assets less current liabilities). Where the company has a bank overdraft which is intended to be a continuing part of its financing structure (in other words a substitute for long-term borrowing—and if the amount is significant in relation to the share and loan capital), then the overdraft figure on the balance sheet should also be included in the total capital employed.

Some managers also incorporate the current liabilities into their calculation of capital employed on the grounds that the amount of credit taken from suppliers is a form of enforced finance at the discretion of general management. The total capital employed would then be equivalent to the gross assets appearing on the balance sheet.

The figure of profit used in the ratio will be the profit before taxation which is available to provide interest and dividends to the suppliers of the capital employed. It will therefore be the profit before charging loan interest. If capital employed is defined as including a bank overdraft, then the comparable figure of profit will be calculated before deducting overdraft interest. In general terms therefore the formula for this ratio is:

$$\frac{\text{Profit before taxation and interest payable} \times 100}{\text{Long-term capital employed}}$$

Extraordinary (nonrecurring) gains or losses could distort the comparison of profitability from period to period and should be ignored.

Return on common shareholders' capital employed. This is a measure of the success of the board in achieving a satisfactory trend of earnings for the common shareholders.

It will normally be calculated by using the following formula:

$$\frac{\substack{\text{Profit after deducting tax,} \\ \text{minority interests and preference dividends} \times 100}}{\text{Issued common share capital and reserves}}$$

As with the return on total capital employed, extraordinary items would probably be ignored. This ratio will be influenced by changes both in total profits and in the amounts needed to pay interest on loan capital, and this gives the board information about the effects of changes in the capital structure.

Return on operating capital employed. The figures of total profit and of total capital employed may include items which are not related to the production of salable goods or services. A common example is the investment of money outside the business either on a long-term basis (trade investments) or as a tem-

porary expedient (funds raised for future expansion which are invested elsewhere until needed for the purchase of additional operating assets). In measuring
the profitability achieved by operational management, such investments should
be excluded from the figure of capital employed, and the dividends or other
earnings received from them should be deducted from total profits. The formula
for this ratio is therefore:

$$\frac{\text{Operating profit before taxation and interest payable} \times 100}{\text{Operating assets employed}}$$

This is the rate of return which can be explained by reference to the other
two key ratios noted as part of the basic system of financial analysis, and now
modified as follows:

$$\frac{\text{Operating profit}}{\text{Sales}} \quad \text{and} \quad \frac{\text{Sales}}{\text{Operating assets employed}}$$

In brief, the rate of return on operating capital employed can be improved
either by achieving more profit per $1 sales or by achieving more sales per $1
invested, or by a combination of both actions.

Whichever of the foregoing measures of profitability is used, it will be
satisfactorily comparable with the budgeted or targeted figure for the period
under review, because the board is fully aware of the company's accounting
conventions and of the figure of profit it is trying to achieve, and it can relate
profit to capital employed on that basis.

When comparing one year's results against another, however, if the historical cost convention is used then consistent results will not be obtained unless
either there is substantial stability in prices and costs or all costs (whether of a
capital or revenue nature) have moved in a similar manner.

Where significant price changes are affecting costs in varying degrees then:

1. For any given physical asset structure the reported value will vary according to the prices at which the various assets happen to have been purchased.
2. The reported profits will be affected by the values at which asset usage is
   reported (as "depreciation" or as the cost of goods sold).

Even for a stable business, therefore, there will be random variations in
the reported rates of return on capital employed. It may be noted in this connection that the five or ten year statistics often included in company reports can
be extremely difficult for the outside user to interpret.

The revaluation of assets (typically in current replacement cost) does not of itself correct this discontinuity, although if it be combined with a restatement of depreciation changes and costs of sales as suggested in contemporary proposals for a system of current cost accounting, it should give rise to greater stability in the required rate of return on capital employed.

In general, however, variances from annual targets are likely to be of greater significance than variations from year to year. The observation of fluctuations in the rate of return is only the starting point for asking the question "why?" i.e., for subanalysis using the *profit:sales* and *capital:turnover* ratios.

Profit Percentage on Sales Value
(Operating Profit:Sales)

Fluctuations in the rate of profit per $1 sales value may be attributable to:

1. Changes in product mix.
2. Changes in market outlet, for example, home or export sales.
3. Changes in selling price.
4. Changes in cost per $1 sales.

Changes in cost per $1 sales could occur because purchase prices were changing at a rate different from selling prices, or because changes in output volume affected the amount of fixed costs attributable to each unit. Such variations could in fact have been built into operating budgets or standards against which comparison would be made. The financial manager should have been involved in decisions on selling prices regarding such factors. He should certainly be consulted on the pricing of major long-term contracts or of overseas business involving consideration of fluctuating exchange rates.

Costs per unit can also vary with the efficiency with which resources are used—a matter for control by operating managers.

Useful indicators of the efficiency of operations include:

1. Sales value per employee, linked with profit per employee, average pay for employee, or added value per employee.
2. Sales per hour worked, or preferably physical output per hour worked (expressed in units or in "standard hours" produced).
3. Statistics linking asset values with numbers of employees or with sales achieved—the subject of the following section.

Capital Turnover (Sales:Capital Employed)

The formula for the capital turnover ratio is:

$$\frac{\text{Sales value for year}}{\text{Operating assets employed}}$$

and the result is expressed as the number of times in the year that the total asset value is "turned over" in sales.

The implication is that any increase in the value of assets employed should be reflected in at least a corresponding increase in sales; though clearly the ultimate objective is an increase in profit, so that this ratio cannot be considered in isolation from the profit:sales ratio.

As with other ratios, the capital turnover ratio for any year will be viewed as part of a trend; and from this point of view it may be satisfactory to use a year-end figure of assets employed provided there are no major fluctuations in the asset value during the course of the year. Preferably, however, the assets employed should be stated at the average value during the year, and this is often approximated by taking the arithmetic mean of the opening and closing values. If this is done then the same average figure should be used in the *profit:capital employed* ratio.

Changes in the ratio can occur if increased sales volume is obtained without any increase in the investment in assets, or if selling prices are changed. The third possible reason is a change in the amount of money tied up in operating assets. This will be obvious from a comparison of consecutive balance sheets.

A subanalysis of this ratio can therefore be obtained by relating the sales value in turn to the values of the various categories of asset employed. Such comparisons, and others related to them, comprise the *asset management* ratios described below.

Asset Management Ratios

The purpose of asset management ratios is to demonstrate the effectiveness of investment in different types of operating assets. This is done mainly by expressing the value of each type of asset in relation to the annual sales value. But other comparisons may be possible, such as sales per square foot occupied.

Sales:fixed assets (fixed asset turnover rate). The sales to fixed assets ratio shows the turnover achieved for each $1 invested in fixed assets. Like other ratios it must be interpreted with care, because a high ratio could mean merely that the fixed assets were old and therefore:

132

1. At a relatively low original cost.

2. Heavily depreciated.

When assets are revalued there will be a discontinuity in the trend of the related ratios. When assets are replaced at inflated prices, or when new assets are added, it must be borne in mind that the additional money invested will be expected to produce a normal rate of return. Therefore, either the sales value should increase correspondingly, or if there is a fall in the *sales:fixed assets* ratio it should be compensated by an increase in the rate of profit to sales value.

Fixed asset investment is normally made in advance of improved operating results, so that the *sales:fixed assets* ratio must be looked at as part of a continuing trend and not in isolation year by year.

Sales:working capital. Working capital for this purpose is normally taken as the figure of net current assets (current assets less current liabilities), and the sales to working capital ratio is expected to show the efficiency with which working capital is being employed. Very great care is needed in interpreting the significance of this ratio, and it is important to remember (as with all ratio analysis) that a ratio that is out of line with past experience or with the ratio in other companies merely highlights an area for inquiry. It does not automatically point to any particular underlying cause.

This point was illustrated in reviewing the various elements of working capital in Chapter 3, but one general point can be made. If a very high ratio of sales to working capital is revealed this may mean that the working capital is being employed effectively. Alternatively it may mean that the working capital figure includes a very low figure of cash, or is after deduction of a high bank overdraft or excessive outstanding debts to creditors—in other words, that the business is relying on short-term finance which should be replaced by more permanent capital. In this condition the business is said to be "overdrafting" in relation to the permanent capital available, and may be putting itself at risk in relation to its creditors.

Liquidity Ratios

The purpose of liquidity ratios is to indicate whether the business is able to meet its short-term liabilities as they fall due. The primary indicator is the *current ratio*, although in some cases (particularly in a manufacturing business) the *quick ratio* may be the more reliable indicator.

These ratios and the further analysis available to the financial manager, in particular the use of cash forecasts and control statements, were discussed in Chapter 2.

Financial Structure Ratios

Although liquidity ratios given an indication of the ability of a business to pay its way in the near future, its long-term survival will depend on the availability of medium- and long-term capital. This may take the form either of equity capital or of fixed-interest borrowing. Loan interest is treated as a business expense for taxation purposes, so that loan capital will always be less expensive than share capital. The analyst will therefore attempt to assess the borrowing capacity of a business, and to compare this with the total borrowing currently outstanding.

Among the factors that affect the extent to which a company can raise loan capital are two which can be checked by ratio analysis:

1. The security it can offer—measured by alternative forms of debt ratio.
2. The profits available in relation to fixed interest charges—measured by the *interest:earnings* ratio.

Such ratios were illustrated during the discussion of capital gearing in Chapter 6.

Investment Ratios

A company's ability to survive is also dependent on its ability to attract additional equity capital when required. A major factor in the assessment of this capability is the relationship between the earnings available for common shareholders and the stock market price of the shares. These relationships were explained in Chapter 7 and were further exemplified in discussing the new issue market in Chapter 8.

Growth

The significance of many of the ratios already discussed will depend on the current rate of expansion of the business. For example, if sales show an upward trend this may help to explain why there is a temporarily disproportionate increase in fixed assets or inventory or an extension of the period of credit allowed or a decline in the liquid ratio.

Growth for these purposes may be measured in terms of the annual percentage increase in sales or total capital employed or total profit before tax, whichever is the most relevant to the desired comparison.

It is important, however, to bear in mind:

1. That growth in money values, however relevant to the general scheme of ratio analysis, does not necessarily imply a growth in physical terms, but may merely reflect a trend of increasing costs or prices.
2. That growth, however defined, cannot be interpreted as good or bad without knowledge of its conformity with the company's strategic plans.

Interdivisional Comparison

The internal use of accounting ratios by a business will be largely concerned with comparisons with targets set in accordance with the firm's own method of accounting, but it should be possible to use the same approach in judging the relative effectiveness of subunits or divisions within the total organization.

Difficulties are sometimes experienced:

1. In deciding how much capital is employed in a particular department of the business. Is it meaningful, for example, to apportion the capital value of premises among departments occupying those premises when none of them has any influence over the total area available?
2. In deciding how much profit a department has made. Here we have the familiar bone of contention—apportioned central charges. Whether these can be treated as genuine costs of a division will depend on whether the divisional manager has had an opportunity of challenging the proposed apportionment and approving it as a fair charge against his activities.

The real question at issue in these cases is the definition of responsibilities. If a department is to be treated as a profit center for control purposes, then the manager must have complete responsibility for all the capital he employs, all the products he sells, and all the costs he incurs. If a manager is to be independent in this way, then if he is selling goods or services internally to other managers, or buying from them, the pricing of those interdepartmental transfers must be realistic. Very often internal "transfer prices" are based on cost (actual or standard) plus a profit markup, sometimes on an outside selling price less a preferential discount. Ideally they should be "arm's length" commercial prices, though in some cases (particularly for partially processed items) no commercial price may be available. However, if outside prices are used for internal transfers there will be no incentive for a manager to make use of internal resources in preference to dealing with outside companies, and this may result in suboptimal utilization of the resources within the business. Transfer prices usually have to be hedged around with rules regarding the circumstances in which outside procurement may be preferred to internal purchases and sales.

In a large organization, some divisions may be occupying premises owned by the business, whereas others are in rented premises. If the divisions are sufficiently similar for their results to be compared with each other, then some means must be found of equalizing the occupancy costs. The normal method is to treat premises as being owned centrally, removing the costs of land and buildings from divisional capital employed, and to make a fair rental charge to each division. If the various divisions are diverse in the nature of their activities, so that they are not expected to make similar rates of return on their capital employed, then the question of ownership or occupancy of premises is just another reason for different rates of profitability to be targeted.

Finally, depreciation charges may be inequitable between different divisions or departments of the company because some department may be using older equipment than others and so suffering lower depreciation charges based on historic costs. This problem would disappear if an inflation-adjusted accounting system were in use. But even in the context of historical accounting many companies choose to make internal depreciation charges based on annually updated asset values. Again, this problem may not be important if each department has its unique rate of return which is not intended to be compared with those of other departments.

In summary:

1. Taking the capital employed and the profit targeted for the business as a whole, it is possible to set divisional target rates of return on capital employed, and to use them in judging the effectivenss of the managers concerned.

2. In most cases it will be sufficient to give each department its unique target rate and to control it against that rate. Where it is desirable to compare departments with each other, it may be necessary to eliminate random distortions by defining a system of transfer pricing and by equalizing such items as occupancy and depreciation charges.

3. Where managers cannot independently influence the value of their capital employed, or where much of the business asset structure is under central control, it will probably be preferable to judge divisional performance on the basis of marginal contribution to central fixed costs rather than by attempting to devise a system of control based on "profits" related to "capital employed."

Interfirm Comparison

The comparison of ratios from one firm to another, even in the same industry, involves a number of difficulties, particularly in:

1. The valuation of fixed assets. Where historical values are used the *fixed*

asset:sales ratio will vary according to the average age of assets held. A common basis of valuation is needed—possibly current cost or replacement cost.

2. Depreciation rates may differ. The accounts need adjusting to include comparable rates.

3. The methods of accounting for inventory (FIFO, average costs, etc.) may vary. It may be best to adjust all the balance sheets to year-end market values.

4. The cost content of work in progress may vary. Some companies will include a share of administration costs; others will cut off at factory cost or include direct costs only. A common method, probably factory cost, would have to be used.

5. If comparison of different items of expense is possible, then there must be consistency in the classification of costs under the main headings of operating costs, marketing costs and administration costs, and also in the method of apportioning common costs.

Shareholders' Use of Accounting Ratios

Apart from reviewing the manager's stewardship of funds, probably most simply seen in a source and application of funds statement, shareholders need to judge the efficiency of the management as evidenced by the company's profitability. Even the funds flow statement will incorporate a figure of profit, so that the correct definition of profit is essential to shareholders' understanding of accounts.

From the point of view of the shareholders the word "profit" has a quite clearly defined meaning. It is that residue of income which is potentially distributable to them. In the case of a business expected to continue as a going concern, therefore, "profit" can be defined only after provision has been made for the maintenance of the future earning power of the business, i.e., for the preservation of the assets employed.

Under conditions of price stability, accounts prepared on the historical cost basis do in fact show profit in this way. Under conditions of significant price change they do not.

Historical cost accounts do not even give the shareholders parity of information with the managers, since in interpreting the results reported the managers have access to detailed operating data and budget plans.

Until some reform of accounting principles is achieved, therefore, published financial statements are of little value to shareholders or prospective investors since:

1. For the company in isolation there is no indication of the extent to which the ability to earn future profits is being maintained.

2. For the purposes of interfirm comparison there is no common basis of asset valuation or profit measurement.

Certain ratios will have a value in their own right, for example, the *accounts receivable:sales* ratio and the ratios of liquidity, but for the rest the shareholder has to trust that a favorable trend of reported ratios does at least indicate positive directorial action.

Ratios for Other Users of Financial Statements

So far as the providers of loan capital are concerned, company financial statements will show the assets of the business at something less than their realizable value, so they do provide some assurance of security, although to the extent that historical values are used the debt capacity of the company may not be fully revealed.

From the point of view of employees, the declaration of profits before full provision has been made for asset replacement is clearly misleading, and can involve the company itself in unsatisfactory explanations of the limitation of funds available for improved employee remuneration.

Summary

For the manager of a business, ratio analysis is a valuable means of progressive investigation of the sources, causes of and responsibilities for the reported results and position. Its validity, however, stems from the fact that the rules of accounting adopted by the business are known, and the analysis is made within that framework.

In surveying the progress of a business over a period of years, corrections are necessary for distortions caused by changes in the structure of prices. Adjustments are also necessary if subunits are to be compared against each other.

For comparison between companies, published financial statements are not on a sufficiently uniform basis for more than very generalized conclusions to be drawn.

For outside users of financial statements, inflationary or deflationary trends throw a high degree of doubt on the usefulness of any analysis based on historical figures.

10

Investment Appraisal and Control

The Nature of Investment Decisions

It is of the nature of business that you must commit resources before achieving gains, and it is because today's outlays are certain whereas tomorrow's gains are only a forecast that business involves risk. As the old saying has it, "money does not grow on trees," so when money must be spent and its recovery will be delayed, the amount unrecovered will be a cost to the business. (We discussed the cost of capital in Chapter 7.)

As money becomes available to the business it must be put to work, so that a great part of the job of managing a business consists in making investment decisions. The balance sheet of the business, within the limitations of its asset valuation conventions, reflects the current state of the investment projects in process of implementation. It shows the fixed assets, the inventories, the credit allowed to customers, and any investments in activities outside the business.

The balance sheet, however, shows effects, not causes or reasons for investment. Among the various projects which gave rise to that position a variety of objectives might have been involved, for example:

1. To improve the efficiency of production, i.e., to reduce costs, perhaps by buying improved machinery.
2. To increase production capacity in order to satisfy sales demand, i.e., to increase profits.
3. To introduce a new profitable product; development, tooling, working capital and marketing cost outlays might all be involved in this project.
4. To open up a new profitable market. The costs of advertising, market research, free samples and so on are incurred before the hoped-for increase in profits can be achieved. So they also are investment outlays.
5. To replace existing equipment which is beyond economical repair—an investment decision in the sense that it provides the opportunity for reviewing the profitability of what is being done at present, and the relative profitability of alternative ways of doing it in the future.
6. To improve the welfare of employees, for example, by the provision of a new cafeteria or recreation facilities.

The constantly recurring theme of all these projects except the last one is that they must result in an increase in profits, and even welfare proposals do have some ultimate cost justification—if we did not provide this facility we should not be able to recruit the employees we need, and therefore the business would suffer.

The purpose of investment is to make a profit, and that profit must be reasonable in relation to the amount of money invested; i.e., the investment must yield a satisfactory rate of return on the capital employed in it. The required rate of return will be based on the company's cost of capital and will thus be a rate competitive with that obtainable from alternative investments which involve similar risks. It will be a rate that satisfies the existing suppliers of capital, and will enable the business to obtain additional capital when it is required.

Procedures for Appraisal of Investment Projects

In appraising any investment project which appears to be compatible with the marketing, technological and other nonfinancial objectives of the business, the financial manager should ensure:

1. That it will provide the required rate of return on the amount invested.
2. That if it represents one out of several alternative ways of investing a

limited amount of money, then it is the best of those mutually exclusive projects.

3. That undertaking the project is more beneficial than doing nothing, i.e., continuing with existing equipment or methods. In many cases the additional ("incremental") outlays and recoveries that make up the project are defined by reference to an existing situation, but even then it is possible to overlook the fact that existing practices will be full of inefficiencies, and to compare this with a supposedly perfect new project is unrealistic.

4. That the project is being undertaken at the right time. In relation to plant replacement projects, for example, the extent to which the second-hand value of the existing equipment varies from year to year may have a bearing on the best time to replace it. Again, if a drop in interest rates is forecast it may be better to delay a project until the marginal cost of capital is reduced rather than to take the operating benefits which would arise in the meantime.

The above considerations apply to the evaluation of a project in its own right. Even when this has been done and a project appears to be acceptable there are other tests to be applied to ensure that the project can be accommodated within the overall long-term plans of the company.

For the moment we will review briefly the various methods of project evaluation. The most common of these are:

1. Return on capital invested.
2. Payback.
3. Discounted cash flow methods:
   a. Internal rate of return.
   b. Net present value.

Return on Capital Invested

This method expresses the average annual earnings of a project as a percentage of capital invested.

EXAMPLE

	Project R	Project S	Project T	Project U
	$	$	$	$
Investment	10,000	10,000	10,000	10,000

	Project R	Project S	Project T	Project U
	$	$	$	$
Profits				
Year 1	–	2,000	1,000	5,000
Year 2	1,000	2,000	2,500	7,000
Year 3	1,500	2,000	1,300	15,000
Year 4	2,500	1,000	–	8,000
Year 5	3,000	1,000	–	5,000
Total	8,000	8,000	4,800	40,000
Average per annum	1,600	1,600	1,600	8,000
Return on investment	16%	16%	16%	16%

In this example the initial investment has been taken as "capital invested" for the purpose of calculating the rate of return. In some cases an average capital employed figure is used, normally a simple average of the initial investment and the residual value. In the above example, if the residual value of the investment after five years (Project T–3 years) was forecast as nil, the average capital employed would have been $5,000 for Projects R, S, and T, and $25,000 for Project U. The reported rate of return would then have been doubled, to 32% in each case.

What does "profit" mean? As a project has to repay the amount invested as well as earning a profit, the figure of profit used will normally be what is left after charging depreciation but before taxation, on the grounds that the company's tax liability will depend upon the outcome of its operations as a whole and is therefore not relevant to the consideration of a single project.

Alternatively it is possible to use figures of profit before depreciation, giving an approximation to cash flow over the life of the project, though not accurate year by year because fluctuations in inventory and credit periods would not be taken into account. If this interpretation of profit is used, then the reported rate of return will include the straight-line depreciation rate appropriate to the project life. Taking the example above, Projects R, S, and U all have five-year lives, so that the depreciation of the capital outlay would be equivalent to 20% per annum. On a before-depreciation evaluation, therefore, these projects would show a rate of return of 16% + 20% = 36%. Project T, however, has only a three-year life, so that taking profit before depreciation would give it a rate of 16% + 33 1/3% = 49 1/3%.

The advantages claimed for this method are:

1. The calculation of the return on capital invested is simple.

2. It deals with "profit," and managers are used to thinking in terms of profit, so they can understand the calculation.
3. It takes account of all profits forecast during the project life. (The payback method described below does not do this.)

Advantages (1) and (2) would only be of interest to us provided the results yielded by the method were reliable guides to investment decisions.

The disadvantages of the method are:

1. There are no universally accepted definitions of "capital invested" or "profit," as noted above, so that different people using the same basic data could report different rates of profitability. This might not matter provided the target rate had been established on the same basis as the project calculations.
2. The method provides for an initial investment followed by a series of profits or losses. It does not provide simply for the case where additional investment, probably in current assets, will take place during the years after initial outlay or adjusted on the "profit" figures, which spoils the simplicity of the presentation.
3. Similarly it does not provide for those instances where the initial investment takes place over a period of time which may extend to a number of years before any profits are received.

This question of time scale has a more general application:

4. The method does not take into account the timing of the profit record. Profits earned in the earlier years, for example, are given equal weight with those earned in later years. Why should they not be treated equally? Two answers are commonly given:
   a. The further ahead you are forecasting the more uncertain your forecast becomes. This of course is true of all estimates, whether for investment evaluation or for any other purpose. There are techniques for compensating for this uncertainty, which we shall discuss later. This answer is not peculiar to the return on capital invested method.
   b. The quicker you get your money back the less you lose in interest charges or the opportunity cost of other projects foregone. This answer of course reveals the weakness of the return on capital approach to investment evaluation. We do not want to know how quickly we get our money back, but the return on capital does not tell us this; it tells us only that if we follow certain accounting conventions we shall be reporting a profit or a loss. This information has its own importance, but it does not tell us how money inflows will be related to the money we invest.

Payback

The payback method tells us the time period required to recover in cash the amount outlaid in cash on a project. Ideally the return cash flows should be calculated in regard to the timing of collections from debtors and payments to creditors, and the impact on tax payments of the implementation of the project. Depreciation would be ignored.

The example on pages 141-142 can be restated in terms of cash flows, and the possible effect of doing this is shown in the following table. Taxation has been adjusted, and since tax is payable largely in arrears it has been necessary to add a sixth year to the tabulation. The annual cash inflow for each project is therefore:

Profit for year + depreciation − tax (50%) on preceding year's profit.

For example, the cash inflow in Year 3 for Project S is:

$2,000 (profit) + $2,000 (depreciation) −
$1,000 (50% of Year 2 profit) = $3,000

It will be seen that Project R does not recover the whole of the $10,000 invested until about halfway through the fourth year. Project S takes exactly three years to recover the initial outlay, and Projects T and U both achieve their payback during the course of the third year. The decision to invest can be based either on accepting any project which repays the amount invested within a chosen period of time (if this is three years then Projects S, T, and U are all acceptable) or on ranking the projects in accordance with the speed of recovery—in this case Project T gives the quickest payback and would be preferred to the other proposals.

	Project R	Project S	Project T	Project U
	$	$	$	$
Cash Investment	10,000	10,000	10,000	50,000
Cash Inflows				
Year 1	2,000	4,000	4,333	15,000
Year 2	3,000	3,000	5,333	14,500
			9,666	29,500
Year 3	3,000	3,000	3,384	21,500
		10,000	13,050	51,000
Year 4	3,750	2,000	(650)	10,500
	11,750			
Year 5	3,750	2,500	–	11,000
Year 6	(1,500)	(500)	–	(2,500)
	14,000	14,000	12,400	70,000

The feature in favor of the payback method is that it concerns itself with cash flows, but having defined these it fails to make full use of them.

The disadvantages of the method are:

1. It makes no effort to identify profitability, which is the object of investment. Very few organizations would have as their primary objective the minimization of payback time.
2. It ignores variations in the timing of cash flows within the payback period. Compare Projects S and U in the above example. Project U has the slightly shorter payback period, yet in periods 1 and 2 it recovers only 30% and 29% of the initial outlay, whereas Project S recovers 40% and 30%.
3. It ignores completely any cash flows after the payback period. Project T above has a shorter payback period than Project S, but the latter project continues longer and yields a further $1,600.
4. As with the return on investment method, there is no means of dealing with the investment buildup period. If, for example, the $50,000 outlay on Project U had been incurred in equal instalments in periods minus-2 and minus-1, one could say that in average the $50,000 outlay had occurred one year before the inflows commenced, so that the payback period was one year plus just under three years, i.e., nearly four years.

   Yet the first outlay of $25,000 in Year minus-2 (say at minus 1 1/2 years) would be paid back in the latter part of Year +2, giving just under 3 1/2 years payback; and the second outlay at an average of minus six months would be paid back before the end of Year 3, thus having a payback of just under 3 1/2 years also.

Despite the disadvantages, payback is widely used in making investment decisions. The point must be made that payback can be used as a simple rough-screening device for eliminating from consideration those projects which are not capable of yielding an adequate rate of return. It might be decided, for example, that in a particular business it would be unrealistic to look further ahead than five years in evaluating projects. The business requires an after-tax rate of return of 20%. If a project had equal annual cash flows, then to achieve a 20% rate of return it would need to have a payback period no longer than 3 years. (You can check this by the net present value method described below.)

Also, in ranking mutually exclusive projects that are fairly similar in size and complexity, the payback method will often give identical results with the more detailed methods of evaluation which we will now consider.

Discounted Cash Flow

Discounted cash flow methods overcome the disadvantage of the methods so far described, because they:

1. Use cash flows such as are calculated for the payback method, but for the whole life of the project.
2. Do not need to differentiate "capital" from income flows, but can accommodate all cash flows inward or outward whenever they occur.
3. Take account of the rate of return on the capital invested in the project by discounting all the cash flows to their present value equivalent.

In order to obtain the present value of a sum to be received or paid at some future date, we take an appropriate discount factor which, when used to multiply the actual amount, produces the relevant present value figure. The discount figure is the reciprocal of the factor used for computing compound interest; therefore as the formula for compound interest is $A = P(1 + r)^n$ (where A is the final value, P the original sum, r the rate of interest and n the number of years), that formula can be reversed to show:

$$P = \frac{A}{(1+r)^n} \text{ or } A(1+r)^{-n}$$

Where $A = \$1$, the value of P (i.e., the discounted value, or discount factor) is $(1 + r)^{-n}$. A table showing discount factors for $1 with various values of n and r is given in the appendix to this chapter.

We will just take one simple example:

A project involves paying out $100,000 now and $80,000 after one year. The return cash flows are $150,000 in Year 2 and $64,900 in Year 3. This project yields a 10% DCF rate of return because using the discount factors for 10% the various cash flows inward are equivalent to the cash flows outward; thus:

Time period $	Cash flows in (or out) $	Discount factors @ 10% $	Present value of cash flows $
0	(100,000)	1.00000	(100,000)
1	(80,000)	0.90909	(72,727)
2	150,000	0.82645	123,967
3	64,900	0.75131	48,760
		Net present value	Nil

It is often helpful, if you are not convinced of the validity of such a solution, to prove that the "net terminal value" of the project, built up from compound interest calculations, is in fact zero. This is done for the above example as follows:

Time Period		Amount
		$
0	Amount invested	(100,000)
	Yield 10% for one year	(10,000)
		(110,000)
1	Further outlay	(80,000)
		(190,000)
	Yield 10% for one year	(19,000)
		(209,000)
2	Received	150,000
	Outstanding	(59,000)
	Yield 10% for one year	(5,900)
		(64,900)
3	Received	64,900
	Net terminal value	Zero

Thus the inward cash flows are sufficient to reimburse the outward cash flows and to give the company a return of 10% on the amounts unrepaid from time to time.

Discounted cash flow calculations can be applied in two ways:

1. To discover the "internal rate of return" of a project, i.e., the rate of return it yields on the money tied up in it.
2. To arrive at the net present value of a project by using a predetermined target discount rate.

Internal Rate of Return

In DCF calculations for finding the internal rate of return (IRR) the object is to discover the rate of interest at which the present value of all the cash inflow will equal the original investment, and normally this can only be done by trial and error. For example, if the first rate of interest you try discounts the cash inflow to a figure below the cost of the original investment, it means that the rate used is too high and you should try a lower rate.

The internal rate of return for a given set of cash flows is that rate at which the present value of the inflow is the same as the present value of the outflow. In other words the "net present value" is zero.

The method is illustrated in the following example.

Year	Cash flows		Discount factors	Amount
	$			$
0	(13,500)		1.000	(13,500)
1	1,000	Try 15%	.870	870
2	4,000		.756	3,024
3	7,000		.658	4,606
4	8,000		.572	4,576
5	5,000		.497	2,485
		Net present value		2,061

The net present value is positive—the actual rate must be more than 15%

			1.000	(13,500)
	Try 25%		.800	800
			.640	2,560
			.512	3,584
			.410	3,280
			.328	1,640
	Net present value			(1,636)

The net present value is negative—the actual rate must be less than 25%

At this stage there are two choices open to us in arriving at the actual internal rate of return:

1. To interpolate from the above two results. Note that we swing from a negative NPV of $1,636 to a positive NPV of $2,061 when we move the interest rate ten points (from 25% to 15%). On the average therefore each 1% change in rate alters the NPV by $(2,061 + 1,636 = 3,697) ÷ 10 = $369.7. To move from minus $1,636 to zero NPV we should have to move 1,636/369.7 = 4.4 percentage points, i.e., from 25% to 20.6%, which is thus our interpolated rate of return.

2. To continue with the trial and error method until we find a rate which gives a nil NPV. As shown by the following calculation this rate proves to be approximately 20%.

Year	Discount factors (20%)	Amount $
0	1.000	(13,500)
1	.833	833
2	.694	2,776
3	.579	4,053

Year	Discount factors (20%)	Amount $
4	.482	3,856
5	.402	2,010
	Net present value	28

The reason why the interpolated rate was slightly (though not significantly) inaccurate is demonstrated on the graph below. This shows net present values on the vertical scale plotted against discount rates on the horizontal scale. The solution rate (20%) can be read off below the point where the NPV value is zero. The NPV line follows a typical compound interest curve, whereas our interpolation assumed a straight line between the 15% and 25% values, as shown by the dotted line on the graph.

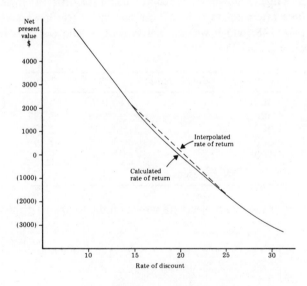

The Net Present Value Method

If a company has already decided what is its required rate of return (the cost of the capital it has to service) then it may not be necessary to discover by trial and error what is the precise IRR from a project. All that is needed is to discount the project at the required rate of return and to see whether its net present value at that rate is zero or positive (when the project would be acceptable) or negative (when the project would be rejected).

Taking the example on page 148, if the company's required rate of return had been 25% we should immediately have discounted the project at the rate and we should have discovered that it did not yield 25%. At that point, therefore, the project could be rejected (unless other considerations outweighed the unsatisfactory rate of return) and there would be no need to make trials at other rates.

If the company's required rate of return had been 15%, then our project would have been acceptable, since at that rate it yields a positive net present value. Now every project has its unique NPV curve because the configuration of the curve is determined by the time pattern of the cash flows. The example we have taken has a clearly evident curvature because the project had relatively heavy cash flows in the later years where the discount factors differ significantly from one rate to another. A project with predominantly early cash flows would show a curve which was less steep and approximated more closely to a straight line. When we are comparing alternative projects, therefore, we shall find that our order of preference (or "ranking") at a low discount rate is different from the ranking at a higher rate—the NPV curves, being at a different angle, will have crossed at some intermediate rate. We can see this effect if we take the same project on page 148 (which we will call Project F) and compare it with the following project (Project T):

Years	Cash flows ($)	Discounted at:	10%	20%	25%
0	(10,000)		(10,000)	(10,000)	(10,000)
1	4,000		3,636	3,332	3,200
2	4,000		3,304	2,776	2,560
3	5,000		3,755	2,895	2,560
4	4,100		2,800	1,976	1,681
		Net present value	3,495	979	1

The NPV curves of the two projects are shown on the following graph:

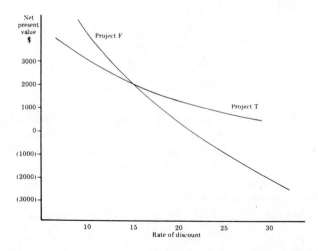

It will be seen that up to a discount rate of about 15% Project F is to be preferred because it gives the higher net present values. Above that rate Project T
gives the better results.

Incremental Rate of Return

The reason why Project F is preferable only at rates up to about 15% is that the
incremental cash flows, in moving from Project F to Project T, show an internal
rate of return of 15%. At and above 15%, therefore, it is worthwhile moving
from one project to the other.

The incremental cash flows [i.e., the amount by which the cash flow of F
is less (greater) than that of T] are shown discounted in the following table:

Year	Incremental cash flows $	14% factor	$	15% factor	$	16% factor	$
0	3,500	1.000	3,500	1.000	3,500	1.000	3,500
1	3,000	.877	2,631	.870	2,610	.862	2,586
2							
3	(2,000)	.675	(1,350)	.658	(1,316)	.641	(1,282)
4	(3,900)	.592	(2,309)	.572	(2,231)	.552	(2,153)
5	(5,000)	.519	(2,595)	.497	(2,485)	.476	(2,380)
	Net present value		(123)		78		271

Discounted at: spans the 14%, 15%, and 16% columns.

An important thing to notice from the above graph is that there is a conflict
between the internal rate of return method and the net present value method
of evaluating alternative projects.

If we had used IRR exclusively we should have concluded that Project T
yielding 25% was preferable to Project F yielding 20%. But if our cost of capital
had been less than 15% we should have been wrong. The reason for this conflict
we will review in the section following.

Therefore if we are using the IRR method, and if the competing projects
are mutually exclusive [i.e., one has to be selected to the exclusion of the
other(s)], then we should always check the incremental rate of return. If the
incremental rate is higher than our cost of capital (our target rate) then we
should select the project which yields that incremental advantage.

A second important point is that if we are using the net present value
method it is not satisfactory to discount at any random rate. The discount rate
used *must* be the company's cost of capital; otherwise our ranking may be
incorrect.

There is another reason why the cost of capital is important, and we will
look at it now.

Reinvestment Assumptions

The discrepancy that sometimes arises between IRR and NPV is caused by the implication in DCF calculations that the inward cash flows arising from time to time can be reinvested at the interest rate used in the calculations. This is a key concept for the correct use of DCF techniques, so we will take time to illustrate it by referring to Project T and using the net terminal value approach. The project can be looked at in any of three ways:

1. Assuming money was borrowed for the project and we want to repay it as soon as possible. The project permits us to pay interest at 25% a year on the balance outstanding at the start of each year.

Year	Transactions		Balance outstanding
		$	$
0	Borrow		(10,000)
1	Interest payable	(2,500)	
	Cash in	4,000	(8,500)
2	Interest payable	(2,125)	
	Cash in	4,000	(6,625)
3	Interest payable	(1,656)	
	Cash in	5,000	(3,281)
4	Interest payable	(820)	
	Cash in	4,100	(1)

Apart from the residual $1 we have paid off the loan with interest at 25% on the reducing balance.

2. Assuming money for the project was borrowed but will not be repaid until the end of the fourth year. We can pay 25% on the whole amount each year provided we can invest all surplus cash from the project also at 25%.

Year	Transactions		Balance accumulating
		$	$
1	Cash in	4,000	
	Interest on loan	(2,500)	1,500
2	Interest earned on $1,500	375	
	Cash in	4,000	
	Interest on loan	(2,500)	3,375

Year	Transactions	$	Balance accumulating $
3	Interest earned on $3,375	844	
	Cash in	5,000	
	Interest on loan	(2,500)	6,719
4	Interest earned on $6,719	1,680	
	Cash in	4,100	
	Interest on loan	(2,500)	9,999
	Repay loan	(10,000)	(1)

The net terminal value is again $1.

3. We have sunk $10,000 in some item of equipment. By the end of its four-year life that investment will have generated cash flows which, if re-invested at 25%, will make available our original $10,000 plus interest at 25% compound.

From your compound interest tables, $10,000 at 25% for four years should amount to $10,000 × 2.4414 = $24,414.

Let us see this happening.

Year	Transactions	$	Balance accumulating $
1	Cash generated		4,000
2	Interest earned on $4,000	1,000	
	Cash generated	4,000	9,000
3	Interest earned on $9,000	2,250	
	Cash generated	5,000	16,250
4	Interest earned on $16,250	4,063	
	Cash generated	4,100	24,413
	Difference as before		1

When we say that a project has an internal rate of return of 25% we are saying in effect that provided the cash flows generated can be reinvested at 25% we shall earn for ourselves 25% on the amounts we have invested in the project, or we shall be able to pay 25% to whoever loaned us the money. Unless our true cost of capital is the same as the IRR, this method can therefore be misleading if we apply it to the comparison of different projects.

Using the net present value method and discounting at our cost of capital, we are implying merely that we can borrow or we can reinvest at that cost of capital rate, which should be somewhere near the truth.

It will be realized that this method of building up to a net terminal value can be a useful method of project evaluation when lending and borrowing rates differ from each other, or when interest rates are forecast to change during the course of a project.

Advantages and Uses of Discounted Cash Flow Techniques

The advantages of any discounted cash flow method are:

1. DCF allows for the fact that a sum of money today is worth more than the same sum of money in the future. It thus takes full account of both the duration of the project and the pattern of cash flows during its life.

   Do remember that the time value of money in this context has nothing to do with inflation. We are talking about the cost of money, not its purchasing power. The effects of inflation must be forecast and included in the cash flows before we start discounting them.

2. Because we are dealing with cash flows we can take proper account of the timing of tax payments and tax reliefs.

3. It is possible to make adjustments for the uncertainty of the data used. Possible methods are described later.

Dangers in the use of DCF techniques are:

1. The minuteness of the calculations sometimes blinds managers to the unreliability of the data on which they are based.

2. There is sometimes a conflict between the results obtained by the IRR and NPV methods, and it is necessary to know when each should be used (see below).

In deciding which of the discounting techniques to use, the following guidelines are suggested:

1. If the company is financially able to implement all projects which show a rate of return in excess of the cost of capital, and if the particular projects under review are not mutually exclusive, then either the IRR or the NPV method may be used. Projects which show an IRR higher than the company's cost of capital, or which have a positive NPV when discounted at the cost of capital, are acceptable.

2. If, having decided that various projects are acceptable, you then want to

rank them in order of the benefit they yield (either because it is not convenient to deal with them all at once or because they are mutually exclusive) then the method of secondary valuation will depend on how you did your original valuation.

If you had started with calculations of net present value, then nothing further is needed. The projects can be ranked in order of the size of the net present value. Is this true even if one project involved a much heavier initial outlay than another? Tread carefully here. At the moment we are *not* assuming that there is a shortage of cash. The assumption is that any project which covers the cost of capital will be implemented eventually. So the initial outlay is not important—what is important is the size of the extra benefit represented by the net present value.

If, on the other hand, your original appraisal has been made by using IRR you should check the incremental rate of return involved in shifting from one project to another to see where the best overall advantage lies.

3. If money is the limiting factor on your choice of projects, i.e., you are in a situation of capital rationing, then the best technique is to calculate the NPV per $1 invested.

EXAMPLE

			Cash flows		
Year	Project	A	B	C	D
		$	$	$	$
0		(4,000)	(10,000)	(2,500)	(8,000)
1		1,500	6,500	750	—
2		1,500	6,500	750	—
3		1,500	—	750	4,100
4		1,500	—	750	4,100
5		1,500	—	750	4,100
		3,500	3,000	1,250	4,300

If the company has only $16,000 to invest, consider the desirability of the various projects under each of the above methods using 6% as the company's minimum desired rate of return.

NPV	@ 6%	2320	1920	660	1760
IRR		25%	19%	15%	11.5%
NPV	per $	0.58	0.19	0.26	0.22

The result of using each method in terms of NPV would be as follows:

Method:	Ranking	Capital cost	NPV
		$	$
a. NPV	A	4,000	2,320
	B	10,000	1,920
	D (¼)	2,000	440
		$16,000	$4,680
b. IRR	A	4,000	2,320
	B	10,000	1,920
	C (4/5)	2,000	528
		$16,000	$4,768
c. NPV per $	A	4,000	2,320
	C	2,500	660
	D	8,000	1,760
	B (3/20)	1,500	288
		$16,000	$5,028

It can be seen that ranking the projects by the NPV per $ method results in the selection of projects in a way which produces the highest NPV. Therefore, in capital rationing the NPV per $ method is a useful guide to the order in which projects should be selected as it takes account of the amount being invested in each project.

Note, however, that fractions of projects have been included in this example. This may be feasible when dealing with investment in inventory and shares, but not when buying industrial hardware.

4. If the choice is between projects having different lengths of life, a common period should be used for assessment purposes if the IRR method is being used. This might mean either cutting back the longer life by inserting a residual value of the project at the earlier date, or alternatively calculating the terminal value of the shorter project and then applying interest earnings to that value for the period necessary to match the life of the longer project. The two methods will obviously not yield the same answer. Where investments are sequential, as where alternative machines would be replaced from time to time but at different intervals of time, it might be possible to identify a point where the two time series coincided—a 2-year cycle and a 3-year cycle, for example, will coincide after six years.

All these methods involve a fairly high degree of guesswork, and if the difference in life between the projects under review is fairly short there may not be any need to evaluate it specifically.

The Validity of the Discounted Cash Flow Approach

It is sometimes argued that in safeguarding the interests of its shareholders the company should aim to maximize its wealth by maximizing current share prices (including current dividends), and that this is not the same as maximizing the present value of future cash flows. Share prices are influenced by a variety of factors, certainly including the profits and the asset backing revealed by published financial statements.

In reply to this contention it must be pointed out:

1. That there may be conflict between the requirements of existing shareholders (both as a body and as between classes of shareholder) and the requirements of potential future shareholders, and that the company should be aiming to improve the wealth available in the long run—which is what DCF analysis aims to achieve.

2. That the factors which influence share prices have not been defined with sufficient exactitude to provide a basis for operational decisions.

3. That it is agreed that even when a project has been proved acceptable in its own right, one still has to review its acceptability in the context of the overall business plan. We will take up this point shortly under the heading "Other Financial Objectives."

Investment Appraisal Methods in Practice

A recent survey of "capital budgeting practices" showed that among the companies investigated the two discounted cash flow techniques were the most widely used methods of investment appraisal, the internal rate of return method being the more common. The payback method (after taxes) was nearly as popular as the NPV method and was very often used for preliminary screening.

Profit as a percentage of funds employed was used in a variety of forms—before taxes or after taxes, based on initial investment or on some calculation of average investment—but taking all these forms together, it has slightly less popularity than either discounted cash flow methods or payback methods. It was clear, however, that there is still no consensus of opinion on the method that should be used.

Defining Cash Flows

In approaching DCF calculations it is important to make a logical analysis of the gains and losses which can properly be related to the project under review. The following three points often give rise to difficulties:

1. *Sunk costs are irrelevant.* This must be interpreted in the light of each

particular case. Where existing equipment and machinery are transferred from an existing purpose to a new capital project, one must assume that at the time of its purchase it was evaluated after credit was taken for some residual value. It is correct, therefore, to charge the new project with a cost of that equipment, probably its current resale value. If the equipment could be used for more than one purpose, then those other purposes should also be reviewed. Possibly a new machine will have to be bought for one of those purposes, and it would be wrong to look at only one project in isolation from others on which the decision now taken could have an impact. This is one particular instance of the need to look at:

2. *Ripple effects.* If a project saves time on a a particular operation, what happens to that time? Will fewer people be employed (in which case, a true cash saving arises) or will they be transferred to another project which has still to be evaluated? If a new machine speeds up a particular operation, what happens to production flows in subsequent operations? If there is no capacity to take increased production (or no sales outlet for it) then either there will be stockpiling of partly completed work or the improved speed of the new machine will not be used. Every business decision alters something which is surrounded by unaltered practices. The ripple effects on those practices must be brought into account in justifying that decision up to the extent where they cease to be significant.

3. *Inflation.* Cash flows must be estimated in the same terms as were used in defining the cost of capital. If the cost of capital rate is extrapolated from experience, which included inflation, or has been adjusted to include an allowance for inflation, then the future cash flows must be forecast as they will occur, including inflationary increases; i.e., the evaluation will be in "money" terms (as opposed to "real" terms). This is the best approach to use because:

   a. The forecast figures should then be more nearly comparable with the actual results as they emerge.

   b. "Inflation" does *not* mean the cost of living. For business planning it means all the particular price increases that are going to affect the revenues and expenses of that business, and these need forecasting in detail.

The obvious objection to this procedure is the uncertainty that must surround such forecasts. We will discuss this in Chapter 11.

Other Financial Considerations

Having established that a project is in accordance with the nonfinancial objectives of the business and that in itself it yields an acceptable rate of return, two further questions have to be asked:

1. Will the return cash flows be received at suitable times for future re-investment, and will years of low cash flow give rise to future liquidity problems?
2. If the project is undertaken, what will be the short-term effects on the profit figures reported in the profit and loss account?

It may happen that a project with a high DCF rate of return over its life as a whole will entail low profits in the early years. For example, a new hotel may take two or three years to approach full profitability and until that time there may be high interest charges and heavy operating costs. Outside investors have no knowledge of the long-term investment appraisals carried out by managers. They can only judge the trend of business performance from the published financial statements. If a project will have such a significant effect on reported profits that it leads to a prolonged reduction in share prices (and thus increases the company's cost of capital) it may have to be rejected on those grounds.

Where major strategies are under review, therefore, it will be necessary to incorporate the proposed projects into company models (probably computer-based) of future profit and loss accounts and cash flow statements.

Authorization and Control of Capital Projects

The control of investment projects falls into five stages:

1. Budgeting.
2. Project authorization.
3. Implementation.
4. Reporting and review.
5. Audit of results achieved.

All short-term operating budgets are in effect abstracts from a continu-ously developing long-term plan. This is particularly true of the capital expendi-ture budget because the major items included in it will not be completed within the bounds of any one budget year.

The main purpose of the capital expenditure budget is to provide a fore-cast of the amount of cash likely to be needed for investment projects during the year ahead. It also indicates what items of equipment, vehicles and so on will be needed for the purpose of implementing the profit and loss budget. It must therefore be submitted for approval at an early stage in the budgeting timetable.

Approval of the capital expenditure budget does not, except possibly for some minor items, constitute authorization to spend money on the items in-cluded in it. Before any project is commenced it must be evaluated and authorized, as described in the following chart. One possible form for a capital expenditure budget is shown on page 160.

CAPITAL EXPENDITURE BUDGET					Year			
								$000's
Project	Original estimate	Revised estimate	Authorized to date	Budget requested	Years of cash outlay 19....	19....	19....	Notes
					Approved by: Date:			

It is preferable to have a standard form of submitting capital expenditure proposals, so that all the items of information necessary to a decision are clearly displayed. One possible form is illustrated on page 161 and would be suitable for the majority of simple projects. In cases where a series of cash outlays is necessary or there is a complex evaluation of cash savings then detailed working sheets could be attached.

The purpose of the expenditure should be described fully and summarized under one of a number of standard headings, such as "cost saving," "volume increase," "replacement" or "welfare."

This is the part of the form where the originator's ability to distinguish between genuinely profitable purposes and often ill-defined desires is clearly indicated, and poor reasoning in describing the purpose can throw doubt on the validity of the estimates of cost and benefits. The evaluation should be in terms of discounted cash flows unless the amount of money involved is insufficient to warrant so much detail. It is in these cases that the payback period can be a useful screening device. The timetable for the project is important, since the rate of return it will yield will be influenced by the relative timing of the various cash flows.

Each application should be recommended by a nominated senior executive, for example:

Executive	Type of project
Executive in charge: Technical	Capital and revenue expenditure related to research and to the design

PROJECT AUTHORIZATION	No.
	Stage

Outline of requirement

Purpose		
	Cost saving	
	Volume	
	Replacement	
	Development	
	Welfare	

Evaluation	Payback
	.... Years
	IRR
	.... %

Reference to budget	Forecast completion date	Charge code

Cash outlay	$	Recommended by:
Year		Approved by:
Year		Date:
Year		Distribution:

Executive	*Type of project*
	and development of company products.
Executive in charge: Production	1. Additions to and replacement of manufacturing machinery and equipment. 2. Deferred revenue expenditure related to manufacturing operations. 3. Engineering expenditure throughout the company.
Executive in charge: Administration	1. Additions to and replacement of motor vehicles (in consultation with the executive concerned). 2. Major administration projects.
Executive in charge: Marketing	Major marketing projects.

In many companies executives of this status will also have power to give final authorization to projects involving limited outlays of cash, say up to $5,000. But in other organizations all project authorizations must be given by the managing officer or the board.

There should be a central distributing point for all copies of approved authorizations, preferably controlled by the accounting department who will ensure that each project is given a sequential capital order number to which all related paperwork can be referenced.

Where a project is subdivided into stages or sections it is desirable to identify each part either with a separate capital order number or with a suffix to the main number.

A project is authorized on the basis that certain results (e.g., cost savings) will be achieved by specified methods.

Provided there is no change in these basis factors, minor variations in the specification of the equipment and in the relative costs of items making up the total project may be permitted.

It should not be permitted to make use of an authorized amount in order to procure assets of a specification basically different from that originally proposed, nor to make any change which would have the effect of reducing the anticipated return on the capital invested.

In such cases, expenditure on the subject should be stopped and a new authorization sheet submitted.

If at any time it appears from costs and commitments already incurred that the eventual total cost of a project is likely to exceed the amount authorized, then a supplementary authorization should be submitted immediately. Expenditure against the original authorization should be limited as far as possible until the project has been reviewed.

It should not be permissible to use an unexpended balance from one authorization to compensate overspending on another project.

A project should not be considered complete until any replaced asset has been sold or disposal otherwise made. If the original authorization sheet included the disposal of an asset, and subsequently it is decided to retain or to defer disposal of that asset, then a fresh authorization sheet should be raised to cover such retention.

There must be a central record of the costs incurred on each project, including expenditure committed (on purchase orders or otherwise) but not yet due. On the basis of this record, periodic reports should be made to managers and the board showing the progress of each project in terms of expenditure against authorization and also of achievement of the approval time scale. (A specimen form of report is illustrated on page 163.) On the basis of these reports, management can review the desirability of continuing the project, considering the expenditure still to be made and the latest estimate of benefits likely to be achieved. It is unfortunate that once a project is under way the residual expenditure can nearly always be justified arithmetically even though the total for the project as a whole will exceed the original estimate.

| No. | Description of project | Authorized | | | Committed on purchase orders | Costs to date | | | Completion | | Notes |
		Previous year	This year	Total		External	Internal	Total	Authorized date	Forecast date	

CAPITAL EXPENDITURE COST REPORT $000's — Period:

As soon as a project is reported as complete, the capital control section should:

1. Ensure that the disposal of old assets has taken place.
2. Initiate fixed asset records.

The main fixed asset accounts in the financial account books will record the cost of completed capital work and purchases under the main headings of asset type, such as land and buildings, equipment and machinery, office furnishings and motor vehicles. This categorization will probably be linked with different methods of depreciation or may be influenced by taxation or statutory information requirements.

For internal management accounting purposes, means must be found of identifying each asset, and its operating costs, with the department or cost center where it is being used.

The normal records for this purpose are a fixed asset register or a series of fixed asset records, one for each item.

These should show:

1. A description of the asset.
2. Information to enable it to be identified physically.

3. Its location, i.e., the cost center responsible.
4. The basis on which depreciation is to be calculated.

Where an asset is identifiable as an entity it may well have a distinctive number applied by the makers, but it is also common for the company which has acquired it to affix a simple sequential asset number. The engineer or the plant department will often control the allocation of such numbers.

The use of such numbers simplifies the task of taking a physical inventory of fixed assets from time to time. This will help to ensure, not only that assets are not lost and that their state of repair is reviewed, but also that plant operating costs are being charged to the correct cost center.

Control of the location of fixed assets should not, however, depend on taking a physical inventory. There should be a system defined for reporting movements of fixed assets, including their eventual disposal.

The final stage in dealing with investment projects is the "post audit"— the examination of the costs, savings, income and other benefits achieved by implementing the project, as compared with those that were forecast at the time it was authorized. Although people accept without question the need for control against operating budgets, it often happens that the corresponding control against project implementation is somehow thought to be either impossible or derogatory of their authority. Clearly unless some audit is carried out, the business can be lumbered for long periods with the results of badly estimated projects. The feedback from audit reports helps to improve the quality of future estimates.

It must be admitted that major projects often become modified as they progress, and it may be difficult to disentangle the ultimate purpose or the ultimate justification for completing the project. This implies a lack of clear thinking at the justification stage, for which the financial manager must bear the greatest share of responsibility.

Present value of 1

at compound interest $(1+r)^{-n}$

Years (n)   Interest rates (r)

n	1	2	3	4	5	6	7	8	9	10
1	0.9901	0.9804	0.9709	0.9615	0.9524	0.9434	0.9346	0.9259	0.9174	0.9091
2	0.9803	0.9612	0.9426	0.9246	0.9070	0.8900	0.8734	0.8573	0.8417	0.8264
3	0.9706	0.9423	0.9151	0.8890	0.8638	0.8396	0.8163	0.7938	0.7722	0.7513
4	0.9610	0.9238	0.8885	0.8548	0.8227	0.7921	0.7629	0.7350	0.7084	0.6830
5	0.9515	0.9057	0.8626	0.8219	0.7835	0.7473	0.7139	0.6806	0.6499	0.6209
6	0.9420	0.8880	0.8375	0.7903	0.7462	0.7050	0.6663	0.6302	0.5963	0.5645
7	0.9327	0.8706	0.8131	0.7599	0.7107	0.6651	0.6227	0.5835	0.5470	0.5132
8	0.9235	0.8535	0.7894	0.7307	0.6768	0.6274	0.5820	0.5403	0.5019	0.4665
9	0.9143	0.8368	0.7664	0.7026	0.6446	0.5919	0.5439	0.5002	0.4804	0.4241
10	0.9053	0.8203	0.7441	0.6756	0.6139	0.5584	0.5083	0.4632	0.4224	0.3855
11	0.8963	0.8043	0.7224	0.6496	0.5847	0.5268	0.4751	0.4289	0.3875	0.3505
12	0.8874	0.7885	0.7014	0.6246	0.5568	0.4970	0.4440	0.3971	0.3555	0.3186
13	0.8787	0.7730	0.6810	0.6006	0.5303	0.4888	0.4150	0.3677	0.3262	0.2897
14	0.8700	0.7579	0.6611	0.5775	0.5051	0.4423	0.3878	0.3405	0.2992	0.2633
15	0.8613	0.7430	0.6419	0.5553	0.4810	0.4173	0.3624	0.3152	0.2745	0.2394
16	0.8528	0.7284	0.6232	0.5339	0.4581	0.3936	0.3387	0.2919	0.2519	0.2176
17	0.8444	0.7142	0.6050	0.5134	0.4363	0.3714	0.3166	0.2703	0.2311	0.1978
18	0.8360	0.7002	0.5874	0.4936	0.4155	0.3503	0.2959	0.2502	0.2120	0.1799
19	0.8277	0.6864	0.5703	0.4746	0.3957	0.3305	0.2765	0.2317	0.1945	0.1635
20	0.8195	0.6730	0.5537	0.4564	0.3769	0.3118	0.2584	0.2145	0.1784	0.1486
25	0.7795	0.6095	0.4776	0.3751	0.2953	0.2330	0.1842	0.1460	0.1160	0.0923
30	0.7419	0.5521	0.4120	0.3083	0.2314	0.1741	0.1314	0.0994	0.0754	0.0573
35	0.7059	0.5000	0.3554	0.2534	0.1813	0.1301	0.0937	0.0676	0.0490	0.0356
40	0.6717	0.4529	0.3066	0.2083	0.1420	0.0872	0.0668	0.0450	0.0318	0.0221
45	0.6391	0.4102	0.2644	0.1712	0.1113	0.0727	0.0476	0.0313	0.0207	0.0137
50	0.6080	0.3715	0.2251	0.1407	0.0872	0.0543	0.0339	0.0213	0.0134	0.0085

Years (n)   Interest rates (r)

Years (n)	11	12	13	14	15	16	17	18	19	20
1	0.9009	0.8929	0.8850	0.8772	0.8696	0.8621	0.8547	0.8475	0.8403	0.8333
2	0.8116	0.7972	0.7831	0.7695	0.7561	0.7432	0.7305	0.7182	0.7062	0.6944
3	0.7312	0.7118	0.6931	0.6750	0.6575	0.6407	0.6244	0.6086	0.5934	0.5787
4	0.6587	0.6355	0.6133	0.5921	0.5718	0.5523	0.5337	0.5158	0.4987	0.4823
5	0.5935	0.5674	0.5428	0.5194	0.4972	0.4761	0.4561	0.4371	0.4190	0.4019
6	0.5346	0.5066	0.4803	0.4556	0.4323	0.4104	0.3898	0.3704	0.3521	0.3349
7	0.4817	0.4523	0.4251	0.3996	0.3759	0.3538	0.3332	0.3139	0.2959	0.2791
8	0.4339	0.4039	0.3762	0.3506	0.3269	0.3050	0.2848	0.2660	0.2487	0.2326
9	0.3909	0.3606	0.3329	0.3075	0.2843	0.2630	0.2434	0.2255	0.2090	0.1938
10	0.3522	0.3220	0.2946	0.2697	0.2472	0.2267	0.2080	0.1911	0.1756	0.1615
11	0.3173	0.2875	0.2607	0.2366	0.2149	0.1954	0.1778	0.1619	0.1476	0.1346
12	0.2858	0.2567	0.2307	0.2076	0.1869	0.1685	0.1520	0.1372	0.1240	0.1122
13	0.2575	0.2292	0.2042	0.1821	0.1625	0.1452	0.1299	0.1163	0.1042	0.0935
14	0.2320	0.2046	0.1807	0.1597	0.1413	0.1252	0.1110	0.0985	0.0876	0.0779
15	0.2090	0.1827	0.1599	0.1401	0.1229	0.1079	0.0949	0.0835	0.0736	0.0649
16	0.1883	0.1631	0.1415	0.1229	0.1069	0.0930	0.0811	0.0708	0.0618	0.0541
17	0.1696	0.1456	0.1252	0.1078	0.0929	0.0802	0.0693	0.0600	0.0520	0.0451
18	0.1528	0.1300	0.1108	0.0946	0.0808	0.0691	0.0592	0.0508	0.0437	0.0376
19	0.1377	0.1161	0.0981	0.0829	0.0703	0.0596	0.0506	0.0431	0.0367	0.0313
20	0.1240	0.1037	0.0868	0.0728	0.0611	0.0514	0.0433	0.0365	0.0308	0.0261
25	0.0736	0.0588	0.0471	0.0378	0.0304	0.0245	0.0197	0.0160	0.0129	0.0105
30	0.0437	0.0334	0.0256	0.0196	0.0151	0.0116	0.0090	0.0070	0.0054	0.0042
35	0.0259	0.0189	0.0139	0.0102	0.0075	0.0055	0.0041	0.0030	0.0023	0.0017
40	0.0154	0.0107	0.0075	0.0053	0.0037	0.0026	0.0019	0.0013	0.0010	0.0007
45	0.0091	0.0061	0.0041	0.0027	0.0019	0.0013	0.0008	0.0006	0.0004	0.0003
50	0.0054	0.0035	0.0022	0.0014	0.0008	0.0006	0.0004	0.0003	0.0002	0.0001

Years (n) Interest rates (r)

Years (n)	21	22	23	24	25	26	27	28	29	30
1	0.8264	0.8197	0.8130	0.8065	0.8000	0.7937	0.7874	0.7812	0.7752	0.7692
2	0.6830	0.6719	0.6610	0.6504	0.6400	0.6299	0.6200	0.6104	0.6009	0.5917
3	0.5645	0.5507	0.5374	0.5245	0.5120	0.4999	0.4882	0.4768	0.4659	0.4552
4	0.4665	0.4514	0.4369	0.4230	0.4096	0.3968	0.3844	0.3725	0.3611	0.3501
5	0.3855	0.3700	0.3552	0.3411	0.3277	0.3149	0.3027	0.2910	0.2799	0.2693
6	0.3186	0.3033	0.2888	0.2751	0.2621	0.2499	0.2383	0.2274	0.2170	0.2072
7	0.2633	0.2486	0.2348	0.2218	0.2097	0.1983	0.1877	0.1776	0.1682	0.1594
8	0.2176	0.2038	0.1909	0.1789	0.1678	0.1574	0.1478	0.1388	0.1304	0.1226
9	0.1799	0.1670	0.1552	0.1443	0.1342	0.1249	0.1164	0.1084	0.1011	0.0943
10	0.1486	0.1369	0.1262	0.1164	0.1074	0.0992	0.0916	0.0847	0.0784	0.0725
11	0.1228	0.1122	0.1026	0.0938	0.0859	0.0787	0.0721	0.0662	0.0607	0.0558
12	0.1015	0.0920	0.0834	0.0757	0.0687	0.0625	0.0568	0.0517	0.0471	0.0429
13	0.0839	0.0754	0.0678	0.0610	0.0550	0.0496	0.0447	0.0404	0.0365	0.0330
14	0.0693	0.0618	0.0551	0.0492	0.0440	0.0393	0.0352	0.0316	0.0283	0.0254
15	0.0573	0.0507	0.0448	0.0397	0.0352	0.0312	0.0277	0.0247	0.0219	0.0195
16	0.0474	0.0415	0.0364	0.0320	0.0281	0.0248	0.0218	0.0193	0.0170	0.0150
17	0.0391	0.0340	0.0296	0.0258	0.0225	0.0197	0.0172	0.0150	0.0132	0.0116
18	0.0323	0.0279	0.0241	0.0208	0.0180	0.0156	0.0135	0.0118	0.0102	0.0089
19	0.0267	0.0229	0.0196	0.0168	0.0144	0.0124	0.0107	0.0092	0.0079	0.0068
20	0.0221	0.0187	0.0159	0.0135	0.0115	0.0098	0.0084	0.0072	0.0061	0.0053
25	0.0085	0.0069	0.0057	0.0046	0.0038	0.0031	0.0025	0.0021	0.0017	0.0014
30	0.0033	0.0026	0.0020	0.0016	0.0012	0.0010	0.0009	0.0006	0.0005	0.0004
35	0.0013	0.0009	0.0007	0.0005	0.0004	0.0003	0.0002	0.0002	0.0001	0.0001
40	0.0005	0.0004	0.0002	0.0002	0.0001	0.0001	0.0001	0.0001	0.0000	0.0000
45	0.0002	0.0001	0.0001	0.0001	0.0000	0.0000	0.0000	0.0000	0.0000	0.0000
50	0.0001	0.0000	0.0000	0.0000	0.0000	0.0000	0.0000	0.0000	0.0000	0.0000

Further
Applications
of DCF Techniques

Evaluation of Decision Data

Managers spend their lives making decisions between alternative courses of action. In many cases one of the possible alternatives will be to do nothing—to maintain the status quo. But in every case there will be the possibility of doing something that will alter the existing state of affairs.

Apart from those decisions which amend selling prices without affecting the volume of sales, all actions will have some effect on the costs of the business, and the incremental or differential costs must be forecast. Even simple decisions, however, can affect the time pattern of cash receipts or payments, thus involving the consideration of changes in interest charges or opportunities for profit. In other words the appropriate method of evaluation will be the use of discounted cash flow calculations.

The purpose of this chapter is to exemplify the application of such calculations to:

1. Optimal life decisions.
2. Lease, buy or installment purchase.

3. Alternative forms of borrowing.
4. Royalties and license agreements.

The chapter concludes with a brief discussion of the problem of uncertainty in forecasts.

Optimal Life Decisions

Calculations of the following all depend on forecasts of the residual or scrap value of the asset year by year into the future:

1. The optimal life of a newly acquired asset.
2. The timing of the replacement of an existing asset.
3. The optimal retirement date of an asset which is not to be replaced.

Because such forecasts are highly suspect at the present time due to changes in price levels, formal evaluation of optimal life is less common than it used to be, but some attempt should be made to give financial guidance on the subject.

EXAMPLE

An item of equipment is purchased for $100 on the basis of the following forecast of cash savings:

Year 1	$50
2	38
3	26
4	15
5	10
6	4

Its scrap value at the year's end is forecast year by year as follows:

Year 1	$20
2	17
3	14
4	11
5	5
6	0

What would be the most profitable period of time to run the equipment before scrapping it? (The company's cost of capital is 14%.)

The answer can be found by taking different possible periods, each with its appropriate residual value, and calculating the NPV in each case at the company's cost of capital. The life period showing the highest NPV would be financially the best.

Year	0	1	2	3	4	5	6	
Factor 14%	1.00	.88	.77	.67	.59	.52	.46	*NPV*
2-year life								
Flow	(100)	50	55*					
Amount	(100.0)	44.0	42.3					(13.7)
3-year life								
Flow	(100)	50	38	40*				
Amount	(100.0)	44.0	29.3	26.8				0.1
4-year life								
Flow	(100)	50	38	26	26*			
Amount	(100.0)	44.0	29.3	17.4	15.3			6.0
5-year life								
Flow	(100)	50	38	26	15	15*		
Amount	(100.0)	44.0	29.3	17.4	8.9	7.8		7.4
6-year life								
Flow	(100)	50	38	26	15	10	4*	
Amount	(100.0)	44.0	29.3	17.4	8.9	5.2	1.8	6.6

*These items comprise the appropriate cash savings for the year plus the relevant scrap value.

The five-year life yields the highest NPV, and would be preferred.

There is an an alternative method (sometimes known as the optimal replacement method) which consists of:

1. Discounting each year's forecast cash flows at the chosen rate.
2. Summing the accumulating discounted amounts year by year.
3. Discounting each year's forecast scrap value and adding that to the previous accumulated total year by year.
4. Deducting the discounted figures each year from the original investment to give a present value.
5. Converting the present value each year to an "annual equivalent" (i.e., an average annual amount) by using annuity tables.
6. Selecting the life which shows the highest annual equivalent.

Using the previous figures, the method can be demonstrated as follows:

1. Year	0	1	2	3	4	5	6
2. Factor 14%	1.00	.88	.77	.67	.59	.52	.46
3. Cash flows	(100)	50	38	26	15	10	4
4. Discounted	(100.0)	44.0	29.3	17.4	8.9	5.2	1.8
5. Accumulated	(100.0)	(56.0)	(26.7)	(9.3)	(0.4)	4.8	6.6
6. Residual value		20	17	14	11	5	0
7. Discounted		17.6	13.1	9.4	6.5	2.6	0
8. Present value		(38.4)	(13.6)	0.1	6.1	7.4	6.6
9. Annuity factor 14%		0.88	1.65	2.32	2.91	3.43	3.89
10. Annual equivalent		(43.6)	(8.2)	0	2.1	2.2	1.7

Notes: 1. Present value (line 8) = line 5 plus or minus line 7.
     2. Annual equivalent (line 10) = line 8 divided by the annuity factor (line 9).

Again the five-year life is the most favorable.

Lease or Buy Decisions

In decisions of this nature, we are reviewing different time patterns of expenditure to discover which is the least expensive.

EXAMPLE

The XYZ Company has decided to install a new milling machine. The machine costs $20,000 and would last five years with a trade-in value of $4,000 at the end of the fifth year. The company's cost of capital is 12%.

As alternatives to outright purchase the company could buy the machine on an installment basis, paying an initial deposit of $6,000, and installments of $4,000 per annum at the end of the next five years; or it could lease the machine at a cost of $4,800 per annum for five years payable at the beginning of each year. Under this alternative there would be savings in insurance and servicing of $500 per annum. What is the better alternative?

ANSWER

On the facts given, the annual cash flows and their present values at 12% would be as follows:

		Outright purchase		Installment purchase		Leasing	
Year	Discount factor	Cash flows	Present value	Cash flows	Present value	Cash flows	Present value
0	1.00	(20,000)	(20,000)	(6,000)	(6,000)	(4,800)	(4,800)
1	.89			(4,000)		(4,300)*	
2	.80			(4,000)		(4,300)	(13,072)
3	.71			(4,000)	(12,160)	(4,300)	
4	.64			(4,000)		(4,300)	
5	.57	4,000	2,280	0**		500	285
Net present value			(17,720)		(18,160)		(17,587)

Notes: *$4,800 less savings $500.
     **$4,000 less residual value $4,000. Leasing has the lowest cost and is the pre-
     ferred alternative.

Where only two alternative methods of financing the acquisition were under consideration it would be possible, of course, to calculate the incremental cash flows and just discount those.

One of the main features of these decisons, the amount and timing of tax relief, has been omitted from the above simple example. In practice this would always be taken into account.

It is assumed that the leasing of this machine is the most profitable way of using the $20,000 outlay; this may not be the case, and one ought to look at the alternative uses of the money before making a final decision.

Alternative Forms of Borrowing

In some cases it will be necessary to incorporate a specific interest charge into the cash flow calculations, and this is illustrated in the following example:

A company is buying a special purpose machine tool for $120,000. A final decision must be made as to how the purchase is to be financed.

There are three available methods:

1. Outright purchase using bank overdraft facilities at an interest rate of 9% per annum.
2. Loan from a bank, covered by a specific debenture. The loan would be repayable by annual installments of $25,000, with interest at 15% per annum on the declining balance.
3. Leasing agreement with a bank who would buy the machine and rent it to the company for $18.30 per $1,000 per month.

The machine attracts annual allowances for tax purposes at the rate of 25% on the declining balance method. The rate of corporation tax has been taken as 40%. All taxation adjustments are made one year in arrears. It may be assumed that the company is making adequate profits to absorb any "loss" adjustments within this project.

The savings, before tax, arising from the use of the machine are estimated at $15,000 in the first year and $30,000 per annum thereafter. The residual value of the machine after six years is forecast at $20,000.

It may be assumed that the bank overdraft and accrued interest would be repaid out of savings and tax benefits received.

You wish to calculate:

1. Which method of financing would be financially preferable over the first six years (plus taxation adjustments in the seventh year) if the opportunity cost of capital employed is 20%. Use annual compounding.

2. The opportunity cost of capital at which the ranking of the overdraft alternative and the debenture alternative would be reversed.

The suggested approach is as follows:

PRELIMINARY CALCULATIONS

1. Savings and tax thereon

Year	Savings	Tax charge at 40%	Net cash flow
	$	$	$
1	15,000		15,000
2	30,000	40% X 15,000 = 6,000	24,000
3	30,000	40% X 30,000 = 12,000	18,000
4	as Year 3		18,000
5	as Year 3		18,000
6	as Year 3		18,000
7	tax charge Year 6	12,000	(12,000)

2. Capital allowances

Year		Cost of machine / allowance	Cash effect of allowances at 40%
		$	$
0	Cost of machine	120,000	
2	Annual allowance 25%	30,000	12,000
		90,000	
3	Annual allowance 25%	22,500	9,000
		67,500	
4	Annual allowance 25%	16,875	6,750
		50,625	
5	Annual allowance 25%	12,656	5,062

Year			Cash effect of allowances at 40%
		$	$
		37,969	
6	Annual allowance 25%	9,492	3,797
		28,477	
	Residual value	20,000	
7	Remaining depreciable base	8,477	3,391

3. Loan account

			Tax relief on interest 40% one year in arrears	
Year			Year	Amount
0	Loan	120,000		
1	Interest 15%	18,000	2	7,200
		138,000		
	Repaid	(25,000)		
		113,000		
2	Interest	16,950	3	6,780
	Repaid	(25,000)		
		104,950		
3	Interest	15,743	4	6,297
	Repaid	(25,000)		
		95,693		
4	Interest	14,354	5	5,742
	Repaid	(25,000)		
		85,047		
5	Interest	12,757	6	5,103
	Repaid	(25,000)		
		72,804		
6	Interest	10,921	7	4,368
	Repaid	(25,000)		
	Assume repaid end Year 6	58,725		
	(Offset by residual value	20,000)		

4. Overdraft

			Tax relief on interest 40% one year in arrears	
			Year	Amount
0.	Initial overdraft	120,000		

		Year	Amount
Year			

1. Interest 9%   10,800   2   4,320

Repaid—this depends on cash flow available, so further calculations on the overdraft will have to be made at the same time as the cash flow calculations in method 1.

5. Leasing charges

The monthly charge is $18.30 per $1,000 on $120,000 = $2,196.

Annual charge 12 × $2,196 = $26,352

Tax relief 40%   10,541

Net   15,811

Year	Amount
1	26,352
2	15,811
3	15,811
4	15,811
5	15,811
6	15,811
7	(10,541) relief on Year 6.

We can now evaluate the three alternatives.

1. Overdraft

Year	Savings less tax	Capital allowances	Interest relief	Net flow			Tax relief 40%
					Advance	120,000	
					Interest	10,800	4,320
1	15,000	–	–	15,000	Repaid	(15,000)	
						115,800	
					Interest	10,422	4,169
2	24,000	12,000	4,320	40,320	Repaid	(40,320)	
						85,902	
					Interest	7,731	3,092
3	18,000	9,000	4,169	31,169	Repaid	(31,169)	
						62,464	
					Interest	5,622	2,249
4	18,000	6,750	3,092	27,842	Repaid	(27,842)	
						40,244	
					Interest	3,622	1,449
5	18,000	5,062	2,249	25,311	Repaid	(25,311)	
						18,555	
					Interest	1,670	668
6	18,000	3,797	1,449	23,246	Repaid	(20,225)	

The cash flows actually affecting the business are therefore:

Year		Amount	Discount factor	Discounted
6	Cash flow in excess of overdraft repayment 23,246-20,225	3,021 ⎫		
	Residual value of machine	20,000 ⎭	0.33	7,597
7	Capital allowance	3,391 ⎫		
	Tax relief on interest	668 ⎭	0.28	1,137
	Net present value			8,734

2. Loan account

Year	Savings less tax	Capital allowances	Interest relief	Loan repayment	Net cash flow	Factor	Discounted amount
1	15,000	–	–	(25,000)	(10,000)	.83	(8,300)
2	24,000	12,000	7,200	(25,000)	18,200	.69	12,558
3	18,000	9,000	6,780	(25,000)	8,780	.58	5,092
4	18,000	6,750	6,297	(25,000)	6,047	.48	2,903
5	18,000	5,062	5,742	(25,000)	3,804	.40	1,522
6	18,000	3,797	5,103	(25,000)	1,900	.33	627
	Balance of loan				(58,725)	.33	(19,379)
	Residual value of machine				20,000	.33	6,600
7	–	3,391	4,368	–	7,759	.28	2,173
Net present value							3,796

3. Leasing

Year	Savings less tax	Leasing charge	Net cash flow	Factor	Discounted amount
1	15,000	26,352	(11,352)	.83	(9,422)
2	24,000	15,811	8,189	.69	5,650
3	18,000	15,811	2,189	.58 ⎫	
4	18,000	15,811	2,189	.48 ⎬	3,918
5	18,000	15,811	2,189	.40	
6	18,000	15,811	2,189	.33 ⎭	
7	–	(10,541)	10,541	.28	2,951
Net present value					3,097

CONCLUSION

At a cost of capital of 20% the bank overdraft method of financing the project yields the highest net present value and would be preferred.

Royalties and License Agreements

This is a specialist field with legal and taxation implications, often involving foreign countries. As illustrations of the principles involved two examples are given.

EXAMPLE 1

A foreign company has requested your company, concerning one of your patented products, to:

1. Grant them the right to manufacture.
2. Make available to them the related manufacturing know-how.

As financial officer preparing the agreement you have to decide:

1. The various forms that payment by the licensee could take and the circumstances most appropriate in each case.
2. The factors you would take into account in deciding the amount payable.
3. The special points to be included to ensure that payment is received in full at the agreed time.

Suggested approach:

1. Payment may be provided for in three ways:
   a. *Lump sum payment.* This kind of payment is particularly apt when it is difficult to ensure the secrecy of the know-how, or when the know-how is competing with other processes which are similar but which for some reason the grantee cannot or does not wish to apply.
   b. *Periodic royalties* based on, e.g., monthly sums at a fixed rate or at an increasing or decreasing rate or on a percentage of products made or sold.

   The payments may be made either at fixed periods or as linked to the production or sale by the grantee of the products covered by the know-how.

   In the latter case, the agreement should provide for periodic returns of products and should state how soon after the return the amounts due should be paid.

   c. Periodic royalties preceded by an initial payment (e.g., on the signing of the contract).

2. The amount imposable as royalties will be based on the grantor's assessment of the profitability to the grantee of the business he will transact under the license. A lump sum or initial payment will represent the discounted value of the whole or part of such royalties during the life of the agreement. Its size will be determined by the grantor's assessment of the risk that later periodic payments will not be forthcoming.

3. See note concerning periodic returns and due dates under (1) above. Also:

   a. Royalties should be expressed free of all dues and taxes leviable in the grantee's country.

   b. The method of deciding the applicable rate of exchange should be specified.

   c. The levy of interest on royalties due and unpaid should be stated.

   d. The agreement should be determined in the event of nonpayment after due notice, and a penalty for breach should be imposed.

We will now look at one possible use of DCF calculations.

EXAMPLE 2

Your manufacturing company has agreed to pay royalties of $2 per unit on a patented component which is incorporated into its products.

The forecast of future royalties payable is as follows:

Month	Amount
December 19X2	2,300
June 19X3	1,460
December 19X3	4,780
June 19X4	9,560
December 19X4	4,780

The company wishes to buy the patent rights by commuting these royalties into one or more lump-sum payments. The licensor has suggested the following alternatives:

1. A single payment in December 19X0.
2. Two equal payments in December 19X0 and December 19X1.
3. Three equal payments in December 19X0, 19X1, and 19X2 respectively.

The marginal cost of capital to the company is 10% per annum, and its opportunity cost is 20% per annum. There is no problem of availability of funds.

You are required to calculate the higher and lower limits within which you would expect to negotiate the amount(s) payable under each of the alternatives given above.

SOLUTION

Month	Amount of royalty payable under existing agreement	Discount at 10% Factor	Discount at 10% Amount	Discount at 20% Factor	Discount at 20% Amount
	$		$		$
December 19X0		1.00		1.00	
December 19X1		.91		.83	
December 19X2	2,300	.83	1,909	.69	1,587
June 19X3	1,460	.79	1,153	.64	934
December 19X3	4,780	.75	3,585	.58	2,772
June 19X4	9,560	.71	6,788	.53	5,067
December 19X4	4,780	.68	3,250	.48	2,294
	22,880		16,685		12,654

Alternative			
1.	16,685 ÷ 1.00	16,685	
	12,654 ÷ 1.00		12,654
2.	16,685 ÷ 1.91	8,736	
	12,654 ÷ 1.83		6,915
3.	16,685 ÷ 2.74	6,089	
	12,654 ÷ 2.52		5,021

You would therefore open negotiations probably slightly below $12,654 for alternative 1; $6,915 × 2 for alternative 2; and $5,021 × 3 for alternative 3.

The maximum prices you could afford to pay would be the corresponding figures listed above under the 10% discount column.

The Problem of Uncertainty in Investment Decisions

All methods of investment appraisal involve forecasting future events, but forecasts by their nature are subject to inaccuracy or uncertainty.

This must mean that there is some degree of risk that the rate of return or the NPV considered most likely will not, in fact, be achieved.

There are four possible ways of dealing with this uncertainty:

1. *Ignore it.* As we have seen earlier in this book, the company's cost of capital, its required rate of return, can never be fixed with high precision.

It is representative of a spectrum of rates which might be regarded as acceptable. The view is sometimes taken, therefore, that imprecision in the rate of return criterion can permit some uncertainty in the data used, and that no specific adjustment for risk need be made. This line of argument, however, can lead to the accumulation of uncertainties to the extent that rational appraisal of projects becomes impossible.

2. *Modify the target requirements,* whether rate of return or payback period. This may be done on a selective basis for those projects that are believed to contain high risks. However it is done, this procedure involves arguing in a circle. By making a specific change in the target requirements the company has put a value on the uncertainty, which of its nature is unknown. Even when used selectively this method can lead to the rejection of good projects.

3. *Sensitivity analysis.* In its simplest form, sensitivity analysis is a desk operation for the accountant with a calculating machine. It consists of:

   a. Breaking down the cash flow data into a number of major variables, in other words, making a usable model of the project. Examples might be initial outlay cost, production hours, wage rates, production efficiency, sales quantities and selling prices.

   b. Taking each variable in turn and modifying it by a fairly arbitrary percentage (say 10%) upward and downward from the original estimate.

   c. Recalculating the DCF rate of return on the project, taking each new estimate in turn.

For example, if the IRR of a project were originally calculated as 15%, and five major variables were defined, each of which was then modified by 10% either way, one could finish up with a table like this:

	Original project rate of return—15%	
	Rate of return when variable altered by 10%	
Variable	*a. adversely*	*b. favorably*
1. Initial outlay	12%	17%
2. Production efficiency	9%	19%
3. Wage rates	13%	16%
4. Sales volume	8%	20%
5. Sales price	12%	18%

It then becomes clear that the rate of return achievable on this project is particularly sensitive to fluctuations in production efficiency and sales volume, and particular attention should be given to improving if possible the quality of those estimates.

It is arithmetically possible to calculate project rates of return, assuming that all variables are affected together, either adversely or favorably, but as this is an unlikely contingency, and as the above caculations were made using an arbitrary 10% swing, this exercise would not have any great validity.

What is needed is some method of establishing:

a. The possible range of variation on each variable.

b. The likelihood of various combinations of these variations. Attempts to do this are covered by our fourth group method:

4. *Risk analysis.* This involves estimators in making forecasts to which probability ratings can be applied.

One way of attempting to get a better feel for the likely results of a project is to go back to each estimator and ask him to forecast for his particular variables, not merely the expected figure, but also the best and worst possibilities. Unfortunately it is common to find that the worst possibility in any situation is catastrophe, and the best that can be envisaged would put some memorable mining prospectuses to shame. The method, therefore, usually fails to add significantly to management understanding of the project.

A modified procedure is to ask each estimator to forecast not the best or the worst possible outcome but a range of probabilities—for example that there is a "10% chance" that the sales figure for a particular year will be below $100,000 and a 10% chance that it might be above say $250,000, the most likely figure being $150,000. If the estimates are expressed in this way then those of you who remember your mathematics will realize that we have a basis for a probability distribution. For each variable, each year, a probability curve can be constructed as shown:

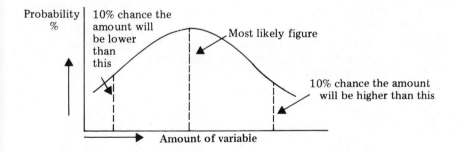

The beauty of this procedure is that it is now possible to use a standardized computer program for taking random samples, to make a sufficient number of sampling runs from the various probability curves and to construct a probability distribution for the project as a whole. This will be expressed in terms of the IRR and could appear as in the following diagram:

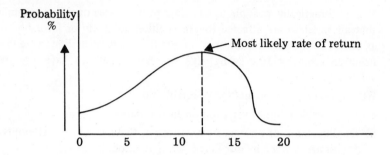

The decision maker now has a much more realistic view of the probabilities of the situation. Whereas, for example, in the chart illustrated, he had originally been told that the project would yield 15%, he now sees that the most likely rate of return is 13%, that the chances of a higher rate of return fall off fairly rapidly and that there are significant chances of lower rates of return and even of loss.

And now for the final, and most important point about the appraisal of investment projects. All the mathematics in the world will not relieve the manager of his proper responsibility—that of making a decision. All the techniques described in this chapter have as their aim to identify possible financial effects if particular decisions are taken. But:

1. Decisions are not taken only for financial effects. All the nonfinancial objectives of the business have to be considered—the welfare of the employees, the responsibility of the company to the community, the need for growth, power and influence and many others.

2. A manager takes risks. Faced with the preceding chart he might ask himself whether, if the project in fact resulted in one of the lower rates of return, that would be disastrous for the business or merely inconvenient. If inconvenient, then his personal and the corporate attitude to risk-taking would influence his decision.

3. Good managers know more about their business than most of their employees individually can do. The project evaluation was built up from employee opinions, using employee skills. The manager may still feel it is right to override those opinions.

12

Investment in Securities

Introduction

We have seen that a business needs to keep cash resources profitably occupied, and funds temporarily surplus to requirements should be invested in such a way as to yield the highest rate of return consistent with liquidity—the ability to realize the investment quickly when cash is again needed.

In various places we have referred to the requirements of the long-term investors in securities, but mainly from the point of view of a business assuming to attract the investor. The business should aim to maximize the wealth accruing to the common shareholders. This can be achieved by ensuring such a balance between distributed and retained profits as would enable the shareholder to obtain the greatest possible total benefit between the time he bought his shares and the time he sold them at the pevailing market price.

In Chapter 7, when discussing the cost of equity for a company we referred to earnings yield (and its converse the price/earnings ratio) and dividend yield as measures of shareholder satisfaction. These ratios were further illustrated and explained in Chapter 8 when considering the pricing of equity issues.

In Chapter 14, we shall be concerned with the purchase of securities, but purely as a means of obtaining control of a particular business.

We must now look at the problems of invesment in securities from the point of view of the long-term investor, whether a private individual or a company formed for this purpose (such as an "investment trust") or one of the financial institutions, like insurance companies or pension funds, for which successful investment is essential to the achievement of some other aim—protection of clients against the risks of loss or the provision of an income after retirement age.

Objectives of Investment

The objective of the rational investor is to choose that portfolio of investments which maximizes his "utility," i.e., the net present value of the cash flow expected to be generated by the portfolio. This objective is precisely the same as that of the company investing in capital projects as described in Chapter 10, and in dealing with securities one has a similar number of basic variables to consider, i.e.:

1. The purchase price of the investment.
2. The interest or dividends it will yield.
3. The price at which it will be realized.
4. The transaction costs of buying and selling.
5. The effect of these cash flows on the investor's liability to taxation.

There are, however, significant differences between investment in securities and investment in other types of capital asset. Among them are:

1. *Flexibility in amount invested.* In buying a machine, a building or a car the initial outlay is dictated by the asset desired. In investing money, the amount to be put at risk is entirely at the discretion of the investor, apart from any minimum amount that may be fixed in particular circumstances (for example, certain bonds are sold in $1,000 denominations).
2. *Variability in purchase price.* The price of an asset will change from time to time, but the price of many investments fluctuates daily in accordance with the balance between supply and demand.
3. *Discretion concerning timing of investment.* If an asset is required for use in a business, then it must be acquired at a time related to production, sales or other conditions of its use. In the case of a security the investor

can buy and sell at times related simply to the availability of funds and the price changes noted above.

4. *Liquidity of investment.* An asset being used in business cannot be disposed of while there is a use for it, and for some assets there may not be a second-hand market. Securities can be sold at any time, and a buyer will normally be available.

5. *Security of income.* Forecasts of income from fixed asset investments are always subject to uncertainty, and so are forecasts of equity earnings, but it is possible to obtain securities yielding a fixed money income.

6. *Security of capital.* Similar comments relate to forecasts of residual or realizable values, and again it is possible to obtain securities which have a fixed capital value or a fixed redemption amount.

The investor, therefore, is ideally looking for the investment that would maximize his utility with complete security and complete liquidity. "Portfolio theory" is concerned with the theoretical means of selecting an optimal set of investments, bearing in mind the anticipated returns on those investments and the risks associated with them. In other words, risk is traded off against returns. Thus, as between two investments with equal anticipated returns the rational investor will prefer the investment with the smaller risk (he will display some degree of "risk aversion"). Between two investments with equal risk the rational investor would prefer the one with the greater anticipated return.

Risk is normally defined as the variance (or standard deviation) of the anticipated return on the investment. This is precisely the definition we used in relation to fixed asset investment when we were looking at probability curves derived from forecasts of a mean value and the "one in ten chances" high and low estimates.

You might like to refer back to Chapter 11 where the following risk profile of an investment was illustrated:

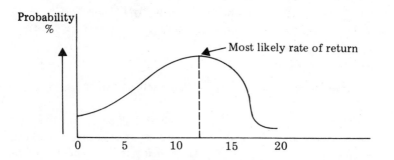

Now suppose that there is a choice between two investments (A and B) and their respective risk profiles are as shown in the following example.

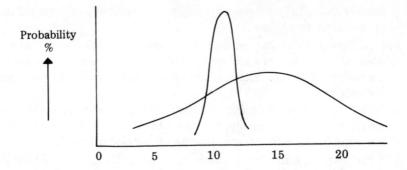

Probability
%

0   5   10   15   20

In brief, Project A has a wide range of possible yields, whereas Project B offers almost complete certainty of a return of about 10%. Which should the investor choose?

Before answering that question we might first ask whether any security could exist with a risk profile like that of Project B. The answer is "yes." There are of course three broad categories of investments:

1. *Fixed capital investments* which guarantee security and high liquidity. Examples are:
   a. Bank deposit accounts.
   b. Savings and loan deposits.
   c. Other investment deposits.
   d. Treasury bonds, bills, and notes.
   e. Savings bonds.
   f. Municipal bonds.

2. *Fixed interest investments* which guarantee a fixed rate of interest. Their price on the stock exchange will fluctuate, but in most cases they are redeemable on predetermined dates and terms. Examples are:
   a. British and foreign government stocks.
   b. Industrial development bonds.
   c. Preferred stock.

3. *Common shares,* variable in both income and capital repayment.

Fixed capital investments are virtually risk-free. So are fixed interest investments if they are dated and well secured. Apart from common shares, preferred shares are clearly the most risky, since their fixed dividend depends on the availability of profits, and they have no security in the event of liquidation.

Reverting then to the question of whether an investor should choose the high-risk or the low-risk investment, this will depend on a number of factors:

1. Whether he can afford to lose his money. If he chose the high-risk investment showing perhaps a 20% possibility of loss, and if in fact he did lose all or part of his investment, would that ruin him, seriously disrupt his future plans, or merely be inconvenient? If there is a 20% chance of ruin one would expect the rational investor to avoid that investment even though the most likely outcome would be a high rate of return (as financial controllers we must continue to assume that we are discussing rational investors and not compulsive gamblers).

2. The constitution of his portfolio as a whole. Assuming a mixed portfolio of high-risk and low-risk investments, so that the low-risk items ensure an adequate income and basic security, then risks of limited losses will fall into the "inconvenient" category and may be accepted.

3. The objectives of the particular investor concerned. We have already said that the general objective of investment was to maximize the net present value of the cash flows generated by the portfolio. Different investors will give different relative weightings to distributed income as opposed to capital growth. To take a few examples:

   a. *Pension funds* need very little distributed income since their short-term liabilities for current pensions and repayments to members leaving the plan are more than covered by current contributions. They look for safe long-term investments, though these should naturally give as high a yield as possible. A large proportion of their investment will thus be in government bonds, with a variable proportion of equity or property investment as and when opportunities for capital growth appear to arise.

   b. *General insurance companies,* on the contrary, have high short-term liabilities by way of claims arising on short-term policies, and their investment must be in securities which are readily realizable without loss.

   c. *Life insurance companies* have similar liquidity requirements to pension funds, but due to the highly competitive nature of their business they must take rather higher risks in order to offer acceptable whole life policies and to minimize their premium charges.

   d. *Mutual funds,* originally established to enable individual investors to share in a better balanced portfolio than they could afford themselves, have in many cases specialized so as to offer either high-income yield or capital growth or a combination of both. The balance of investments will thus depend on the major objective.

4. The duration of the investment. This was partly illustrated above. The return obtainable from common shares is uncertain not only in amount but in its timing. The investor in common shares must be prepared to wait until he judges he has obtained the optimal return.

5. The prevailing economic conditions. When there is the expectation that interest rates will rise, the prices of both fixed interest and, to some extent, variable income securities are likely to fall. At that time the investor would be best protected if he were holding fixed capital investments which he could realize without loss and then reinvest elsewhere after the rise in interest rates had occurred.

If business recession is expected then a switch into fixed interest securities would be beneficial before the drop in equity earnings and prices occurs, and when signs of recovery appear the investor should buy equities while prices are still relatively low. There are even times of general economic, financial and political uncertainty when cash appears to be the only safe resort.

These guidelines are only helpful if the investor has the facility to switch investments. This means having an investment fund sufficiently large to bear the expenses of the switch transactions, but in many cases the large fund cannot switch at will because the large sales or purchases involved would have their own disruptive effect on the price of the securities traded. (Note that this is one reason why institutional investors are not, in general, providers of funds for the smaller business, and why the growing dominance of institutional investment has contributed to stagnation in the capital investment sector.)

To summarize, the investor is aiming to maximize his yield from his portfolio. This will be the present value of anticipated income and capital gains from his investment. In taking an investment decision, therefore, the investor must ask not only *what* security to buy but *when* to buy it (and eventually to sell it) so as to take full advantage of fluctuations in price.

The Yield on Fixed Interest Investments

The yield on fixed interest investments can be considered under two aspects—the "interest yield," which is the relationship between the nominal rate of interest and the current market price, and where a redemption date and amount are fixed, the "yield to redemption," which is the internal rate of return generated by future interest flows and the eventual redemption proceeds.

An actual set of calculations is illustrated below for one particular security. Terms are 8½% 1984/86, based on the price at a particular date. The method is straightforward and familiar from your previous work on DCF calculations. In this example discount tables with annual compounding have been used.

In practice the calculations would take account of the actual half-yearly timing of the interest payments.

EXAMPLE OF YIELD CALCULATIONS
Terms 8½% 1984/86

Quoted in the *Wall Street Journal* on April 7, 1976, as follows:

Market price (per $100)	: 85 3/8 (i.e., 85.375)
Yield–Interest	: 10.20%
Yield to redemption	: 11.28%

Calculations

1. Interest yield

Market price as above	$85.375
As interest is payable on this security on January 10 and July 10 each year, the above price will include interest accrued between January 11 and April 7 = 88 days. 88/366 × $8.50 =	2.044
Net price	$83.331

On the net price of $83.331 the annual interest of $8.50 gives a yield of $\frac{8.50 \times 100}{83.331}$ = 10.20% as quoted above.

2. Yield to redemption

The future cash flows resulting from investment now, and the approximate discounted value (based on tables with annual compounding), are as follows:

Year		Cash flow $	Discount factors @ 11%	Discounted Cash flow $
0	Purchase price now	(85.375)	1.000	(85.375)
1	Interest to April 1977	8.500	.901	
2	Interest to April 1978	8.500	.812	
3	Interest to April 1979	8.500	.731	
4	Interest to April 1980	8.500	.659	
5	Interest to April 1981	8.500	.593	50.065
6	Interest to April 1982	8.500	.535	
7	Interest to April 1983	8.500	.482	

Year		Cash flow $	Discount factors @ 11%	Discounted Cash flow $
8	Interest to April 1984	8.500	.434	
9	Interest to April 1985	8.500	.391	
10	Interest to April 1986	8.500	.352	
10¼	Interest July 1986	4.250	.344	35.862
	Redemption at par	100.000		
	Approximate net present value at 11%			0.552

The actual yield is thus slightly higher than 11%. *The Wall Street Journal,* using actuarial tables, arrives at 11.28%.

The market price of a fixed interest security will tend to move toward the redemption price as the date for redemption approaches, but with long-term securities this will not be the predominant influence on price. The long-term investor will attempt to buy at a price that maximizes the yield to redemption, always assuming that this is not below expected future rates of interest. The short-term investor will be more concerned with the interest yield and will buy when this is above the yield offered by other forms of investment.

The Value of Common Shares

What are the equivalent decisions in the case of the investor in common shares?

On these there is no fixed rate of interest, and the equivalent calculation is the dividend yield, which is based not on future knowledge but on past history. In the comparison of one share with others having different dividend dates, there is an implication that the past trend of dividends will be continued into the future. Except for very high-risk companies this may be a reasonable assumption since one of the board's main concerns will be to maintain a stable dividend policy. At some stage in the company's life, however, if it is successful, there should be an increase in dividends. To assess the likelihood of this, one needs to look at the trend of available earnings.

There is no exact equivalent of yield to redemption because common shares are not redeemable. The two alternative substitutes are:

1. An assets valuation which can be based on estimates of the realizable value of the business assets. This is in the nature of a "liquidation" valuation, since if the business is profitable the value of the assets in their present use should be greater than their value on realization or in any alternative use. One of the basic ideas of accounting for inflation is that balance sheets ought to reflect the use-value of the assets to the business.

2. A valuation representing the present value of the future stream of earnings, since the whole of these will in due course belong to the common shareholders. The price/earnings ratio is an indicator of investors' opinion about the future earnings potential of a company, not necessarily in absolute terms but certainly in relation to other companies offering alternative investment opportunities.

In approaching equity investment decisions, investors generally make use of one or both of two evaluation techniques:

1. *Fundamental analysis.* Fundamental analysis relates to the historical performance of particular companies, and in particular, from the study of past earnings and dividend trends attempts to forecast what future earnings and dividends will be. From these studies conclusions are reached about:

   a. The "true value" of the shares concerned.
   b. The likely future trend of the share price, which is believed to be heavily influenced by earnings and dividends.

   Armed with this information, the analyst decides when is the right time to buy these shares, i.e., when they are undervalued in relation to the true value and the future trend of the share price is likely to be upward.

   Many statistical studies have shown that future share prices are not in fact predictable from past share prices, as would be the case if prices were closely lined with predictable earnings. In fact the movement of stock market prices over time approximates a "random walk."

   A random walk is generated by drawing random numbers and plotting them in the order they are drawn, the dimensions of the series being limited by choosing a mean and standard deviation.

   Other studies suggest that the theory of random walks applies also to the growth of company earnings, and the term "higgledy-piggledy growth" was coined by Little and Raynot to describe their findings that in the short run it is virtually impossible to find any consistent growth in earnings in a given company, and in the long run it is hard to discover any repetition of earlier growth behavior.

   Although *growth* in earnings may not be predictable from past records, it may well be possible to identify a *level* of earnings for a company relative to other companies since there is often some continuity in good management. It may therefore be possible also to predict the level of the share prices of that company relative to those of other companies. Unfortunately this does not identify clearly when to buy or sell the particular share, and in consequence it becomes necessary to look for some more general pattern in the movement of stock market prices.

   The national income of most developed countries is subject to cyclical fluctuations. The profits of companies also fluctuate through these business cycles, and there is thought to be a relationship between overall business activity and the level of stock market prices. If one could forecast the level of business activity it would thus be possible to forecast at least some part of share price movement, and in particular the "turning points" at which the direction of price movements may be changed because of changes.

The most comprehensive approach to such a forecast is the econometric model, which aims to represent the economy by a series of mathematical equations dealing with key factors—a vastly more complex application of the approach to sensitivity analysis and risk analysis described in Chapter 11. Another approach is to extrapolate from past aggregate profit levels, making allowances for forecast changes in economic factors.

Another way of predicting turning points is simply to forecast the level of stock market indices—the approach of the technical analyst.

2. *Technical analysis.* If investors expect a certain thing to happen, the actions they take can make sure that event does come about. The technical analyst (or "chartist") studies the movement of share prices over time (either in the aggregate or for a particular company) and looks for recurring patterns of price movements or recurring interrelationships between stock price movements and other market data. From past cylical patterns he predicts future price movements.

One technique that has been shown to be useful for prediction purposes is the study of advances and declines. Calculations are made from stock exchange records of the proportions of shares traded which advance or decline in price on any day. From this it is possible to predict the number of advances and declines for the next day.

Over a series of days the cumulative net advances or declines are calculated (the "breadth" of the market). The breadth statistics would normally be expected to move in line with changes in the related index of stock market prices. If, for example, the index and cumulative number of price advances have both been rising and then the index continues to rise while the number of advances slows down, this is taken as an indicator that the index may soon reach a peak and begin to turn downward. The indication is most accurate when based on a limited number of companies.

Successful Investment

Many selected portfolios do not show a performance better than the market average, but this should not be surprising because market averages are dominated by price movements in the shares of the larger companies, and it is in these companies that institutional investors are most active. The market average is therefore to some extent the outcome of the application of portfolio judgments.

The conclusions reached in a study by M. G. Kendall many years ago are probably still valid; i.e., success in investment is largely attributable to:

1. Chance.
2. Economic circumstances in which all prices are moving together.
3. Inside information.
4. The ability to make switches very quickly.
5. A scale of operations at which transaction costs are not significant.

Among these factors the only one normally applicable to the small investor is "chance."

13

Methods
of Business Valuation

Purposes of Business Valuation

There are times, unfortunately, when one has to estimate the liquidation value of a business—what proceeds may be obtained from the disposal of its assets in order to meet the claims of the various classes of creditors. If this is the only course of action available, then the financial manager's role is rapidly approaching its termination.

However, the purpose of this chapter is to review the various methods of valuing a business as a going concern.

In this context the value of a business means its value to its proprietors. Admittedly the providers of debt capital will be interested in the total asset value as an indicator of the security for their loans. But asset values, as we shall see, do not exhaust the value of the business as an operating entity, and it is this total value which concerns the proprietors—it is their business.

When we have established this total value we can then apportion it among the individual owners, normally in relation to the amount of capital each has contributed, which in the case of a company limited by shares will be represented by their various shareholdings.

194

The main reason why we should want to value the business is as a basis for agreeing to a price at which the whole or part of a proprietor's interest may be transferred to someone else. There are three common aspects of such transactions:

1. The transfer of shares in unquoted companies. It is one of the distinguishing features of closely held companies that the right to transfer shares is restricted by the Articles of Incorporation, commonly at the absolute discretion of the directors. Linked with this provision there may be regulations governing how a "fair value" for such transfer shall be established. In the case of listed companies shares will of course be bought and sold at the current market price and (except in very special circumstances) no other valuation will be needed.

2. Taxation of capital transfers, on death or otherwise. Again in the case of the listed company the market price of shares would normally be used.

3. The amalgamation of businesses or the takeover of one business by another. Here a large-scale transfer of ownership occurs, so that even for the quoted company the market price of shares ceases to be a valid basis for the transaction. A special valuation will be needed.

Methods of Valuation

In the case of an amalgamation or takeover the companies involved are undertaking a very large-scale capital investment or disinvestment, and one would expect the method of evaluation to be of the same nature as those found to be most suitable for the investments discussed in Chapter 10, in other words, to be based on the present value of future cash flows. We will look at this possibility in a later paragraph, but it is a matter of fact that DCF techniques have not been widely used for business valuation, even for mergers and acquisitions. For small share transfer and taxation purposes the work involved in cash flow analysis would rarely be justified.

The methods in common use, which will first be described, are based on:

1. Asset values.
2. Earnings.
3. Some combination of these two.

It must be emphasized that any method will rely on estimates that will be subject to uncertainty. If alternative methods are applied to the same company it is likely that they will give rise to different valuations. For these two reasons it is never possible to arrive at a valuation which is uniquely "correct." The purpose of making valuations is to provide a framework within which it may be possible to agree to an acceptable solution to the problem in hand—whether it be the establishment of a share transfer price or an amount of tax payable or the negotiation of terms for the combination of two businesses. In the examples that follow we shall never be fixing a price—we shall be suggesting a range of possible values or a starting point for further discussion.

Valuation Based on Asset Values

There might be some occasions when the book value of the assets would be acceptable. In most cases, however, and particularly if the business were being valued for the purpose of sale, it would be necessary to revalue the assets on a more appropriate basis. This is likely to be the value of the assets to the business as a going concern.

The value to the business of freehold land and buildings would be their open market value for their existing use, and this should be established by a professional appraiser. Such a valuation would automatically take account of any deterioration in the condition of the buildings.

In the case of leasehold property, the unexpired portion of the lease would also have an open market value. It is conceivable that the open market value would be excessive in relation to the discounted future earning power of the business, in which case an earnings-based valuation for the business as a whole would be more appropriate than an asset valuation. Alternatively, if a prospective buyer had the intention of altering the nature of the business, one might substitute an open-market valuation of the land and buildings based on that alternative use.

If the intention was to dispose of the land and buildings, then they should be valued at the net amount they would realize if sold.

Readers who are familiar with the proposals for accounting methods based on "current costs" will recognize their similarity to the above valuation methods.

In the case of inventory and work in progress the relevant valuation would be their historical cost, although if the business were being valued for sale then it would be reasonable to substitute some approximation to their replacement value. From this starting point it would be necessary to make deductions for damaged or defective inventory and for any inventory which is not readily salable or which could be sold only at prices below the basic valuation.

Provisions for debts unlikely to be collected would presumably have been made in the accounts of the business, but their adequacy would need to be reviewed.

Any figure of goodwill in the company's balance sheet would be ignored, since goodwill emerges from a valuation based on earnings and has no part in the valuation of assets.

The asset value method of valuation might be the most suitable for a property company, but even in this exceptional case it is unlikely that it would be used as the only method. Applied to the calculations of a salable value of a business it implies that the purchaser is just buying a collection of assets without regard to their earning power.

Valuations Based on Earnings

A very popular method of assessing the value of a company is to use some predetermined rate of return an investor would expect on this particular type of investment. This is customarily the simple rate of return on capital employed such as is used in the ratio analysis of accounts. The rate is applied to the earnings of the company to arrive at the capital sum which would yield those earnings at that rate.

The earnings figure required is that which will be maintainable in future years. The valuation would be highly misleading if it were based on past experience, and immediately afterwards, there was an acceleration or a falling-off in the rate of earnings. You will read sometimes about takeover offers which have proved excessive because after the acquisition, the earnings of the acquired company failed to reach the forecast figure.

This can happen in spite of independent investigation by accountants, because it is of the nature of forecasts to be unreliable. However, every effort must be made to make a reliable forecast of future earnings as the basis of valuation. In most cases the forecast will be to some extent an extrapolation from past experience, and in those cases where a takeover aggressor has to make a valuation without help from the target company he will be almost entirely reliant on the past history of earnings.

If earnings have not been consistent in the past, this may be because this is the type of business which naturally has fluctuating profits (some types of jobbing and contracting work are of this nature) or is affected by a recognizable cycle of business activity. We should then take an average figure of profit over a suitable number of years as our starting point. If the profits had been showing a steady increase or decrease, then we might calculate a weighted average over perhaps three or five years, giving the heaviest weighting to the most recent results.

In every case it is important to adjust the reported profits for individual items which relate purely to past exceptional circumstances (such as abnormal remuneration to the founders of a private company) or which are dealt with differently by other companies from which the proposed capitalization factor is being derived. The ownership or leasing of assets would fall into this category.

Instead of using a bookkeeper's rate of return it is sometimes possible to use a price/earnings ratio. A listed company will have its own P/E ratio, and one only has to decide whether the same ratio will continue to apply under future business conditions. The chances are that it will unless there is an unforeseen major change either in the economic environment or in the management of the business. The ratio may be high in relation to current earnings because investors believe that earnings will increase—and vice versa. Using a P/E ratio therefore means that you can jump directly from today's earnings to a valuation which takes account of a consensus opinion on what future earnings will be.

If we are dealing with an unquoted company, then we should look for a quoted company (or preferably a group of quoted companies) in the same field of business and apply its P/E ratio, or a representative ratio, to the private company's results—but not without adjustment. Experience shows that the P/E ratio to be applied to a private company's results should be about half the ratio which exists for a comparable public company. If, for example, the P/E ratio of a quoted company was 12:1, then in valuing a similar private company a ratio of about 6:1 would be used.

The following example illustrates the use of an average figure earnings and also the application of a P/E ratio.

The following is the balance sheet of Loafers Inc., a private wholesale bakery:

LOAFERS INC.
Balance sheet at December 31, 19X6

	$		$
1,600,000 common shares of 25¢ each	400,000	Goodwill	100,000
		Fixed assets	445,000
		Current assets	955,000
Capital reserve	75,000		
Revenue reserve	225,000		
	700,000		
250,000 7% preferred shares of $1 each (redeemable in 20 years)	250,000		
	950,000		
Current liabilities	550,000		
	$1,500,000		$1,500,000

The P/E ratio for public companies in the industry is approximately 15. Mr. Cakebread, the chairman and managing director, has received a bid of 35¢ each for the common shares, and he seeks advice as to whether this is a reasonable price to recommend his shareholders to accept.

The following information is relevant:

1. Included in fixed assets are premises valued at $300,000 in January 19X0.

A fair rental, for the premises would be $40,000 a year at 19X6 rates, which on an estimated yield of 10% would make them now worth $400,000.

2. On a review of the current assets it now seems desirable to make further provisions for doubtful debts of $15,000 and obsolete inventory worth $17,000.

3. Profits/(losses) before taxation have been:

19X3	120,000
19X4	(10,000)
19X5	100,000
19X6	150,000

The forecasted profit before taxation for 19X7 is $180,000.

4. The purchaser would redeem the preferred shares at par.

Method of approach:

	$	$
Assets basis		
Fixed assets	445,000	
Add: Probable appreciation of property to give current yield of 10%	100,000	545,000
Current assets $(955,000 - 17,000 - 15,000)$	923,000	
Less: Current liabilities	550,000	373,000
		918,000
Deduct: Preferred shareholders' entitlement		250,000
Net asset value		$668,000

Net asset value per common share $\dfrac{\$668,000}{1,600,000} = 41.75\cancel{c}$

Without revaluing the property the net asset value per common share would be $\dfrac{\$568,000}{1,600,000} = 35.5\cancel{c}$

Earnings basis

	3-year weighted average $000	3-year average $000	5-year average $000
Profits/(losses)			
19X3			120
19X4			(10)
19X5	100 X 1 100	100	100
19X6	150 X 2 300	150	150

	3-year weighted average $000	3-year average $000	5-year average $000
19X7	180 X 3 540	180	180
	6 940	430	540
Average per annum	156.7	143.3	108.0
Taxation at, say, 50%	78.3	71.7	54.0
	78.4	71.6	54.0
Preferred dividend	17.5	17.5	17.5
Net earnings	60.9	54.1	36.5
Capitalized at P/E ratio 7.5	$456,750	$405,750	$273,750
Value per share	28.5¢	25.3¢	17.1¢
P/E ratio at bid price 35¢ approx.	9.2	10.4	15.3

One is not aware of the reason for the loss incurred by the business in 19X4, nor why the 19X5 profit was below what appears otherwise to be a steady upward trend. The 19X7 forecasted profit of $180,000 has not yet been achieved, of course, and without it one might not assume any trend but rather a series of random results. If the forecast is achieved, does this suggest even higher profits in later years without any need to introduce more outside capital?

Assuming that $180,000 is a realistic figure of maintainable future profits, then the earnings valuation would be:

	$000	$000
Maintainable annual profit		180
Less: Taxation 50%	90	
Preferred dividend	17.5	107.5
Net earnings		72.5
Capitalized at P/E 7.5		$543,750
Value per share		34.0¢

One would have thought that a P/E ratio of 7.5 on a forecast of profit never before attained was not commercially realistic in the baking industry. If it be accepted, however, that $180,000 profit is a realistic forecast, it is worth considering how the buyer proposes redeeming the preferred shares. If he were able to do this by a loan at 12½% the above calculation could be revised as follows:

	$000
Maintainable annual profit	180
Less: Loan interest $25,000 @ 12½%	31.25

	$000
	148.75
Taxation (50%)	74.375
Net earnings	74.375
Capitalized at P/E 7.5	557.8
Value per share	34.9¢, which is approximately the amount of the offer

To summarize, the bid of 35¢ appears generous in relation to earnings so far achieved, but may be no more than adequate if there is a real prospect of the 19X7 forecast being achieved and maintained. In either case the bid is far below what one would believe to be a realistic value of the assets, and in fact, corresponds closely with the existing book value. It is possible that by making what appears to be a fair offer in relation to profits, the bidder is hoping to gain possession of valuable assets, which he might plan to sell, and to take the business into his own existing facilities.

The bid should not be accepted, and efforts should be made during the course of further negotiations to discover the real objectives of the bidder.

The above example was worked out in some detail not merely to give an illustration of particular methods of calculation but also:

1. To show the difficulty of trying to arrive at a valuation based on past earnings.
2. To reemphasize that there is no such thing as an exact value for a business. There will always be a range of possible values, and which of these will be nearest to a final agreed-upon value will depend among other things on the purpose for which the valuation is being made.

A point worth making at this stage about the earnings basis of valuation when the purpose is the sale of a business is that the existing profits may be attributable to some extent to the efforts of the management team. If this team does not stay with the business after its change of ownership there may be difficulties, at least in the short term, in running the business and in achieving the profits which had been forecast.

It will have been noticed that Loafers Inc. in the above example had incurred a loss in one of the years under review. Although in this case the loss had been more than compensated for by later profits, it will often happen that a business which is subject to a bid will have unrelieved tax losses at the date of transfer. If the purchaser will be able to offset these losses against future profits and so reduce the future tax bill, then they have a salable value related to that future tax relief, and this must be taken into account in arriving at a valuation of the business. It will be borne in mind that such losses can only be used by the purchaser against future profits earned from the transfered business.

Combined Methods of Valuation

Because the assets valuation and the earnings valuation of a business are likely to differ, attempts are sometimes made to combine them into a composite valuation. This is not a scientific procedure. It seems to stem from the fallacy that there must be "a valuation" for a business, and in most cases the effect is merely to give some spurious justification for an already negotiated value.

For the sake of completeness, the two main methods are:

1. The Berliner method:
   a. Capitalize maintainable earnings at an acceptable rate of return.
   b. Value net tangible assets on a going concern basis.
   c. Take an arithmetical average of the two figures.
2. Dual capitalization method:

   This method relies on the possibility of defining two acceptable rates of return—one on tangible assets of the class existing in the business under review and one on intangible assets (this would be a higher rate because of the lack of tangible security).

   If this step is possible at all then the subsequent procedure can be illustrated in the followng example:

EXAMPLE

A business has tangible assets valued at $668,000. Its maintainable earnings are $72,500. The expected yield on tangible assets is 10% and on intangible assets 15%.

a. Tangible assets of $668,000 with an expected rate of return of 10% means that the amount of profit attributable to the tangible assets is $66,800.

b. The profit attibutable to intangible assets is therefore
   $72,500 − 66,800 = $5,700.

c. The value of the intangible assets is
   $$\frac{\$5,700 \times 100}{15} = \$38,000.$$

d. The total value of the business is
   $668,000 + $38,000 = $706,000.

The Superprofit Method

The superprofit method, which has some similarity to the method just described, used to be very popular and still has some adherents, probably because it starts with the simple concept of the accountant's rate of return and finishes up rather like a Dutch auction.

We will again take an example to illustrate the steps in this method.

EXAMPLE

The information needed is:

Value of net tangible assets, say	$145,000
Normal rate of return from an investment of this type	20%
Maintainable earnings estimated at	$29,500

The method then is as follows:

1. Calculate the expected annual profits, i.e., 20% × $145,000 = $29,000.
2. Calculate the superprofits, i.e., the difference between the profits at the required rate of return and the profits as actually forecast @ $29,500 − $29,000 = $500 per annum.
3. Decide how many years' superprofits shall be included in the purchase price—say 3 years—and thus the "value" of the superprofits, i.e., 3 × 500 = $1,500.
4. Add the value of the superprofits to the value of the net tangible assets to arrive at the total business valuation—in this case $145,000 + $1,500 = $146,500.

The superprofit values can be regarded in two ways:

1. As a value of "goodwill"—the business yields more than the rate of return that the buyer expects normally, so he is willing to pay more than the market value of the assets in order to get the extra profit.
2. As a subdivision of the earnings valuation of the business. In this instance we could have said that the value of the business was $29,500 maintainable earnings capitalized at 20% = $147,500, but in doing that we should have implied that the above-average performance of this business was going

to continue indefinitely. The superprofits method identifies how long these high profits are expected to last, i.e., three years, and to the extent that the number of years is realistic this is a better method than the straight capitalization of earnings.

Discounted Cash Flows

Following this last thought about the duration of benefits, it would have been possible to apply the discounted present value approach to the example above. We have here an annuity of $29,500. By equating it to an outlay of $147,500 we have implied a discount factor of 5.000. Look at your annuity tables under 20% and you will find that for 50 years the discount factor is 4.995. In fixing a value of $147,500, therefore, we are buying more than 50 years' profits, indeed we are buying $29,500 in perpetuity. In how many business situations would a buyer deliberately do this, or a seller expect it? (There are some, obviously, like leasing premises, but in this case we are looking at a firm of builders' merchants.)

Admittedly in negotiating prices many factors will be taken into account, including the relative strengths of the negotiators, but it is desirable that negotiations should not start from the exaggerated valuations implicit in the use of the simple rate of return on capital employed.

Suppose in this instance we had started with the assumption that the earnings of $29,500 would continue for ten years. At 20% our ten-year annuity discount factor is 4.1925, and this would have given a value to the business of $29,500 × 4.1925 = $123,680 approximately, a difference of $23,820 or 16% from previous valuation. This is significant.

The discounting method also enables us to deal with:

1. Nonconstant earnings, since each year's forecast earnings can be evaluated at its own discount factor.
2. Outlays connected with company acquisition—not only the initial legal and other costs, pension payments, and new recruitment and training costs, but also any additional finance required after the original purchase.
3. Realization of surplus assets.
4. The effect of the amalgamation on the cash flows of the bidding company.

What is needed is a comparison of combined cash flows over the years ahead—first of the two businesses as at present constituted and then of the new combined business. This differential cash flow should be discounted at the cost of capital (however defined) of the bidding company.

Discounting methods have not so far been widely used because of:

1. The complexity of the data to be handled and its sheer volume.
2. The difficulty of forecasting reliably.
3. Lack of clarity about the appropriate cost-of-capital rate.

The third point is the most difficult. The other difficulties are rapidly disappearing with the ready availability of computer models and developed techniques of risk analysis which we have already discussed. In time the simplistic approach to cash flow analysis that we have today will in turn be replaced by more dynamic models. But for the moment the techniques described in detail in Chapter 11 are the best we have, and we are certain to see them applied more and more to the problems of business valuation.

Pricing Businesses for Merger or Acquisition

Although we started by discussing business valuation, it is inevitable that, in thinking about valuations for acquisition, we should have tended to look ahead to fixing a price. At this stage, therefore, we will summarize briefly the various factors that mgiht influence the determination of a merger or acquisition price.

In the case of the sale of a private business, the price eventually settled will in general terms be determined by:

1. The enthusiasm of the shareholders (or proprietors) for disposing of their shares.
2. The benefits envisaged by the purchasing company as arising from the amalgamation.

The vending company may be prepared to consider a merger or offer for a variety of reasons, which may include:

1. Difficulty in ensuring adequate *management* ability in the future, particularly where the business has been built up by the skill and vision of one or two individuals.
2. Difficulty in obtaining *finance* from the limited sources available to a private business, whether for expansion or diversification, or for the replacement of assets, particularly when replacement costs are increasing significantly. This may include the inability to expand on the existing site, and inadequate finance to move elsewhere.
3. Difficulty in recruiting *labor,* either because employment in a small business may not be attractive to skilled people or because the possible scale of remuneration is inadequate.

4. Declining *prospects* for the traditional line of business.
5. *Taxation* disincentives in the existing form of organization, possibly because of "close company" regulations or because of potential problems in the valuation of shares for estate tax purposes.

The advantage of a solution to these problems may be considerably offset, however, by the vendors' reluctance to see radical changes made by a purchaser to the traditional form, reputation and prestige of the old business, or by a fear that long-service employees will not be fairly treated.

The benefits sought by a purchasing company will be discussed in Chapter 14, but in the context of the acquisition of a private business, it is likely that the acquisition of tangible assets will not be of major significance. The main objective will probably be the right to a future stream of profits resulting from the amalgamation.

Turning to the public company, the value of a small holding of shares to their owner will, in the absence of a bid, be measured by the stock exchange price. Many investors, however, would not be prepared to sell at that price because either:

1. Their investment objectives or tax status makes their particular valuation of the security different from the market value.
2. They hold a controling interest in the business.

Apart from private investors of savings, the investors in a company may include:

1. Professional individual investors, seeking to make either revenue or capital speculative gains, or both.
2. Investment trusts concerned with secure growth in income and capital values.
3. Insurance companies and pension funds probably looking more for secure long-term growth than high immediate income.
4. Other institutional investors, with varying requirements for security, growth, and steady income.

Where a controling interest exists in the share capital, the value of those shares to the holders may be below the market price, because they would be unable to dispose of a large block of shares without depressing the market price.

On the contrary, the controling shareholders might be able to command a higher price in a bid situation because:

1. The holding confers the ability to influence the policy of the business.
2. In particular they may have the power to arrange mergers with other companies in which they are interested.

3. They may be able to exercise powers of patronage and to ensure that existing staff are given continuity of employment.
4. They may regard themselves as guardians of a long family tradition.
5. Their voting power gives them personal status and prestige.

Certain special classes of companies may have a high takeover value to particular bidders. The company with accumulated tax losses has already been mentioned.

Apart from pure valuation considerations, the price negotiable for a takeover or merger can be influenced by such factors as:

1. The importance of the acquisition to the offering company, as part of its long-term strategy.
2. The urgency of a sale for the offeree shareholders, whether for the purpose of avoiding estate taxes, obtaining cash resources or for some other reason.
3. The skill with which the case for or against the amalgamation is presented by the respective companies.
4. The influence exercised by institutional investors for purposes related to their own development policies.
5. The economic or political environment at the time of the negotiations.

Paying the Acquisition Price—Share-For-Share Deals

When the price at which a business is to be acquired has been finally settled, a further decision is required as to how it shall be paid. The main alternatives are:

1. In shares of the acquiring company.
2. In cash.
3. In fixed interest securities.
4. In convertible securities.
5. By a combination of these methods.

Where payment by the issue of shares is decided, then the number of shares required will be calculated from the purchase price divided by the market price (or other agreed-upon price) per share of the acquiring company's shares.

For example if A Company were buying B Company for $240,000 and the market price of A Company shares was 80¢, then the number of shares to be issued for the purchase price would be:

$$\frac{\$240,000}{\$0.80} = 300,000 \text{ shares}$$

If the business being acquired is a company with share capital, then its shareholders will exchange their existing shares for shares issued by the acquirer. In the above example, if B Company had 400,000 shares outstanding the shareholders would relinquish their 400,000 shares in exchange for 300,000 new A Company shares. The offer would be expressed as 3 new shares for every 4 now held.

How are the interests of the existing shareholders in the aggressor company affected by the creation of these new shares? It is important that the earnings obtained through the acquisition should be sufficient in relation to the new shares issued to ensure that there is no fall in the average earnings per share, i.e., no "dilution" of the earnings per share of the aggressor company's shareholders.

If dilution does occur the share price is likely to fall. Dividends may be reduced, and the old shareholders will not have gained but suffered in consequence of the acquisition.

Let us suppose that Alpha Company is to acquire 100% of the common share capital of Beta Company by issuing its own shares. Alpha Company's authorized share capital is 4 million shares at 25¢ each, of which 3 million are already outstanding. Its profit and loss account for the year to December 31, 19X0, showed:

	$
	$
Profit before tax	240,000
Corporation tax @ 50%	120,000
Earnings	$120,000

$$EPS = \frac{\$120,000}{3,000,000} = 4¢$$

If the stock market price of the share is 40¢, the value of the company on a P/E ratio is 10.

Beta Company has 1 million shares at 10¢ each outstanding. Its profit and loss account for the year ending December 31, 19X0, showed:

	$
	$
Profit before tax	60,000
Corporation tax @ 50%	30,000
Earnings	$30,000

$$EPS = \frac{\$30,000}{1,000,000} = 3¢$$

If the stock market price is 24¢, the P/E ratio of Beta Company is 8.

With the market price per share of Alpha Company and Beta Company standing at 40¢ and 24¢ respectively, on acquisition Beta Company's shareholders would receive $\frac{1,000,000 \times 24}{40}$ = 600,000 shares in Alpha Company.

Assuming that profits would be sustained after the acquisition:

$$\text{EPS} = \frac{\$150,000}{3,600,000} = 4.2¢$$

As the result of the acquisition, Alpha Company has increased its equity capital by 20% and its earnings by 25%.

What has happened to the old shareholders in Beta Company? They used to be entitled to earnings of $30,000 on 1,000,000 shares, i.e., 3¢ per share. They now hold quoted shares which they realize, probably for more than they could have obtained for their old unquoted shares, and which in view of the increase in earnings per share for Alpha Company may well increase in price.

For Beta Company shareholders there has been a trade-off between loss of earnings (but again with hopes of increase due to the combined strengths of the new group) and other benefits.

What could be done if Beta Company wanted a better deal?

In the above example, Alpha Company's EPS has increased because it acquired with its own shares another company (probably a nonlisted company) on a lower multiple of earnings than that applicable to its own shares. If, on the other hand, Beta Company had been bought out on a P/E ratio of 12 [giving that company a value of $360,000 (i.e., $30,000 × 12)], then Alpha Company's earnings would be diluted; namely:

$$\text{Number of shares outstanding} = 3,000,000 + 900,000 \ (\$360,000 \div 40¢)$$
$$= 3,900,000$$
$$\text{Earnings} = \$120,000 + \$30,000 = \$150,000$$
$$\text{EPS} = \frac{\$150,000}{3,900,000} = 3.8¢ \text{ per share}$$

Alpha Company's EPS has been reduced because, in order to acquire Beta Company, it has increased its equity capital by 30% while increasing its earnings by only 25%. This is due to the fact that Beta Company has been valued on a higher multiple of earnings than Alpha Company.

In order to avoid the dilution of the earnings of the present members of Alpha Company, some other method must be devised to acquire Beta Company on a higher multiple of earnings. Possible alternatives would be to offer the present shareholders of Beta Company a mixture of cash, debt securities, convertible debt securities, and shares. Let us see how these alternatives work if Beta Company is valued on a multiple of 12 at $360,000.

Cash or Debt Securities

Alpha Company raises $360,000 in cash at an interest rate of 12%, or it issues at par $360,000 of 12% debt securities. Alpha Company is therefore issuing no additional equity but has to pay $43,200 (12% of $360,000) interest every year, such interest being allowed as an expense for corporation tax purposes. A pro forma consolidated profit and loss account based on this proposal would show:

	$
Profit before tax and interest	300,000
Less: Interest	43,200
	256,800
Corporation tax @ 50%	128,400
Earnings	$128,400

$$\text{EPS} = \frac{\$128,400}{3,000,000} = 4.3¢ \text{ compared to the existing } 4.0¢$$

Debt Securities and Shares

Alpha Company issues at par $180,000 of 12% securities and $180,000 worth of shares which will involve the issue of 450,000 shares valued at 40¢ each. A pro forma consolidated profit and loss account based on this proposal would show:

	$
Profit before tax and interest	300,000
Less: Interest (12% of $180,000)	21,600
	278,400
Corporation tax @ 50%	139,200
Earnings	$139,200

$$\text{EPS} = \frac{\$139,200}{3,450,000} = 4.03¢ \text{ compared to the existing } 4.0¢$$

Beta Company's shareholders now get a high price for their shares and an improvement in their earnings (interest $43,200 subject to personal tax instead of potential maximum dividends of $30,000 subject to personal tax), but they have surrendered their voting power and any possibility of future earnings or share price growth.

Convertible Debt Securities

The advantage of receiving convertible debt securities from the viewpoint of the shareholders of Beta Company is that the debt securities should provide them with a better income than before while at the same time providing them with potential capital growth if conversion into equity takes place.

As far as Alpha Company is concerned, the interest payable on the debt securities should not dilute the earnings of the company in the initial years, and if (as is hoped) the earnings of the company, together with the savings of interest, has increased by the time the debt securities is converted into equity, the additional equity can be absorbed without reducing EPS.

As a rule of thumb, convertible debt securities should be convertible over a two-year period (commencing three years after the date of issue) at a premium of 10-20% above the existing share price. With that in mind, let us examine the effect of Alpha Company's issuing $360,000 of 10% convertible debt securities which can be converted in three years' time into equity on the basis of 20 shares for every $9 of stock. A pro forma consolidated profit and loss account based on this proposal would show:

	$
Profit before tax and interest	300,000
Less: Interest (10% X $360,000)	36,000
	264,000
Corporation tax @ 50%	132,000
Earnings	$132,000

Basic EPS $= \dfrac{\$132,000}{3,000,000} = 4.4\cent$ compared to the existing $4.0\cent$

On the assumption that all the debt securities are in due course converted into equity (in which case 800,000 additional shares (being $360,000 ÷ 9 X 20) will be issued), the fully diluted EPS will be:

$$\frac{\$150,000}{3,800,000} = 3.95\cent$$

However, it is to be hoped that in three years' time the group's earnings will have increased to a figure well in excess of $150,000, so that there should be no dilution in earnings.

When Earnings Dilution is Acceptable

It might be concluded from what has been said above that dilution of earnings must be avoided at all cost. However, there are two cases where a dilution of earnings might be accepted on an acquisition if there were other advantages to be gained.

The first of these cases involves a trading company with high earnings, but with few assets, which may want to increase its assets base by acquiring a company which is strong in assets but weak in earnings, so that assets and earnings get more into line with each other. In this case, dilution in earnings is compensated for by an increase in net asset backing.

EXAMPLE

Earnings Company has an issued capital of 2,000,000 $1 common shares. Net assets (excluding goodwill) are $2,500,000 and earnings average around $1,500,000 per annum. The company is valued by the stock market on a P/E ratio of 8. Assets Company has an issue capital of 1,000,000 common $1 shares. Net assets (excluding goodwill) are $3,500,000, and earnings average around $400,000 per annum. The shareholders of Assets Company accept an all-equity offer from Earnings Company valuing each share in Assets Company at $4. Calculate Earnings Company earnings and assets per share before and after the acquisition of Assets Company.

Before acquisition of Assets Company:

$$\text{Earnings per share (EPS)} = \frac{\$1,500,000}{2,000,000} = 75\cent$$

$$\text{Assets per share (APS)} = \frac{\$2,500,000}{2,000,000} = \$1.25$$

After acquisition of Assets Company:

Assets Company's EPS figure is 40¢ (i.e., $400,000 ÷ 1,000,000), and the company is being bought out on a multiple of 10 at $4 per share. As the take-over consideration is being satisfied by shares, Earnings Company's earnings will be diluted because Earnings Company is valuing Assets Company on a higher multiple of earnings than itself. Earnings Company will have to issue 666,667 shares valued at $6 each (earnings of 75¢ per share at a multiple of 8) to satisfy the $4,000,000 consideration.

$$\text{EPS} = \frac{\$1,900,000}{2,666,667} = 71.25 \text{ (which is lower than the previous } 75\cent)$$

$$\text{APS} = \frac{\$6,000,000}{2,666,667} = \$2.25 \text{ (which is higher than the previous \$1.25)}$$

If Earnings Company is still valued on the stock market on a P/E c
share price should recede by approximately 30¢ [8 × (75¢ − 71.2
because the asset backing has been increased substantially the comp
probably be valued on a higher rating than 8.

The second case where a company might be willing to accept earn
tion involves an acquisition whereby the "quality" of the acquired c
earnings is superior to that of the acquiring company.

Listed companies in different industries are given different rating
department store like Macy's is valued on a higher price earnings (P/E)
an industrial company like Inland Steel. The reason for the former
higher rating is that its profits are stable and consistent (because i
necessities like food and clothing), whereas the profits of the latte
depend very much on the economic climate and fluctuate in accorda
The "quality" of earnings is therefore of paramount importance v
mining the rating of a company.

As another example, breweries are valued on higher multiples t
companies. If, therefore, a tobacco company acquires a brewery,
earnings will take place. However, the share prices should not suff
of the takeover because the overall quality of earnings compre
dilution of earnings.

14

Mergers
and Acquisitions

Note. The subjects covered by Chapters 14 and 15 have many legal and taxation implications upon which expert advice is essential, and we have therefore confined these chapters to a broad outline of the matters which might be of interest to the financial manager in the preliminary stages of amalgamation or reorganization proposals.

Definition of Mergers and Acquisitions

A merger or amalgamation is the fusion of two or more existing companies, the resultant single company being either one of the existing companies or a completely new company. In the latter case the fusion operation may be referred to as a consolidation. A merger is normally brought about by an exchange of shares.

An acquisition is the purchase by one company of a controling interest in the share capital of another existing company. An acquisition may be effected:

1. Agreement with proprietors of the business being acquired, or with the holders of sufficient shares to command a majority of the voting power or to give effective working control.
2. The purchase of shares on the open market.
3. A takeover offer to the general body of shareholders.

In the United States, there are various constraints on the manner in which mergers and takeovers can be effected. The Securities Exchange Commission and the Antitrust Division of the Justice Department often become involved if the possible combination is of sufficient size.

In common parlance, the terms "merger" and "takeover" are often used interchangeably and even to cover forms of partial cooperation, such as joint trading.

Purposes of Merger or Acquisition

Although the mechanics of combination differ to some extent between mergers and acquisitions, the objectives of the company playing the leading role are likely to be similar in all cases. As a first step toward successful negotiations, the acquiring company needs to think out carefully and express in specific terms, its own:

1. *Corporate objectives*—what it is aiming to achieve, in particular as a result of the proposed combination.
2. *Acquisition criteria*—what attributes it is looking for in the type of company with which it seeks to combine.

Among the possible purposes of acquisition are those listed below. It is important that the acquiring company should decide which specific advantages it is seeking in order to establish the criteria by which it will judge the desirability of companies available for acquisition.

1. *Procurement of supplies*
   a. To safeguard a source of supply for materials.
   b. To obtain bulk purchase discounts or to improve negotiating strength in dealing with suppliers.
   c. To obtain cost economies in the buying department.
   d. To standardize materials and thus share the benefits of the suppliers' economies of scale.

2. *Production*

   a. To amalgamate production facilities and thus achieve economies of scale (e.g., more intensive utilization of equipment and labor, longer runs and lower setting-up cost per unit). Such economies will not always be possible, and may be offset by, for example, increased transportation costs.

   b. To standardize product specifications, enabling value analysis to be applied, giving economies in tooling costs or improving aftersales service.

   c. To obtain improved technology and know-how from the company acquired.

3. *Marketing*

   a. To obtain new products—for diversification or substitution or to complete a product line.

   b. To obtain new market outlets, possibly overseas.

   c. To eliminate competition or protect an existing market.

   d. To unify sales departments.

   e. To rationalize distribution.

   f. To reduce total advertising costs.

   g. To diversify the business.

4. *Finance*

   a. To obtain direct access to cash resources.

   b. To acquire assets surplus to the needs of the combined business and dispose of them for cash.

   c. To obtain greater asset backing which will assist in obtaining loans.

   d. To obtain tax benefits, including the acquisition of tax losses.

   e. To improve earnings per share.

5. *General*

   a. To buy management talent.

   b. To buy time while the development plans of the acquiring company mature.

It will be noted that some of these objectives are "defensive" on the part of the acquiring company, e.g., eliminating competition, buying time for development, safeguarding a source of supply. Others are aggressive, and many of these will yield gains as a result of "synergy"; i.e., the combined companies working as a whole will obtain greater total benefits than would have been possible while each was operating separately. The benefits of synergy, however, tend to decline the further a company moves away from the area of technology or the type of market to which it has been accustomed. It may be noted also that economies of scale often take longer to emerge than was expected when an acquisition was planned.

Preliminary Screening Criteria

When the reasons for merger or acquisition have been established, the next stage is to institute a search for suitable candidates.

In some cases, a potential candidate will already be known to the managers of the aggressor company, possibly from personal contacts during the ordinary course of business, and it is possible that the idea of amalgamation will have arisen even before a policy of expansion has been worked out or given formal expression. In other cases, a company, having decided that growth by acquisition is desirable, may be prepared to wait for suitable opportunities to emerge, possibly from a direct approach by another business in need of managerial or financial aid. Even in these instances, however, it is important to survey a wider field of possibilities, and in the majority of cases where no one candidate is immediately obvious, it will be necessary to institute more positive search methods. This wider survey can be undertaken either by making known the company's requirements to its brokers or merchant bankers or to selected business associates or by setting up a research team within the company's own organization. The task of research will be simplified if the main characteristics of the type of business to be acquired are defined in advance, including the size of activity which the acquirer is capable of managing and the price it can afford to pay.

Among the characteristics on which decisions may be required are:

1. The trade or industry in which the potential candidate company should be operating.
2. Any especially desirable characteristics in its products or the service it offers.
3. Whether it should be centered in a particular area or be serving a particular market.
4. Whether a public or a private company would be preferred.

The size of the company being sought could be defined in terms of profit or sales, numbers of employees, or the market value of its share and loan capital.

In some cases, there will be quite specific requirements for, perhaps, a business with modern premises or with surplus cash resources.

The search should cover as large a field as possible because among the businesses reviewed, only a very small percentage will be suitable for further investigation, and of these perhaps two or three will actually be available for acquisition or merger.

The trade or industry required having been defined, the starting point for investigating candidate businesses within that industry could be:

1. Classified trade directories or telephone directories.
2. Trade journals.
3. Trade associations or chambers of commerce.

In many cases, the company's own suppliers or customers will be in the type of business specified, and may either themselves be potential candidates or may be sources of information about other companies. Rarely, a candidate may be found among newspaper advertisements of businesses for sale.

These investigations may give a general idea of the size, and in some cases, of the profitability and liquidity of the business concerned, but these aspects will need to be researched in greater detail for a selected short list of candidates.

In the case of private businesses, the sources of information are likely to be confined to personal contacts, supplemented by reports on credit status, such as may be obtained through banks or credit agencies. For public companies, Standard & Poor's or Moody's will give information about the company's history, its directors, its capital structure and dividends paid. For all public companies, access is possible to annual reports, financial statements and reports to the Securities Exchange Commission (form 10-K). When a potential candidate is a customer of the investigating company, it is possible that unpublished accounts will be available on the credit assessment file.

Whenever a company has a normal policy of expansion by acquisition, it should maintain files of newspaper cuttings, patent office search reports, catalogs, price lists, and other material of potential value for acquisition studies.

The Contested Offer

Where the board of a public company is likely to resist any approach for merger or takeover, the information outlined above would be discussed with the bidding company's merchant bankers, who would contribute their own knowledge of the situation and would collaborate in a full analysis of the information available. On the basis of the developed information, a decision would be taken either to buy shares in the candidate company or to frame an offer to the shareholders.

The Uncontested Offer

Where the management of the candidate business is likely to be receptive to the idea of a merger or takeover, then it should eventually be possible to achieve an analysis in depth of their existing business and of the future prospects for a combined organization. Before this stage is reached, however, there will be a period of discussion, sometimes prolonged, during which the parties involved move from the general idea of business cooperation to the more specific idea of merger, and then to the point of willingness to investigate in detail the advantages, disadvantages, and risks involved.

Any attractive company known to be interested in selling is likely to have the choice of a number of offers which are reasonably attractive financially. It is important, therefore, to interest the seller in the nonfinancial aspects of the acquisition. There are no general rules about which of these will be most relevant in any particular instance. They might include:

1. Continuing status and employment for the proprietor or managers.
2. Guarantees of continued employment and suitable remuneration for employees.
3. Preservation of existing trade names.
4. Growth opportunities for the company acquired.

The buying company, however, should not enter into serious negotiations without having in mind some preliminary calculations of possible future combined profits and of the upper and lower purchase prices, assuming alternative methods of payment (i.e., for cash, by the issue of common shares or convertible debentures, or by a combination of methods). The relationship between price and profits would have to satisfy such evaluation criteria as:

1. Prospective return on investment, calculated on a discounted cash flow basis.
2. Annual rate of return on shareholders' equity.
3. Annual growth rate in earnings per share.

In arriving at the upper limit of offer price, one would include the value of those assets to be acquired which would not be required for use in the business but would be available for conversion into cash. The lower limit might be the net liquidation value of all assets to be acquired, or it could be related to the current market valuation of the candidate company's shares if this were below the underlying asset value. These early calculations, however, would undoubtedly be modified progressively as further information became available.

Investigation of the Candidate Company

The investigations necessary in the approach to a merger or acquisition fall typically into four stages:

1. The analysis of information available in published form or otherwise without access to the records of the candidate company, leading either to the commencement of negotiations or to an immediate bid.

2. Joint investigations by the managers of the companies involved into products, markets, technology and the status of research projects, as a means of defining more clearly the advantages which might emerge from an amalgamation of activities. The precise details of such an investigation would depend on the nature of the business involved.

3. A full investigation into profitability and intrinsic value of the companies concerned, normally carried out by independent experts, including a report by investigating accountants, the form of which would be influenced by legal requirements.

4. Forecasts of the investment necessary and the yields obtainable under proposed action plans, leading to the definition of a merger contract or agreed-upon bid. These forecasts would also be subject to independent review.

Alongside, or arising from, the accounting investigation of past history and the current position, and a necessary preliminary to the forecast of future results, the management of the companies concerned will need to gather information for the following purposes:

1. To plan in detail how the product lines and production facilities of the two companies could be integrated.

2. To plan the integration of administrative functions.

3. To highlight anomalies in pay and conditions of work and to consider how they can be reconciled.

4. To ensure that the companies' conditions of purchase and sale are compatible.

5. To review cost and profit structure and prepare an outline plan for profit improvement.

6. To tackle any legal difficulties in integration.

Profit Forecasts

One of the most important sections of any prospectus or takeover bid document is the one that sets out the directors' estimate of the current year's results and the dividend that they propose to recommend in the event that this estimate is realized.

Possible assumptions in a profit forecast might include:

1. Current management policies will continue (for a company being acquired).
2. Interest rates and the bases and rates of taxation, both direct and indirect, will not change materially.
3. There will be no material change in international exchange rates or import duties and regulations.
4. Turnover has been forecast on the basis that sales will continue in line with levels and trends experienced this year to date, adjusted for normal seasonal factors—a reduction of $100,000 in turnover would result in a reduction of approximately $—— in the profit forecast.
5. Trading results will not be affected by industrial disputes in the company's factories or in those of its principal suppliers.
6. A new factory will be in full production by a specified date.
7. Increases in labor costs will be restricted to those already agreed upon.
8. Increases in the level of manufacturing costs for the remainder of the year will be kept within the margin allowed for in the estimates.
9. The provision for outstanding claims in respect of the group's products will prove adequate and no further major claims will arise.

Valuation of Companies for Merger or Acquisition

The various methods of business valuation were explained and illustrated in detail in Chapter 13, and examples were also given of various "packages" of shares, cash, debt securities, and convertible debt securities for the purpose of settling an agreed-upon price with benefit to both parties to the deal.

Methods of Takeover or Amalgamation

The main possible methods of combining two companies are as follows:

1. *Acquisition of all outstanding equity capital* of the candidate company, either for cash or by exchange of shares. The share-for-share offer is the most common method of achieving a merger. It may be effected by the bidder directly or through the creation of a new holding company. In some cases, the desired result may best be achieved by a "reverse bid" by the offeree company.
2. *Acquisition of the assets* of the candidate company is one of the ways noted in the foregoing paragraph.
3. *A partial bid,* i.e., the acquisition of less than 100% of the equity of the candidate company, either for cash or by exchange of shares.

Other possibilities are *an issue of new shares in the candidate company* to the offering company, giving working control, or *the purchase of candidate company shares in the open market.*

The acquisition of minority-held shares in an existing subsidiary company can involve additional legal formalities, and this will be discussed later.

Among the factors that could influence the choice of method would be:

1. Whether to obtain 100% ownership of the capital or undertaking of the offeree company is desirable.
2. Whether either company has preferred share or debenture holders whose consent to the chosen plan would be necessary.
3. The taxation consequences of the various methods, from the point of view of the companies or of the shareholders involved.
4. The possibility that preacquisition profits of the candidate company may not be available for future dividends.
5. The existence of important contracts which could not be transferred from one company to another.
6. The preservation of the status of existing directors.

Acquisition of All Outstanding Equity Capital

The bidding company offers to acquire from the shareholders of the offeree company all the shares except those already held by the bidder or its subsidiaries.

The offer may be either:

1. At a stated cash price.
2. In exchange for the issue as fully paid of shares in the bidding company on a stated basis (for example, three shares in the bidding company for every two shares held in the offeree company). The offer is generally made conditional upon its acceptance by a specified date by the holders of not less than 90% (or some other percentage) in value of the shares concerned. This percentage entitles the bidder to acquire compulsorily the shares of any shareholders who do not accept the initial offer (depending on state law). This procedure is a common method of achieving a merger. The effect is that the offeree company becomes a wholly owned subsidiary of the bidding company. The balance of control in the board of the bidding company will depend on the size of the blocks of shares now held by the former shareholders in the offeree company.

The terms of a bid or amalgamation will take account of:

1. The pre-existing market prices of the shares in the two companies.
2. Recent dividend yields and cover.
3. Growth prospects.
4. Voting strength.
5. Underlying asset values.

In some cases, a straight share-for-share offer may not achieve a reasonable balance between shareholders under one or more of these headings, and the consideration may then be a combinaton of shares and cash or shares and debentures.

In some cases, it may be desirable for the candidate company to become the holding company, and the original "aggressor" should be its subsidiary. Possible reasons are:

1. When the candidate company is a public company and maintaining the status is desirable.
2. When it is preferable for the aggressor to become the operational or trading company, and the candidate company be the administrator of the new group.

In such cases, by agreement between the two boards, the candidate company may make a "reverse bid" for the whole of the capital of the aggressor.

Where a merger is envisaged, as distinct from a takeover, the two boards may arrange for the registration of a new company which will then offer its own shares in exchange for the shares of the shareholders in the two pre-existing companies.

Acquisition of the Assets or "Undertaking" of the Candidate Company

By agreement between the boards of the two companies, the assets of the offeree company may be purchased by the bidding company, for cash. The bidder then carries on the business previously carried on by the offeree company, which is then left as a "shell" company holding only cash. The shareholders in the offeree company remain the same.

Alternatively, the whole or selected assets of both companies may be acquired by a new company in exchange for shares. This procedure is particularly useful for merging the similar activities of the two companies, while leaving them to carry on individually any dissimilar activities. If equal, it could be that neither of these companies would be a "subsidiary" of the new company. A further possibility is to liquidate the two original companies and to distribute the shares from the new company among the original shareholders.

Partial Bids and Purchases of Shares

If the bidding company wishes to have legal control over the offeree company, it will need to acquire shares giving only 51% of the voting power, or less if there are no predominant blocks of shareholding. It will therefore offer to acquire, for cash or on a share-for-share basis, only that limited number of shares. This can avoid some of the detailed requirements for an offer document and the accounting requirements relating to subsidiary companies. In a cash offer the amount of cash required is limited, and in a share offer the risk of control by the new shareholders is reduced.

Provision must be made in the offer document for the action to be taken if acceptances are received in excess of the desired number. Alternative possibilities are:

1. To scale down all the acceptances pro rata.
2. To take acceptances in date order of receipt.
3. To leave the choice of acceptances to the discretion of the bidder.

When a few blocks of shares, possibly held by the directors of the candidate company, can give effective working control of the business (though not the legal control), the aggressor may attempt to purchase those shares by a private deal.

If there is sufficient authorized, but unissued, capital under the control of the directors of the candidate company, they have the power to issue such shares to the aggressor company for cash. If it is necessary to create more capital for this purpose, an ordinary resolution of the shareholders may be required.

Position of the Board and the Shareholders
in the Bidding Company

Provided the proposed merger or acquisition falls within the company's articles of incorporation, the necessary decisions are entirely within the powers of the board. Where new capital is required to implement the transaction, however, its issue must be approved by ordinary resolution of the shareholders in a general meeting.

If there is evidence that the directors have failed in their duties of care and skill in relation to any matter, or have breached their fiduciary duties (for example, by accepting private benefits or by making a bid at a price which they do not truly consider to be justified), an aggrieved shareholder can apply to the court for an order restraining such action.

Position of the Board and the Shareholders in the Offeree Company

The position of the board in relation to the sale of assets, or to the issue of shares or the sale of their personal shareholdings, is similar to that outlined for the board of the offering company in the previous section. Whether the board can sell the company's assets or liquidate the company without shareholder approval depends on state laws.

Acquiring the Minority-Held Shares of a Subsidiary

Apart from offers in similar form to those previously outlined, the minority interest in a subsidiary company may, subject to state law, be dealt with by a specific reduction of capital and repayment to the selected shareholders at an appropriate price.

If the company concerned is a private company, its articles of incorporation will often empower (or may be altered to empower) the directors to require certain shareholders to sell their shares at a price determined in accordance with the articles.

Regulatory Agencies

Federal Trade Commission—legal advice concerning antitrust laws should be obtained at an early stage in order to avoid later difficulties that could prove to be very expensive. Antitrust legislation has been in existence since the latter part of the nineteenth century. The purpose of such legislation is to limit the growth of monopoly (although a monopoly is not illegal per se), prevent unreasonable trade restraints and to prevent small businesses from being devoured by larger companies.

These laws are administered by the Department of Justice's Antitrust Division as well as the Federal Trade Commission (FTC). The FTC has the authority to initiate investigations, make regulatory law and issue cease and desist orders.

Antitrust laws may be applied to restrict three different types of merger or acquisition. The most common use of the antitrust laws is to restrict or prevent a horizontal merger, if the result would be a lessening of competition or an unreasonable restraint of trade. A horizontal merger occurs when two or more companies in the same line of business (such as two steel companies) agree to merge.

Vertical mergers may also be prevented if the effect would be to lessen competition or unreasonably restrain trade. A vertical merger occurs when a customer and supplier (such as a steel company and an automobile manufacturer) agree to combine operations.

The third type of merger is called a conglomerate merger. This type occurs when a conglomerate (a company involved in many different lines of business) acquires another business. Generally, a conglomerate-type merger will not unreasonably restrain trade, and so the Justice Department will not interfere with this type of merger as a general rule, although there is a significant number of Justice Department officials who believe that size alone should be sufficient to prevent a merger. If this view becomes the accepted view, conglomerate mergers could become a thing of the past.

Not all acquisitions are friendly. Often, shareholders, management or competitors of either the target company or the acquiring company will issue a formal complaint either to the Justice Department or to the FTC, in which case an investigation may be launched. The complaining party may seek damages if damages have been suffered as a result of a violation of the antitrust laws. Even if the acquisition is successful, a subsequent challenge could force the acquiring corporation to divest itself of the recently acquired corporation.

A corporation contemplating an acquisition can notify either the FTC or the Justice Department. If the Justice Department is notified, it will give an opinion concerning the legality of the acqusition. If advice is requested from the FTC, the means and details of the proposed acquisition are made public and the public has thirty days to comment on the proposal.

If the proposed acquisition involves a large corporation, prior FTC notfication is mandatory. This rule applies where one of the corporations has net sales or assets of at least $100 million and the other corporation has net sales or assets of at least $10 million.

Securities and Exchange Commission—The Securities and Exchange Commission (SEC) administers the federal securities laws. The Securities Act of 1933, passed during the Depression, requires full and fair disclosure for all public offerings of securities. However, the SEC has no authority to determine the quality of an offering, and the fact that the SEC has not prevented an offering from being made does not mean that the offering is a good investment. Certain disclosure requirements must be met even if the acquisition is to be gained by a cash tender offer as soon as five percent of the securities are acquired.

A detailed registration statement must be filed with the SEC before a public offering of securities can begin. The SEC then declares the registration statement effective, provided no further information is first necessary. Upon approval, the securities can then be issued.

A prospectus containing financial, historical and other information is included in the registration statement. Separate financial statements for each company must be included if the securities are intended to be exchanged for other securities. These statements must be audited by a firm of independent CPAs and must generally be for a period of at least three years.

Finding the Necessary Finance

Finding finance for an offer wholly or partly in cash is subject to the problems ordinarily associated with fund raising, particularly concerning the asset cover for long-term borrowing and the means of ensuring the servicing of the funds acquired.

In some cases, an issuing broker will undertake to provide the cash needed under a "shares or cash" offer, or to buy for cash any shares issued to the offeree company's shareholders under a share-for-share transaction.

These arrangements should be finalized before the bidder commits itself to any offer.

Problems of Integration

Once the merger or takeover has been effected, there will begin the problems of getting the two businesses working together as a new entity. These problems will affect every functional area and every level of employment.

An important step toward effective central management is to unify the accounting systems and financial control. Even when the accounting systems inherited by the new group are adequate in themselves, it is likely that there will be differences in costing methods, budgetary control systems and accounting practices. In some cases the accounting periods of the various companies will be different, either in month-end dates or in the subdivision of the year into reporting periods.

Until accounting systems are integrated, it will be difficult to obtain reports, particularly on profitability and asset control, which can be used either by central management or for operational decisions.

Among matters needing action will be:

1. Definition of accounting terminology.
2. Uniform coding systems.
3. Uniform application of principles, for example, in defining "fixed" and

"variable" costs, in overhead absorption, and in setting standard product costs.

4. Uniform estimating procedures in relation to selling prices.
5. Uniform forms of report.

There will undoubtedly be opposition to changes in well-established procedures, and it may be advisable to establish a coordinating committee through which the members of the various accounting organizations can meet each other and reach mutually acceptable decisions.

The management of cash resources impinges on every other activity of the group, and among the matters requiring attention will be:

1. Integration of credit policy in relation to customers. The increased size of the new entity may enable it to be more rigorous, both in the assessment and review of creditworthiness and on the terms of credit it may allow.
2. Integration of terms of credit taken from suppliers. Here again, the enhanced buying power of the group may permit better purchase prices and also the ability to take longer credit on a consistent basis than was previously possible.
3. Integration of inventory policies regarding the marketing objectives of the group and the ability to centralize certain production facilities.
4. Integration of the methods used in evaluating capital projects and of decisions on the methods of financing such projects.
5. Negotiations with banks to concentrate transactions with a limited number of banks, and thus obtain better terms of credit. The relative advantages of central or decentralized banking facilities will have to be investigated, and linked with this, the role of the central office as the coordinator of cash resources and overdraft facilities.
6. Simplifying the financial structure by replacing loan capital of the merged companies or the company taken over with a new loan issue by the group, if this can be done on favorable terms.

Legal Formalities

Among the legal formalities associated with a merger or takeover will be:

1. The adoption of resolutions at shareholders' meetings.
2. If a new holding company is formed or amendments are necessary to the constitution of either company, drafting new articles of incorporation and making any necessary modification to the articles.

3. Structuring the change in a manner that will take advantage of tax attributes.

4. Registration of any new company with the appropriate state agency.

5. Modifying contracts in the name of the new company.

6. Issuing new conditions of employment.

7. Altering company names on signboards, vehicles, etc.

8. Printing new letterheads, billforms, and other stationery.

The relevant formalities will vary from case to case, but the most simple are the most easily overlooked.

15

Business Law
for the
Financial Manager

Laws Affecting Employees

A multitude of federal and state laws affect the employer-employee relationship. The most important of these are outlined below.

Fair Labor Standards Act (FLSA)—This law is primarily concerned with wages and hours and is, therefore, commonly referred to as the Wages and Hours Law. It established a minimum wage that must be paid to every worker covered by the act, which includes almost all employees. Some exceptions are newspaper carriers, agricultural workers (to some extent) and actors. The minimum wage required increases periodically, rising with changing economic conditions. The obvious reason for the minimum wage requirement is to provide every worker with a minimum income. Many economists argue, however, that this creates unemployment because workers who are not worth the minimum wage will either be laid off or never hired in the first place.

The equal pay provision requires that workers be paid equal wages for equal work. Wage discrimination because of sex is prohibited. The overtime provision requires that certain employees be paid time and one-half for overtime, which is defined as all hours worked in excess of forty per week. The law does not require that time and one-half be paid for hours in excess of eight per day, although union contracts or company policy may allow this. The child labor provision prohibits an employer from employing a child under sixteen years of age.

Social Security—The Federal Insurance Contribution Act (FICA), commonly referred to as social security, was passed in the 1930s. The FICA tax is withheld from the employee's paycheck and the employer pays an equal portion. Failure to withhold the employee portion of the tax can result in severe penalties for the employer; many employers in financial difficulty will use these funds to pay their own expenses, which is the primary reason a company will find itself in trouble with the Internal Revenue Service. Independent contractors who are paid by a company do not have any FICA taxes withheld, although they are liable for self-employment tax. There is often a fine line between who is classified as an employee and who is classified as an independent contractor. If a company pays an individual based on independent contractor status and it later turns out that the individual should have been classified as an employee, the company (not the employee) is liable for FICA taxes that were not withheld (in addition to the company portion, which was never paid in the first place). The employer will also be liable for income taxes that were not withheld and may be subject to interest and penalties as well.

Workmen's Compensation—The general rule is that all employment-related injuries are covered even if the injured employee was grossly negligent. The employer pays a certain amount for each employee into an insurance fund, and the fund pays the individual who is injured. The fund may be a state fund or that of a private carrier. An employee who receives workmen's compensation may not sue the employer even if workmen's compensation was not sufficient to cover the injuries received.

Employment Discrimination—An employer may not discriminate on the basis of sex, race, color, religion or national origin. This rule applies to hiring, layoffs, compensation, hours and conditions of employment. However, based on recent Supreme Court decisions, it is not illegal to hire or promote certain minorities under certain conditions—although many people have argued that this is, in effect, reverse discrimination. Persons between the ages of forty and sixty-five may not be discriminated against unless there is a legitimate reason for doing so. For example, a frail, sixty-four-year-old applicant need not be hired to fill a vacant position on a loading dock if the work involves heavy lifting, which he would not be able to do because of age.

Occupational Safety and Health Act (OSHA)—This law, which requires that employers provide a safe and healthy place to work, applies to any employer who is engaged in commerce. The Labor Department promulgates regulations in this area and carries out inspections. Whether an unwelcome inspector may enter a plant without a search warrant is an issue that should be discussed with counsel. Because the regulations are lengthy and often contradictory, there is much room for abuse by an overzealous inspector.

Employee Retirement Income Security Act (ERISA)—This act became law in 1974 and was enacted to correct some pension plan abuses. Pension plans must comply with strict funding, disclosure, participation and vesting requirements. The Department of Labor and the Internal Revenue Service administer the law jointly.

Antitrust Laws

The antitrust laws go as far back as 1890, when the Sherman Antitrust Act was passed. The purpose of the antitrust laws is to prevent unreasonable restraints of trade and increase competition. Agricultural organizations, stock exchanges, labor unions and professional baseball (but not football) are exempt from the federal antitrust laws.

Illegal Agreements

Certain types of agreement are illegal per se. That is, there is no justifiable reason for entering into the agreement, and any such agreement is automatically in violation of the antitrust laws. The most common types of agreements that fit this category are the following.

Price-Fixing—Competitors sometimes attempt to fix prices. Maximum or minimum prices may be set, or a negotiable list price may be agreed upon. Competitors may enter into an agreement to limit production or purchases. Any agreement between competitors that fits one of these categories is illegal per se, and no rationale may be used to justify such an agreement, even if it would actually benefit the average consumer.

Regulated industries may be allowed to fix prices, provided such price-fixing is deemed to be in the public interest.

Division of Markets—Competitors may agree to divide a market. For example, two manufacturers, one located in California and the other in New York, may decide not to compete for customers since such competition would result in receiving a lower price for their product. They enter into an agreement whereby the New York manufacturer will sell only to those customers located east of the Mississippi river, and the California manufacturer will sell only to those customers located west of the river. Not only will both manufacturers be able to reduce their shipping expenses by doing this, but they will also eliminate price competition. Because potential customers will have only one supplier, they will have to pay whatever price the supplier wishes to charge.

Agreements of this sort are always illegal per se, and no excuse, no matter how reasonable, may be given to alleviate the impact of the antitrust laws.

Tying Arrangements—Tying arrangements involve at least two products, the tying product and the tied product. A tying arrangement exists if a seller refuses to sell a certain product unless the buyer also agrees to purchase a second product as well. For example, a computer company may be the sole supplier of a certain computer software device. The company will agree to sell this device only if the purchaser also agrees to purchase a second item, which is readily available elsewhere.

A tying arrangement is illegal per se if the effect is to create a monopoly or to substantially lessen competition.

Group Boycotts—A group boycott exists when a group of competitors agrees not to do business with a certain person or firm, or agrees to deal with such person or firm only if certain conditions exist. For example, a group of American manufacturers might agree not to sell to (or buy from) a certain Israeli arms manufacturer. This agreement might be entered into because of pressure from certain Arab governments. The result is a restraint of trade and is illegal per se under the antitrust laws.

Resale Maintenance Agreements—In the past, certain manufacturers would agree to sell their products to retailers only if the retailers would agree not to resell the product for less than a certain amount. In states that had "fair trade" laws this arrangement was perfectly legal. However, fair trade laws no longer exist, and any manufacturer that enters into such an agreement with a retailer will now be in violation of the antitrust laws. However, this does not prevent a manufacturer from suggesting a retail price, provided the retailer is not bound to offer the merchandise at that price. It is not illegal for an auto manufacturer to have a suggested retail price for each model, provided this price is only suggested and not required.

The Securities Laws

The securities laws were enacted during the Depression. It was thought that one of the prime causes of the Depression was securities manipulation, and the securities laws were enacted to prevent or minimize future abuses. Whether securities manipulation had anything to do with causing the Depression has been hotly debated, but the securities laws remain with us to this day and have been amended several times since they were first enacted. A major effect of these laws is to prevent or minimize security fraud, since publicly traded securities must meet stringent requirements.

Taxation
for the
Financial Manager

The field of taxation is both diverse and complex, but there are certain concepts that every financial manager should be familiar with.

Tax Rates

Tax rates change often and are subject to several exceptions. However, the basic tax structure is as follows:

1. The first $25,000 of taxable income* is taxed at 17%.
2. The second $25,000 is taxed at 20%.
3. The third $25,000 is taxed at 30%.
4. The fourth $25,000 is taxed at 40%.

*The definition of taxable income involves many concepts and is subject to many exceptions. Basically, taxable income equals all revenues taken in (whether actually or constructively) less all deductible expenses.

5. Any taxable income in excess of $100,000 is taxed at 46%.

6. Capital gains may be taxed at either the regular corporate rate or at 28%, at the option of the corporation.

How tax liability is computed may be illustrated by the following example: The JM Corporation has taxable income of $240,000, which consists of $190,000 that is taxable at ordinary rates and $50,000 that is taxable as capital gains. There are two methods used to compute the tax. The method used will be the method that results in the lower tax liability.

Method 1

1st $25,000 @ 17%	$ 4,250
2nd $25,000 @ 20%	5,000
3rd $25,000 @ 30%	7,500
4th $25,000 @ 40%	10,000
Excess ($140,000) @ 46%	64,400
Total tax liability	$91,150

Effective tax rate = 38% ($91,150/$240,000)
Marginal tax rate = 46% (any additional income
                               will be taxed at this rate)

Method 2

1st $25,000 @ 17%	$ 4,250
2nd $25,000 @ 20%	5,000
3rd $25,000 @ 30%	7,500
4th $25,000 @ 40%	10,000
Excess ($90,000) @ 46%	41,400
Capital gains ($50,000) @ 28%	14,000
Total tax liability	$82,150

Effective tax rate = 34% ($82,150/$240,000)
Marginal tax rate = 46% (any additional income
                               will be taxed at this rate,
                               except for capital gains,
                               which will be taxed at
                               28%)

As can be seen, if capital gains are taxed at 28% rather than 46% the tax liability is reduced by $9,000 ($91,150 − $82,150). Another way to compute the tax saving is to multiply the amount of capital gains by the difference in marginal tax rates: $50,000 (46% − 28%) = $9,000.

If the capital gain rate (28%) is less than the marginal tax rate for ordinary income, it will always be more beneficial to tax capital gains at the capital gain rate rather than the ordinary rate. If the marginal tax rate for ordinary income is less than 28%, it will always be more beneficial to tax capital gains at the ordinary rate.

The Subchapter S Corporation

The Subchapter S corporation, also called a tax option corporation or a small business corporation, combines the flow-through advantage of a partnership with the limited liability advantage of the corporate form. A partnership is not a taxable entity. The owners of the partnership (the partners) are taxed on the partnership income as if the income were earned by the individual partners. In effect, the partnership's income "flows through" directly to the partners. Corporation owners, on the other hand, pay a double tax, once at the corporate level and once at the shareholder level, when the earnings are distributed as dividends. The possible tax savings may be illustrated by the following example:

> John and Bob own a business called the J & B Partnership. They want to reduce their personal liability (partners are personally liable for partnership debts etc.) so they decide to form a corporation, but they cannot decide whether a conventional corporation or a Subchapter S corporation would better suit their purposes. The business is expected to generate $200,000 in taxable income annually. Both partners are in the maximum (70%) tax bracket and would like to receive all of the aftertax proceeds that the newly formed corporation is able to generate.

If a conventional corporation is formed, two taxes will be paid, once at the corporate level and once at the shareholder level when dividends are paid. John and Bob stand to save thousands in aftertax income if they choose to incorporate under Subchapter S. The exact amount of tax savings is determined as follows:

Option 1 Conventional Corporation

Taxable income	$200,000
Less: Tax at corporate level	
1st $25,000 @ 17%	$ 4,250
2nd $25,000 @ 20%	5,000

Taxable income		$200,000
3rd $25,000 @ 30%	7,500	
4th $25,000 @ 40%	10,000	
Excess ($100,000) @ 46%	46,000	72,750
Amount available for dividends		$127,250
Less: Tax at individual level		
(70% of $127,250)		89,075
Amount Bob and John will be able to spend after taxes		$ 38,175

Under Option 1 the effective total tax rate is 81% ($161,825 taxes paid/ /$200,000). Bob and John will be able to spend only $38,175 on taxable income of $200,000.

Option 2 Subchapter S Corporation

Taxable income	$200,000
Less: Tax at corporate level	-0-
Less: Tax at individual level	
(70% of $200,000)	140,000
Amount Bob and John will be able to spend after taxes	$ 60,000

Bob and John can save $21,825 ($60,000 − $38,175) annually by forming a Subchapter S corporation rather than a conventional corporation, and still have the benefit of limited liability that goes with the corporate form.

Several requirements must be met in order to qualify for Subchapter S status. The corporation must be a domestic corporation; that is, it must be incorporated under the laws of one of the states rather than some foreign country. The corporation must have only one class of stock; corporations having more than one class of stock, such as preferred stock, do not qualify. There may not be more than fifteen shareholders (a husband and wife or a surviving spouse and estate may be treated as a single shareholder), none of whom may be nonresident aliens, corporations or partnerships. Passive investment income (rents, royalties, dividends, interest, etc.) must constitute less than 20% of total gross receipts of the business. At least 20% of gross receipts must be from sources within the United States.

Shareholders of a Subchapter S corporation are taxed on the corporation's income whether it is distributed or not, so taxes cannot be avoided or deferred by retaining earnings.

Dividends Received Deduction

A corporation receiving dividends from domestic corporations is entitled to an 85% dividends received deduction. In other words, 85% of dividends received from domestic corporations is not taxed at all. The remaining 15% is taxed at ordinary rates, so a corporation in the 46% bracket receiving $100 in dividends from a domestic corporation is taxed at an effective rate of only 6.9%!

Dividend income	$100
Less: Dividends received deduction	85
Taxable dividend income	$ 15

Tax is 46% of $15, or $6.90

$6.90/$100 = 6.9%

The rationale for this is that the corporation paying the dividends has already been taxed, and dividends are paid out of after-tax income. If dividends are taxed, to the recipient the effect is double taxation, and allowing the 85% deduction minimizes this double taxation effect. A comparable tax break exists for individual taxpayers, where the first $100 of domestic dividends received goes untaxed. There are occasional rumblings in Congress (generally in an election year) calling for the repeal of taxes on dividends, since this is double taxation, and such taxation is inherently unfair and reduces incentives to invest. To date, such measures have not been passed, partially because it is argued that eliminating taxes on dividends would benefit only the rich. Whether this statement is valid has been argued for years.

If corporations pay an effective rate of only 6.9% on dividend income, why don't individuals in the 70% bracket transfer their stocks to a wholly owned corporation in order to save taxes on their dividend income? Wouldn't this save substantial taxes?

The rules for personal holding companies prevent this. A personal holding company is a company whose stock is owned (50% or more) by five or fewer individuals, provided at least 60% of adjusted ordinary gross income is from personal holding company sources. Personal holding company income consists of passive source income such as interest, dividends, rents, and royalties. Personal service income is also considered personal holding company income.

The personal holding company tax is 70% and is imposed in addition to the regular corporation tax. Basically, the corporation is taxed as usual (up to 46%), and any remaining income that is not distributed as dividends is taxed at

70%. This is a severe penalty and effectively prevents individuals from establishing a personal holding company for the purpose of avoiding taxes.

Accumulated Earnings Tax

As was previously noted, a double tax results if a corporation distributes dividends to its shareholders. The corporation is first taxed on its income, and then the shareholder is taxed when the remaining income is distributed in the form of a dividend. If shareholders do not need the dividend income the second tax can be postponed indefinitely by not distributing dividends. Doing this enables the corporation to retain more earnings, which can be used for expansion. Over a period of years this added income has a snowballing effect on growth. In effect, the corporation is using Uncle Sam's tax money to expand the business!

There is nothing illegal about doing this. However, an extra tax may be due, depending on the circumstances. If the corporation is accumulating earnings beyond the reasonable needs of the business and does not pay dividends for tax avoidance reasons (the burden of proof is on the government), the corporation may accumulate an excess of $150,000 without penalty. Any additional accumulation is taxed. The first $100,000 of excess is taxed at 27½%. Any additional excess is taxed at 38½%.

If the corporation is able to give a good business reason for the accumulation, such as business expansion or retirement of debt, no accumulated earnings tax need be paid. In practice, this tax has never been imposed on a publicly held corporation. The only type of corporation that need be concerned with this tax is the closely held corporation.

Section 1244 Stock

The general rule is that a person who incurs a loss on the sale of stock is limited to taking a capital loss, which means that he will be able to offset a maximum of $3,000 in ordinary income for any one year. However, if the stock qualifies under section 1244 of the Internal Revenue Code, the taxpayer will be able to offset up to $50,000 of ordinary income ($100,000 on a joint return) if the stock is sold or exchanged at a loss or if the stock becomes worthless. The rationale for this rule is to give the small businessman a tax break when his business fails. Many small businesses fail each year, and giving the small businessman a tax break will enable him to salvage something out of what might otherwise be total disaster. Only small businesses (capital not in excess of $1,000,000) qualify for this tax break.

Postscript

The concepts mentioned in this chapter cover only a few of the most common tax rules affecting a business. The intent is to make the reader aware of these rules, not to make him an expert. Tax laws are in a continual state of flux. The content and scope of our tax laws are being changed daily as a result of congressional action, court decisions (three distinctly different courts are involved in this process—the federal district and appellate courts, the Court of Claims, and the Tax Court), executive order, and interpretations of administrative law and regulations. Obviously competent accounting and/or legal counsel should be retained if a question or problem arises.

Index